Lives of the Great Languages

Lives of the Great Languages

ARABIC AND LATIN IN
THE MEDIEVAL MEDITERRANEAN

Karla Mallette

THE UNIVERSITY OF CHICAGO PRESS
CHICAGO AND LONDON

The University of Chicago Press, Chicago 60637
The University of Chicago Press, Ltd., London

Published 2021
Printed in the United States of America

30 29 28 27 26 25 24 23 22 21   1 2 3 4 5

ISBN-13: 978-0-226-79590-4 (cloth)
ISBN-13: 978-0-226-79606-2 (paper)
ISBN-13: 978-0-226-79623-9 (e-book)
DOI: https://doi.org/10.7208/chicago/9780226796239.001.0001

Library of Congress Cataloging-in-Publication Data

Names: Mallette, Karla, author.
Title: Lives of the great languages : Arabic and Latin in the medieval Mediterranean / Karla Mallette.
Description: Chicago : University of Chicago Press, 2021. | Includes bibliographical references and index.
Identifiers: LCCN 2021007622 | ISBN 9780226795904 (cloth) | ISBN 9780226796062 (paperback) | ISBN 9780226796239 (ebook)
Subjects: LCSH: Arabic language—History. | Latin language—History. | Mediterranean Region—Languages.
Classification: LCC PJ6075 .M35 2021 | DDC 492.709—dc23
LC record available at https://lccn.loc.gov/2021007622

♾ This paper meets the requirements of ANSI/NISO Z39.48-1992 (Permanence of Paper).

This book, about languages that neither live nor die,
is dedicated to the living and the dead.

For A. G. Rigg, Latinist
1937–2019

For Michael Bonner, Arabist
1952–2019

For Evangeline, native informant on
the English of the living

Contents

[PART ONE]

∵

Group Portrait with Language

[CHAPTER 1]

A Poetics of the Cosmopolitan Language

The story that I will tell in this book is, in a sense, a tragedy. Modernity has not been gentle with the cosmopolitan language systems whose trajectories I follow, Latin and Arabic. Arabic survives today as lingua sacra, and it maintains a notional identity as a unified cosmopolitan language. Most Arabs believe that the language they speak is the same as the language they write and the same as the language that was written in the ninth century of the Common Era, although they recognize that it has changed substantially over time. Extensive training is required in order for a speaker of colloquial Arabic to be able to read any of the written registers: Modern Standard Arabic, the classical Arabic of the ninth century, or Qur'anic Arabic.[1] Latin is (by any standard used to measure language vitality) dead as a doornail. The website Ethnologue, a resource that tracks the vitality of all languages, spoken and written, in use on the planet, has posted its epitaph. "No known L1 speakers," it says of Latin—no one, that is, speaks Latin as a first language or mother tongue; "no ethnic community."[2] Literary historians typically describe the passing of Latin in another mode, since its demise made way for the triumph of vernacular literatures. Partisans of vernacularity have perceived the cosmopolitan languages as deadwood to be cut away so that local genius may flourish, the stifling weight of history and convention that must be shifted in order for innovation to emerge. My aim in this book is to construct a counterweight to such descriptions of the megalanguages of literary history: to describe and (for the most part) to eulogize languages that modern men and women of letters often view with suspicion, contempt, or disdain. This book is a ballad for a language that is dead.

Why celebrate linguistic instruments that (literary modernity teaches us) can only alienate the writer's creations from the lives that inspired them? My aim is to honor writers who worked to take on languages that were not their birthright but rather *became* theirs, slowly and by grace of sustained effort. I describe language that gives provincial intellectuals equal footing with cosmopolitan elites, because neither provincials nor cosmopolitans learn the language effortlessly as infants; rather, they earn it by the sweat of their brow. I sing the praises of the cosmopolitan language as a way to opt into empire. I watch the arcane maneuvers of Alexandrian languages whose structure was formalized millennia ago, whose vocabulary has a musty glamour: a foundation cut into living rock. I recognize the allure of writing in an acquired language: a whetstone that hones thought. I admire the cosmopolitan language for its capacity to demand an ethical commitment and an ethical stance from the language worker. By taking on the cosmopolitan language, as we will see, the writer or reader, copyist or printer takes on a way of being in the world, an ethics of engagement that is baked into that language and the texts that carry it through the world.

The framing of this book may appear atypical, even eccentric. Literary historians typically focus not on *languages* but rather on the *texts* created in language. Those who study language as such typically are not literary historians but linguists, trained to deploy research methods and strategies designed to study language. This book takes a different approach. I take languages themselves as objects of analysis, but I study them as literary historian. My aim is not to produce sustained philological analyses of specific texts, although I advance my argument using philological strategies. At times, too, I use other approaches: I describe languages as historical actors and as agents of historical change. Or I sketch a quick portrait of language in its natural habitat: the choreography of behaviors and investments that link author, tongue, and text. Because we typically know languages—we hear, interpret, love them, and sometimes hate them—as they are instantiated in texts and in the mouths of speakers, I use emblematic texts and exemplary speakers as stand-ins for the languages themselves. Yet in a sense speakers and texts are incidental to the story I tell, part of the background noise that language generates in its labors to articulate and sustain itself. As we zoom out from language workers to the global span of the language, as individual humans fade from view, the language itself emerges in greater relief.

The geochronological focus of this book is in part suggested by the languages I take as objects of study, Arabic and Latin. Both languages have a vast chronological range (both, in fact, like to think of themselves as immortal). This study will focus on a particularly eventful moment for both of them: what the Christian West refers to as the Middle Ages, when these two languages connected more writers and readers than ever before or since. The geographical valences of the languages are equally impressive (both, in fact, fancy that they are universal). This book studies the heartland of Arabic and Latin during the Middle Ages. My discussion ranges from Abbasid-caliphate Baghdad and Basra—where the Arabic language was refined and standardized as literary medium—to early modern Italy, where Latinity made its last stand as the common tongue of literary life. Arabic and Latin were blithely unaware of each other for most of their history. Each interacted with other languages: each translated from Greek, for instance; Arabic had a special relationship with Persian and, later, with Ottoman Turkish; Latin was symbiotically connected to the Romance vernaculars that would supersede it. But the Arabs knew little and cared less about Latin letters. Latin did acquire scientific texts from Arabic, and I address this translation movement below. I also discuss those places where writers of Arabic and Latin and speakers of Arabic colloquials and the European vernaculars came into contact: the port cities of the Mediterranean. Thus, the geochronological coordinates of this book stretch from the Abbasid East (mainly between the eighth and tenth centuries CE, with a special emphasis on Baghdad and Basra) to the sixteenth-century Mediterranean (focusing on the Italian Peninsula).

Arabic and Latin are incommensurate languages in so many ways, and it is part of the aim of these opening chapters to spell out how they differ. Despite their differences, however, Arabic and Latin shared one quality: they had the ability to draw men of letters (and the occasional woman) to them. This book studies the attractions of the Alexandrian languages, which inspired writers to set aside the mother tongue as literary vehicle and to embrace them as the truest expression of the truest thought. Because of this conceptual focus, the argument doesn't track chronologically: writers and books are chosen to illustrate attributes and behaviors of the language they used as medium and thus are not arranged in historical order. In this chapter, I outline the structure of the argument, with an abundance of internal references to aid the reader in navigating the nonlinear organization of the book. In the next chapter, Bashshār ibn Burd—an Arabic poet of the Abbasid age—and in chapter 3, Petrarch, who is remembered for his Italian poetry but wrote most of his works in Latin, appear to introduce the languages they served. I begin with a concession to chronology: thumbnail histories of the two languages.

The Latin language, emerging from the murky depths of history as the Romans consolidated their power at the heart of the Mediterranean (ca. third century BCE), developed its literary chops through translation from Greek.[3] Carried out of Rome on the pathways of empire, it spread through the imperial capitals and made some headway in the countryside. But in parts of the empire—in the eastern and the southern Mediterranean, in particular—it struggled, because of competition from other languages (Greek, Syriac, and Armenian) in the east, and because of the sparseness of human settlements along the southwest quadrant of the Mediterranean shore. Following the collapse of the Roman Empire, as the institutions of empire failed, the language suffered considerable entropy. Scholars disagree on the precise timing and mechanics by which Latin lost the hearts and minds of the population.[4] Most scholars believe that, although literacy rates were low, the general public understood the formal language orally in much of western Europe (what is now France, Germany, Italy, Spain, and parts of the UK and Ireland) through the seventh century. In 782, Charlemagne invited poet and grammarian Alcuin (ca. 740–804), who got his Latin in York, to join the palatine school. Alcuin would write a number of treatises on Latin and become a central figure in the language reforms of the Carolingian era. When a young scholar from a land where a Germanic language was spoken had to correct the Latin used by speakers of Romance languages derived from spoken Latin, scholars agree that the umbilical cord between written Latin and the spoken tongues had been severed.

From the ninth century onward, formal, written Latin and the vernaculars were distinct languages, even in Romance-speaking parts of Europe, and written Latin had to be learned through study.[5] French, Occitan, and Italian were no longer spoken registers of the formal language but, rather, independent languages. *Grammatica*, the first topic studied at school, taught Latin as the foundation of the trivium—grammar, logic, and rhetoric—and as point of entry for all future study. Breakaway vernaculars challenged the hegemony of Latinity: first in the north (parts of the oldest treatise on Irish grammar may date to the seventh century), then in Mediterranean Europe (Occitan poetry first appeared in southern France around the turn of the millennium; see chapters 5 and 11 below for the rise of the vernaculars). Latinity endured longer in the Italian Peninsula than most other parts of the Latin West, for a variety of reasons: because the Italians felt ownership over it and over the city of Rome, its sentimental capital; and because the language was identified so closely with the Catholic Church, which was also felt (within Italy, at least) to be a peculiarly Italian possession. Petrarch's championing of Latin and his reforms of the language, bringing it once again into line with classical practice, would do much to extend the life of the language in Italy (see chapter 3). During the fifteenth century, the century of humanism, when most other European regions had happily negotiated the transition to vernacular composition, Latin flourished in Italy.[6] The end game of the venture of Latinity—the competition between Latin and the Italian vernacular(s) for literary dominance during the era of humanism—marks the end of the vitality of Latin in the Italian context, although Latin survives still in Italy as the idiolect of the Roman Church.[7] Scholars trace the neo-Latin tradition from the Renaissance, with its reconsolidation of Latinity on the foundation of classical Latin, through the nineteenth century (at least).[8] But most readers look elsewhere for early modern and modern European literary milestones.

The trajectory of Arabic was quite different.[9] Following the death of the Prophet Muhammad in 622 CE, it burst forth from the Arabian Peninsula, carried with the armies of Islamic expansion. At this early stage, the language had little real-life experience. The literary record consisted of a corpus of pre-Islamic poetry and the Qur'an, both known and transmitted primarily orally (although the caliph 'Uthmān [d. 655] gathered scholars and witnesses to correct the text of the Qur'an and spread copies to all corners of the Islamic world).[10] Under the Umayyads (661–750), following this period of rapid expansion, the domain of Muslim rule extended from the Iberian Peninsula and Morocco in the West to the shores of the Caspian Sea and central Asia in the East. Administering this vast empire put a great deal of pressure on the language; Arabic grew up quickly. Following the Abbasid revolution in 750, the explosive rate of territorial expansion slowed, and Arabization and Islamization slowly transformed the population. The emergent language and the new religion both drew converts to themselves; the Arabic language grew apace, fueled by a burgeoning literary life, intensive grammatical self-examination (the topic of chapter 6), and a vibrant translation movement (chapter 8), which taught the language new behaviors. The Arabic language faced peculiar challenges in certain times and places. In the eastern Mediterranean, for instance—where Latin stumbled, in part because of the daunting linguistic complexity of the region—it had to learn to share territory with a plethora of other languages. The Arabs' genius for coalition building (exemplified in their extension of most of the rights of citizenship to non-Muslim monotheists—mainly to Christians and Jews) served them well, too, as a language policy. The eastern Mediterranean remained a place where multiple languages coexisted but the language of record—for science, literature, and imperial bureaucracy—was Arabic.

Inevitably, given the enormous burden placed on the Arabic language, Abbasid language policy was not monolithic. The territorial extension of the lands of Islam, the quantity of spoken and written languages that coexisted with Arabic, and the portfolio of literary, bureaucratic, and diplomatic duties imposed on it made the language at times magnanimous and at others churlish. With one hand, Abbasid men of letters welcomed the philosophy of non-Arabs into the language and accepted the contributions of non-Arabs to the establishment of its grammatical sciences and its literature. With the other, they snapped at those non-Arabs, who did so much to promote the vitality of Arabic as literary language and who wielded their Arabic as a tool of social and cultural mobility (see chapter 8). The duality of ethnic Arabs' attitudes toward non-Arab litterateurs who used Arabic as literary register was mirrored in the attitudes of non-Arab Muslims. Some were silent about their lives outside the reach of the Arabic language (like Sībawayhi; see chapter 6). Others took the occasional snipe at Arabs, even as they deployed Arabic as cosmopolitan language (like Bashshār; chapter 2). Finally, some opted out of Arabic and chose to bushwhack a literary path in New Persian, for instance, or (later) in Ottoman Turkish.[11] The earliest recorded debates around ethnicity and language choice in the Arabophone world emerged around what is termed the *shuʿūbiyya* movement (discussed in chapters 2 and 6). Those debates never disappeared; at times they become more fraught and charged, at other times less. In the face of this background noise of competition over ownership of the language, however, the Arabic language never stopped being an object of desire for non-Arabs and non-Muslims. Muslim Arabs never had a proprietary hold over the language. It was an important literary language for Mediterranean Jews throughout the Middle Ages. Christian Arabs, too, used it (and still do) as a literary instrument; Lebanese Christians contributed to the modernization and codification of the language during the nineteenth century (see chapter 10). Despite the battles over legitimacy occasioned by the use of Arabic by writers from such diverse linguistic origins, from so many different lands, and for so many different purposes, Arabic retains a promise of openness and remains a powerful literary instrument to the present day.

Or one could tell the story differently, emphasizing the entanglements of the actors rather than separating them for the purpose of analysis:

When Arabic burst onto the scene, in the seventh century CE, Latin had already passed the first bloom of youth. It had flowered and faded in the eastern and southern Mediterranean. It thrived now only in the corridors of power and the monasteries of its former heartland; we are in the chasm between "Late Latin" and "Medieval Latin." Arabic was (and is) buoyed by its status as lingua sacra (see chapters 2, 7, and 13). But Latin had a relationship with scripture that can only be described as complicated, reserving a fuller discussion of the question until later (chapter 7). In 711 CE, Muslim armies reached the Iberian Peninsula. There, Latinity had already faltered, thanks to the expansion of the Visigoths—no litterateurs, they. The Iberian Peninsula was thoroughly Arabized, although (as was true almost everywhere in the Arabophone world) the Arabic language coexisted with regional tongues—including pockets of Latinity and, over time, an emergent Romance vernacular culture. A further wrinkle of complexity: the Muslims who reached the Iberian Peninsula were not themselves necessarily Arabs. Many of the warriors were Berbers, who carried another mother tongue to the northern shores of the Mediterranean.

The armies of Islamic expansion, Arabs and Berbers, settled Iberia and, in the early ninth century, conquered Sicily. They established colonies in southern Italy and even (in 846) threatened Rome, but they never gained a lasting foothold on the Italian Peninsula. Yet around the turn of the millennium the Italians developed extensive mercantile engagements with Arabs, and as a result the Arabic language and Arabic-language culture were not entirely unknown in Italy. The diverse entanglements between Arabic and Latin culture on the Iberian and Italian Peninsulas would flower in the Arabic-to-Latin translation movement of the late Middle Ages (see chapter 9). Over time, the casual contact of merchants, pilgrims, corsairs, captives, and other professional, occasional, or accidental travelers generated a contact language used to communicate between speakers of Arabic, the Romance vernaculars, Greek, and other Mediterranean tongues: a pidginized Romance used in the port cities and bagnios and on the ships that traversed the sea, known as the lingua franca (or "language of the Franks"; see chapter 12). The lingua franca flowered during the twilight centuries of the Mediterranean, between the seventeenth and nineteenth centuries. It vanished with the end of cabotage, trade, and pilgrimage across the sea.

Or, finally, one could start the story with a question:

What bait did the cosmopolitan languages dangle to lure generations of writers away from the bosom of the mother tongue?[12] From the perspective of modernity the cosmopolitan language system appears flawed, thanks to its perceived incapacity to speak to contemporaneity. Latin may boost thought above the travails of the quotidian, but where does that leave Petrarch's Laura (see chapter 3)? Before the vernacular revolutions of European modernity, it seems, writers must accept the estranging filter of the learned language, in an equation that links intimacy to the ephemeral, degrading the language that bubbles spontaneously from the throat as unworthy of literature. The Arabic literary tradition remains permanently alienated from the popular voice that alone grants vivacity to the work of literature.

In this book, I aim to capture the vitality of the cosmopolitan language, to describe the qualities that allowed men like Francesco Petrarch and Bashshār ibn Burd to invest in it their ambitions, their dreams, and even the ambitions and dreams and desires of their most intimate moments. I do not promise a survey of the cosmopolitan language, nor even an exhaustive description of a single cosmopolitan language. Only a truly small-minded philologist would propose such an enormity: the cosmopolitan language is, by definition, as big as the world itself. Rather, I propose a comparative poetics of the cosmopolitan language, a conceptual account of the strategies that language uses to transcend the boundaries that language creates, and a defense of it that might satisfy those men and women who loved their literary lingua franca as the medium of their art. I rely upon vignettes. Group portraits with language capture the texture of the language and its choreography: the network of connections and associations that drew pen to paper and linked writer to writer, text to text, city to city (weaving the hinterlands into its tapestry as well), century to century, and language to language. I am fundamentally interested in the cosmopolitan language systems of the premodern Mediterranean. But it is one of the presuppositions of this book that language, in the twenty-first century, is reaching toward a kind of globalization that to a medievalist looks familiar.

European modernity accustomed us to a series of notions that would appear puzzling at best and outrageous at worst to premodern men and women of letters (and, in truth, to many non-European writers during the centuries of modernity). In the closing decades of the twentieth century, anthropologists began to study national language ideology, as it was defined in modern Europe and is currently understood in many parts of the world. Susan Gal, a pioneer of anthropological study of national language ideology in modern Europe, defined it most succinctly and most effectively: It teaches that language is a nameable, countable property, she wrote ("one can 'have' several"). Monolingualism is normative and natural. Languages are interchangeable; anything that can be said in one language can be translated into any other. Each language has "charming idiosyncrasies that are typical of the group that speaks it." Languages are internally homogeneous, obedient to rules that can be abstracted and laid out as normative. Boundaries between languages—geographical and conceptual—are clearly delineated by lack of mutual intelligibility.[13]

The contrast with national language ideology clarifies the nature of the cosmopolitan languages I analyze in this book. First, the national language, like the nation-state, claims territorial sovereignty. But the cosmopolitan language is transregional and recognizes the presence of multiple linguistic actors in all of the territory where it is used (see chapter 4). Second, according to modern language ideology, the mother tongue—the language we learn as infants from our mothers and from the linguistic surround, without formal grammatical instruction—is the natural and normative language of literature. But the cosmopolitan language system insists on the necessity of linguistic education in part as instrumental (because the language is not learned in daily life) and in part as ethical formation (the language teaches the student how to think). Third, modern language ideology proposes ontological continuity between the spoken and written forms of a language: the language we speak and the language we write are one. But for premoderns, as we will see (in chapter 5), writing a language changes its essential nature, fixing on the page what in its true form is ephemeral and defined by variation and discontinuity. Finally, the national language—because of its association with the mother tongue—represents itself as the language that is always there, always accessible and waiting to be activated, hardwired into the brain. It's the memory palace we return to, when we crave the comforts of home. The cosmopolitan language, on the other hand, because it must be studied and learned, must first be desired. Language workers use the cosmopolitan language not because they are born to it but because they crave the access it grants. It requires labor to construct, but it rewards that labor with its own pleasures. Like the nomad's tent, it gives shelter to the language worker far from the precincts of his *native* tongue (see chapter 2 and part II).

So entrenched is our belief in the validity and legitimacy of the modern language system that it is difficult to articulate and appreciate the power of the Alexandrian language model: the capacity of a learned language of literature to tempt the writer away from her mother tongue. National language ideology asserts that only the mother tongue can express the urgency that compels the writer to set pen to paper (and that compels her public to buy her books). But the allure of the cosmopolitan language is embedded in the DNA of that descriptive adjective itself—*cosmopolitan*—in particular in a specific late twentieth-century and early twenty-first-century regional usage of the word. In the years leading up to the turn of the millennium, *cosmopolitan* became a buzzword that described a particularly dense knot of intellectual affections and visceral emotions. In the popular press, it connoted nostalgia for the ethnic and linguistic density of certain cities of the eastern Mediterranean—Beirut, Alexandria, Izmir, Istanbul—viewed through a sepia-toned lens.[14] Conversely, in scholarly usage, it signified an intentionally dissonant critique of that nostalgia. Scholars criticized cosmopolitan universalism as a cover for the global export of Western values. They saw cosmopolitanism as an old ideology in new clothes: an attack on particularism and local identities in the name of a "universal" humanism that was nothing more than the Enlightenment ideology of western Europe in disguise.[15]

But in American usage in particular, the word retained or revived a glossy veneer, a flirtatious quality. It came to suggest the edgy pleasure associated with big cities, people in motion, and the anonymity of crowds. It connotes (in a word) naughtiness, and in particular the kind of naughtiness that urban centers and human mobility make possible. *Cosmopolitan* magazine has become a supermarket checkout lane banality in the twenty-first century. It's easy to forget how risqué the magazine was during its heyday: it printed the first male nude centerfold (Burt Reynolds) in 1972, and it continued to publish the occasional centerfold thereafter (Arnold Schwarzenegger, for instance, appeared in 1977). The cosmopolitan cocktail is of obscure origin, but it seems to have been created in South Beach in 1985 by a bartender, Cheryl Cook, who understood that people feel sophisticated when holding a martini glass, even if they don't like the taste of gin. It became the last word in turn-of-the-millennium urban sophistication as the favorite cocktail of the character Carrie Bradshaw on the HBO series *Sex in the City*. In the early 2010s, the Cosmopolitan Hotel in Las Vegas—a sumptuous resort property that epitomized the most recent iteration of the new Vegas—promised its clientele "just the right amount of wrong."

In an academic context as in the popular press, *cosmopolitan* connotes human mobility and the networked layering of languages that supports the global movement of people. To American ears, the word suggests the casual hedonism of a particularly urbane and mobile segment of the population. In this vernacular usage, one form of rhizomatic complexity has replaced another. The sense of mobility remains. But linguistic connectivity is replaced by social and sexual connectivity. Most useful for our purposes is the cocktail of connotations that informs both vernacular and scholarly uses of the word: circulation and connectivity are constants. The cosmopolitan language in particular is a linguistic tool that serves as an instrument of human mobility, rather than (like the literary languages of modern Europe, rooted in the soil of the nation) a deterrent to mobility. The cosmopolitan language is a code that must be learned, the price of entry into a far-flung cultural community, rather than our birthright. For this reason, it separates the speaker from his neighbors and even from his own household.

To be clear, the distinction that I am arguing between cosmopolitan language and national languages is not taxonomic. I do not claim that some languages by nature function as cosmopolitan and others as local languages of daily life, or that languages can be categorized as one or the other by virtue of clear genetic differences. Today, for instance, those who use global English or Modern Standard Arabic (MSA) in a formal setting may believe that they write or speak in the vernacular of everyday life. But linguists or attentive readers might insist that the distance between MSA and colloquial Arabic on the one hand, and between global English and a local register on the other, is wider than language ideology admits. I sidestep these niceties. The writer must be trained to write in the formal languages I celebrate in this book. A language system that privileges immediacy and accessibility as the loftiest of virtues may view its disconnection from geographic and historical coordinates as a fault. The Alexandrian languages, however, exalt other qualities: geographic and historical heft and scope; a capacious lexical reservoir that can express the subtlest of concepts; a sophisticated grammar that allows the writer to describe potentiality and actuality, speculative futures and deep history—or, if you prefer, the deep blue future and a speculative past.

It is the premise of this book that, while the opposition between "mother tongue" and "cosmopolitan language" might at times be artificial, the opposition between the *cosmopolitan language system* and the *national language system* is not. The latter presumes an intimate and exclusive relation between language and the nation-state that alone has the capacity to legislate political, legal and cultural identity. The former demands a conversion experience of sorts—the writer must come to it, taking it on as the price of entry to literary life—but, outside this elective affinity, allows a wide field of play. For this reason, the term *Alexandrian languages* may seem a better designation than *cosmopolitan languages*. Like the term *gramatica* (discussed below, chapter 3), *Alexandrianism* names languages that are formally difficult, with abstruse grammar that must be studied at school; complex, with a deep literary history; and—at least as regards use as spoken instrument—extinct. Or we could adopt a term coined by Philip of Harveng (see chapter 11), who wrote around the time of the emergence of vernacular cultures in Romance-speaking Europe, and use the moniker *legittera*, the *letters* or *language* (*littera*) bound by *laws* (*leges*).[16] We may speak one or many languages at home or in the streets. The cosmopolitan language or the Alexandrian language or the *legittera* or the *gramatica* is the one that the author chooses for his most ambitious communications.

The cosmopolitan language, alas, lacks one quality promoted in the national languages' portfolio as an essential charm: it is not a living language. It is a literary convention to describe certain languages as *living*: those that are still spoken in daily life, those that infants learn from their mothers (see chapter 13). In the twenty-first century, activists work to protect those languages that are *living* today but are threatened with *extinction*. The website Ethnologue, for instance, publishes updates on language vitality as part of its report on the health of languages worldwide. Wikitongues aims to record all languages spoken globally, in an effort to protect them from extinction. UNESCO maintains a list of the world's endangered languages and declared 2019 the "Year of Indigenous Languages" in order to protect those languages—and all the cultural memories and aesthetic practices embedded in them—from annihilation. It is not my intention to scorn micro-languages. Seen from this perspective, the cosmopolitan language is not a victimless crime. It sweeps local languages away in its ruthless advance, leaving them no room to flourish.

This book, obviously, subscribes to a different view of language. I come not to bury the cosmopolitan language but to praise it. I also aim to curate the metaphors I use to describe the language. Language does not live or die. The humanity of the cosmopolitan language extends far beyond this mortal coil. It may be (as we will see) vibrant, possessing qualities that observers could describe as emergent.[17] By virtue of this fact, it may appear to have autonomy and agency, and at times in this book I refer to the cosmopolitan languages as actors. In its sensitivity and responsiveness as well as its wide geohistorical reach, the cosmopolitan language often appears to have a heartbeat: it is tempting to speak about such languages as if they had the rudiments of consciousness. Yet it might be more appropriate to describe them using the vocabulary of systemic connectivity and emergence, in order to capture their ability to possess agency without consciousness. This book is a ballad for a language that is dead—and yet lives, in the mouths of its practitioners, wherever literary life is pursued.

∴

In the chapters that follow, I investigate the qualities that distinguished two Alexandrian languages from their local competitors: Arabic (particularly but not exclusively in the Abbasid East) and Latin (especially but not solely in late medieval and early modern Italy). Part II, "Space, Place, and the Cosmopolitan Language," focuses on the psychogeography of the cosmopolitan language: its territorial range and the paths that it travels, linking the far-flung places in which it is known. It isn't true, as they like to tell us, that the megalanguages are coextensive with the physical world. However, they do have remarkable geographical breadth. Perhaps more intriguing, they don't possess exclusive territorial sovereignty wherever they are used. The chapters in part II study the *territory* of the cosmopolitan language: a terrain defined by human circumambulation and (more to the point) by the circulation of words, languages, and texts. A city is a world, a snow globe in which each swirling flake is a book. Yet, paradoxically, cities are less important to the life of the cosmopolitan language than historians sometimes assume they are. The cosmopolitan language creates its own geography (chapter 4). It can act as such wherever its practitioners carry it, whether to the metropole or the provinces. In the chapters of part II, I watch two language workers as they move (unwillingly) between cities: Dante, exiled from Florence (chapter 5), and Sībawayhi, cast out of Basra (chapter 6). Like many before me, I use the biographies of these two men as ethical model, studying the cosmopolitan languages that sustained them through the lens of their lives.

Exodus, in a sense, is the modus operandi of the Alexandrian languages: they are engineered to enable communication across distances, and they guarantee that their practitioners will be understood wherever they find themselves. I use the term *language workers* to refer to these ardent disciples of the language, all those engaged in the production and dissemination of texts: writers, translators, commentators, copyists, editors, publishers, bookdealers, and the occasional saint who invents an alphabet in order to record scripture in a new tongue (chapter 7). But I reserve the term *nomad* for the writers themselves, those who live in the language and are able to move with it from place to place throughout the *logomenē* of the Alexandrian language. In part II, I describe the movement of the language that serves as a structure to house thought through physical space. My aim is to characterize the sensuous appeal of the languages for the nomads who worked to sustain them while being sheltered by them, the haptic and vibrant charm that draws language workers to them.

In part III, "Translation and Time," I discuss the temporal breadth of the cosmopolitan languages. Again, it is my difficult duty to point out that the cosmopolitan languages occasionally give themselves too much credit. They see themselves as eternal and declare themselves to be unchanging and self-identical throughout their long history. But, in fact, they change over time; their character arc demands it. The translation movement, a period of particularly intense change, occurs at a moment when the cosmopolitan language needs to scale up: when circumstances offer it a larger stage than those on which it has performed in the past, and it needs to learn new behaviors or speak to a new public. This transformative moment often occurs near the beginning of the lives of the great languages, as it did in the Abbasid East when the Arabic language absorbed the sciences of the ancient Greeks and literary traditions from the Sanskrit and Pahlavi. But it may also mark a moment when a language self-adjusts, recognizing that it needs to absorb new information or practices in order to remain current. This happened in late medieval Europe, when voracious translation movements brought scientific texts (and the occasional imaginative narrative) out of Arabic and into Latin, then the vernaculars, in response to a swiftly changing intellectual climate. These translation movements have much to fascinate the historian of literature. They allow us to watch as texts move between languages, and to trace the transformations that occur in the process. They are what gamblers call a *tell*: they mark a moment when the cosmopolitan language unwittingly tips its hand. In its most confident moments, the cosmopolitan language proposes that it is coextensive with the known and knowable world. But in the translation movement, it reaches beyond what its own language workers have produced in order to import knowledge discovered and disseminated in adjacent languages.

In part III, I describe episodes in discrete translation movements that show us texts moving through time, passed hand to hand in translation, and that reveal languages striving to learn new behaviors. I look first at a snapshot of language beyond the geochronological focus of this book: the creation of a new alphabet in order to bring Christian scripture to the

Slavonic-speaking Moravians (chapter 7). Cosmopolitan languages often sustain their privileged position by identifying themselves (and behaving) as sacred languages. Both Arabic and Latin have a long, at moments conflicted history as languages with a special relationship to scripture, liturgy, and worship. I use Old Church Slavonic as a cheat shot both to historicize language—it marks the birth of a new written tongue—and to think about the lingua sacra, because its history is much more compressed and much less familiar than either of the two languages that are my focus. The next two chapters follow the winding trail of a somewhat quixotic philosophical treatise through the centuries: Aristotle's *Poetics*. The treatise was translated from Greek via Syriac into Arabic toward the end of the Abbasid translation movement (chapter 8). Then, during the Arabic-to-Latin translation movement, it made its way into Latin (chapter 9). I use this history in order to think about how the Alexandrian languages responded to a uniquely challenging task: translating a work *about* language *from* language *to* language.

The translation movements allow me to examine the strategies that the cosmopolitan language uses to give itself temporal (as well as territorial) breadth. I argue that in place of *haecceity*—the quality of immediacy, urgency, and vivid realism privileged by the modern European languages and often celebrated in modern literature—megalanguages like Latin and Arabic forward another quality, which I call (repurposing an Arabic literary term) *hikaya*. This quality allows the writer to play in the fields of the language, unconcerned with the adjacency of reality. The aim of the language is not to create a vivid, lifelike portrait of the world: your life, memory by memory, flickering by like an old newsreel. I argue that the strength of the cosmopolitan language is not mimesis but performance: the creation of a world parallel to but separate from this one, an arena in which writers and readers meet and tango and spar, one that changes over time but much more slowly than the sublunary world. In the final chapter of part III, I discuss two nineteenth-century language workers who were both besotted by the Arabic language and its ability to sustain precisely this quality (chapter 10). This chapter traces the hikaya of the Alexandrian language—its emphasis on play, using the tool kit provided by the grammatical and lexical structure of the language itself—from the Arabian Peninsula during the era of revelation to nineteenth-century England. I argue that the behaviors I study in this book are possessed by any language willing to disassociate itself from mimesis as literary logic, to differentiate itself from the spoken tongue, and to embrace another portfolio of attitudes and behaviors. With its robust grammar and lexicon, its deep literary history, and above all its charisma, the Alexandrian language can draw the nomads who use it as artistic medium away even from the comfort and pleasures of the mother tongue.

In part IV, the final section of this book, I look at the aftermath of the cosmopolitan language regime in Europe and the West. At the end of the Middle Ages and the early centuries of modernity, the cosmopolitan language of Europe slowly went dark. How has it happened that literary historians represent the collapse of the European common tongue as a liberation and depict the ongoing vitality of the cosmopolitan language in the Arabic-Islamic world as a weakness?[18] In an effort to circumambulate this question, if not to answer it, I describe the moment when the Alexandrian language of literary history fell silent in the Christian West (chapter 11). It retreated into texts as its public grew resentful of its position as a register of communication staved off from daily life, a code that demanded significant study to crack. At roughly the same time, a stunted, parodic shadow image of the Latinity of western Europe emerged in the Mediterranean: the lingua franca (chapter 12). The lingua franca mimicked the grasping range of the cosmopolitan language, but on a much smaller scale. As cosmopolitan language manqué, it is good to think with.

The final chapter of the book provides an outro for the cosmopolitan languages: exit music, to play them off the stage of world letters. Of course, in truth, cosmopolitan languages remain very much the currency of business and culture in the new millennium. They are what organizations like Ethnologue, Wikitongues, and the UNESCO Year of Endangered Languages seek to protect us from. I reflect on the diverse paths followed by Latin and Arabic in the last chapter, and on some of the fundamental questions raised by this book: How do we recognize the nomad's choice of the language she uses to write? How do we honor the *cura litterae*—the care of and for the written tongue—that sustains the *fuṣḥā*, the purest or clearest language? The Alexandrian language is both an aesthetic strategy and an ethical stance. It furnishes a bulwark for trolls and language police. But it also gives poets and storytellers and philosophers and readers a citadel for thought and a fastness in which to shelter. It is the aim of this book to celebrate their labors and achievements and to suggest new ways to think about both their medium and what they accomplish with it.

My decision to focus on Abbasid Arabic and the late medieval Latin of Italy inevitably colors the argument I make and the texts I read. In part these comparanda are selected in order to tell a story that will be comprehensible to a wide audience. I write about both Arabic and Latin for nonspecialists. Writers like Bashshār, Sībawayhi, and al-Jāḥiẓ may not be household names, but the fabled Abbasid East rings familiar from children's versions of *The Arabian Nights* and Hollywood movies spun from those tales during the 1930s, '40s, and '50s, and the Abbasid caliph Harun al-Rashid and his vizier Jaʿfar are known quantities. By the same token, general readers may know little about the vast sea of medieval Latin, but Dante and Petrarch have recognition value—even if nonspecialists know little about their lifelong hovering between vernacular and cosmopolitan languages. These two focal points—the Arabic of the Abbasid East; late medieval Italian Latin—also provide a useful contrast: on the one hand, a language in the bloom of youth; on the other, a language approaching its dotage. But (spoiler alert) the Alexandrian languages have impressive resources. Even when they are young, they seem to possess lexical and archival bounty (or to be able to compensate for their shortfalls through translation). Although elderly, they often retain the possibility to reinvent themselves.

My narrative focuses on Latin and Arabic, but I want to make it clear from the outset that I am not a specialist in either language. I have admired and loved both and have grown exasperated and bored with both. In order to be able to decipher texts written in them, I have spent long hours chanting paradigms and memorizing vocabulary lists. I have scratched notes in the margins of texts in order to avoid the humiliation of failure in reading classes. Both have been objects of fascination and frustration for me. But this book is not about languages that one possesses but rather about languages that one desires. The cosmopolitan language is a tongue that one covets and seeks to win: a mistress tongue (in a formulation that has been used by more than one enamored and unfulfilled author), rather than a mother tongue.

This book, however, could not be written by a specialist or expert. Latin and Arabic are each (like any cosmopolitan language) as big as the world itself. *Only the dead know Brooklyn,* Thomas Wolfe wrote; in the same way, true knowledge of a cosmopolitan language could be achieved only beyond life, only beyond the limitations of mortality. One can be in full command of one's mother tongue, for usage dictates grammar in the case of the mother tongues. But prescriptive grammar must precede descriptive, in the case of the cosmopolitan languages,[19] and the lexical pool of the cosmopolitan language far outreaches the knowledge and scope of any individual speaker or writer of the tongue. If each of these languages is greater than any one writer, the notion of writing a comparative study of the two of them together must seem a fool's errand. Make no mistake: there are specialists and experts in Latin and in Arabic, and any one of them may possess a thorough command of the language. However, it is the aim of this book to pay tribute to languages that exceed any individual's knowledge of them, and to validate the imperfect yet sufficient knowledge of a linguistic and literary tradition—the justification for both these assertions being that the cosmopolitan language is greater than any single student (or ardent lover) of it. I write about languages as chimeric object of desire and pragmatic tool of communication at once. For this reason, the comparative lens is necessary, and a scholar who has made one of these languages the primary object of her study may find it difficult to step back and study the language as comparandum.

I take liberties, too, with geography. Although this book is not set solely in the Mediterranean, Mediterranean history provides the conceptual scaffolding for the story I tell in this book. The shores of the sea, at whose edges great world civilizations perch, isolated from their hinterlands and connected by the ships that sail in cabotage from port to port, each port a meeting point for populations so similar in some ways, so much at odds in others: Mediterranean history gathers together these narrative elements and reworks them again and again.[20] The annual cycles and the grand narratives of Mediterranean history provide what Hollywood scriptwriters and studio executives call the *beat sheet* of this book: an outline that coordinates the dramatic twists of a narrative, isolating the moments at which individual characters and their relations to each other become clear.

Chronology, finally, becomes entangled, baffled by the vast historical scale and the dynamic recurrence of event characteristic of the story I will tell. Without a clear narrative trajectory (as any scriptwriter or studio mogul can testify), no story is worth the telling. But how to tell the story of languages that themselves defy time? The cosmopolitan languages that are the subject of this book detach themselves from time and place. They lift human thought above the hurly-burly of everyday life. Do they, in so doing, put themselves beyond the reach of human affections? Can we truly cathect (to use a word created and sustained, momentarily, by the contact between languages) a tongue that we must learn as adults in the same way that we do the mother tongue, in which we have invested so much: love and memories, the tastes and smells and sounds of infancy and youth?[21]

The chapters that follow aim to describe the power and the allure of the cosmopolitan language model, and in so doing to demonstrate why a writer might turn to a cosmopolitan language *in preference to* her mother tongue. In order to sketch a portrait of the cosmopolitan language, I have chosen a series of vignettes, tableaux vivants of the learned language of literature in characteristic moments. My goal is not to connect the dots between anecdotes but, rather, to draw the circle tight around the language in each case, to draw close to the flickering light cast by the language in order to capture its warmth. I use comparatism as a wedge against the perils of universalism. This work focuses on two traditions that accounted for a significant portion of the literary life of the medieval Mediterranean: the Arabic and the Latin. The result may appear eccentric—where is Aramaic, ancient Greek (or Byzantine Greek, for that matter), Hebrew, Armenian,

Turkish, or Persian?—but only if one expects that totalizing approach to literary history now viewed in most quarters as suspect. In the same way, I use chronotopes as a scholarly convenience, situating my readings of literary texts in specific times and places in order to grant them a measure of philological precision. I do not intend to represent eighth-century Baghdad or sixteenth-century Venice as emblematic of the Arabophone world or the Latin West as a whole but, rather, to locate specific historical moments and geographical coordinates that allow me as reader to dig in my heels and study a cosmopolitan language in its interactions with the life of given geochronological coordinates.

In so doing, I aim to create a stereoscope portrait of the literary language before the nation and beyond the mother tongue. The cosmopolitan language—to sketch a quick definition, a point of reference for the discussions that follow—is a megalanguage that asserts its unity and singularity, while resting upon a foundation of linguistic multiplicity. It has a dynamic, combinatory genius. It does not (as modern languages do) claim exclusive rights to the speaker's identity but, rather, is always relational and intersectional. All those who use it, whether as literary or as spoken tongue, possess multiple languages; the cosmopolitan language represents itself as one among these: *a* literary register (albeit, in many cases, the language proclaims itself to be *the best* literary register). Paradoxically, it assumes a terrain of linguistic multiplicity both outside its own speech community and within that community. It understands that other communities possess a special relationship with a distinct language, and (in some cases) it recognizes the capacities of those languages in those parallel contexts. The cosmopolitan language promises great things to the writer: with it, her words have heft, vitality, permanence; beyond it, all is babble.

[CHAPTER 2]

My Tongue

Arabic in the Arabian Peninsula, seventh century CE, and Baghdad, eighth century CE

The Arabic language has a unique origin story. Epigraphy demonstrates the existence of a northwest Semitic language, forerunner of Arabic, as early as the ninth century BCE.[1] But Arabic became a textual language only during the early decades of the seventh century CE. The Qur'an, revealed between 609 and 632, carried it out of the Arabian Peninsula with a propulsive speed that differentiates it from the counterexample I use in this book, Latin. The Qur'an has no literary precedents. Poets composed in Arabic before the revelation to the Prophet Muhammad, but theirs was a largely oral tradition. The effort to record, transmit, and interpret the Qur'an, then to sustain the bureaucracy of a rapidly expanding empire, gave impetus to the development of written Arabic. In this chapter, I use the Qur'an to introduce the Arabic language. Bashshār ibn Burd, ethnic Persian and Arabic poet, presents the secular, literary face of the language. Finally, a resistance movement on the part of non-Arabs, the *shuʿūbiyya* movement, represents the counterweight of other languages in the Abbasid heartland (present-day Iraq) during the eighth century. I use these elements—the Qur'an, Bashshār, *shuʿūbiyya*, and the backdrop of linguistic complexity in western and central Asia—to capture the complexity of the choice the language worker makes when he embraces the cosmopolitan language, sometimes in preference to other linguistic options present in his environment.

The Qur'an is a self-aware text. It talks about itself, its own exceptional status, and the language in which it is written, in a number of passages.[2] The word "language"—*lisān* in the singular, *alsina* in the plural[3]—appears twenty-five times in the Qur'an.[4] Etymological roots in Arabic are wonderfully productive machines, capable of generating nouns, adjectives, and verbs, along with participles (active and passive), adjectives that act like adverbs, and verbal nouns, in a splendid variety of forms. The root from which *lisān* derives, however—as is standard in the Arabic language, a three-consonant root: *l-s-n*—is a meager source of lexica; it supplies only a single Qur'anic etymon, a single fish swimming in the great reservoir of language that is the Qur'an. This word appears in singular and plural forms, with vocalic supplements that indicate grammatical function as well as an array of attached personal pronouns: *lisānu, lisānun, lisāna, lisānī; alsinatukum* ("your languages"), *bi-alsinatikum* ("with your tongue"), *bi-lisānin* ("in language"), and so on. But in each of the twenty-five occurrences, the word is a noun and means "language" or "tongue"; in Arabic, as in Latin (*lingua*) and Greek (*glōssa*), the word for language derives from the anatomical term for the human tongue.

When the word appears in the plural—*alsina*—it regularly refers to the voices of disputation, which baffle the minds of believers and twist the truth.[5]

> There is among them a faction who distort the Book [i.e., the Qur'an] with their *tongues*. (3:78)

> If they were to get the better of you, they would behave to you as enemies, and stretch forth their hands and their *tongues* against you for evil. (60:2)

In contrast, when the singular form of the word appears, it typically refers to Arabic, often to a clear and beautiful Arabic:

> So, [O Muhammad,] We have made the Qur'an easy in your *tongue*, so that with it you may bring good news to the pious and with it you may warn a hostile people. (19:97)

> Indeed, this is a revelation from the Lord of the worlds: the trustworthy Spirit has brought it down to your heart, that you may be a warner, in a clear Arabic *tongue*. (26:192–95)

In a concise and beautiful image, Moses prays to God to strengthen him and ease his difficulties:

قَالَ رَبِّ اشْرَحْ لِي صَدْرِي
وَيَسِّرْ لِي أَمْرِي
وَاحْلُلْ عُقْدَةً مِّن لِّسَانِي
يَفْقَهُوا قَوْلِي

> [Moses] said: "O my Lord! Expand my breast for me
> and ease my task

and loosen a knot from *my tongue*
so they may understand my speech."
(20:25–28)

Here, the word *tongue* (*lisānī*, "my tongue") refers to a physical tongue: Moses, in the Islamic tradition as in the Jewish, struggles to speak clearly. Moses does not specify the language in which he speaks. Because of the poetic power of this passage, *lisānī* expands to mean at once the tongue, the words it speaks, and the meaning of those words. Moses prays for eloquence and for unity and clarity of message. In the passage that follows, God grants his prayer and sends Moses and his brother to Pharaoh to fulfill their mission as messengers.

Viewed from a narrowly linguistic perspective, the Arabic language itself is both the linguistic medium and the protagonist of the Qur'an. Islamic scripture elevated the Arabic language above the traders of Mecca and Medina and the Bedouins who used it on the trade routes of the Arabian Peninsula and formalized it in the poetic contests that took place in Mecca, sending it out with the Arab tribes who conquered (in a brief span of time) territory from the Strait of Gibraltar to the Indian Ocean. Against the confusion of tongues symbolized by the plural form of the noun—the *alsina* of the conquered peoples—the singular *lisān* of the Arabs would assert unity of message and strength of spirit. The story, of course, is more complicated than that: there are substantive differences between the language of the Qur'an and the literary tongue of the Arabs, as the scholars and litterateurs of Baghdad and Basra would give it shape. The colloquial forms of Arabic spoken in the Arab world fall even farther from the inimitable standard set in the Qur'an and from the carefully crafted instrument of the Arabic literary tradition. Modern Standard Arabic, the formal language of the Arab world today, represents yet another linguistic register—different from both the classical written Arabic of the literary past and the spoken Arabic of the present. Finally, many see this narrative not in a triumphalist mode at all but as a story of conquest and oppression: not the apotheosis of Arabic but rather the annihilation of a polyvocal literary environment that would take centuries to recover and that still struggles to assert itself in many parts of the Islamic world. My discussion in this book recognizes this context, while emphasizing the degree to which literary Arabic was (during the years that are my focus here) an effective tool for global literary and scientific communication.[6]

What does it mean to call a language like formal, literary Arabic *lisānī*: "my tongue"? Written Arabic is no one's mother tongue. Rather, it must be studied and learned by those who hope to use it as literary instrument.[7] In order to establish itself, it must push away the myriad varieties of competitor languages, including the spoken mother tongues and parallel cosmopolitan languages like itself. Those who aspire to participate in cultural life must put on the Arabic language like a suit of clothes—stiff and formal at first, becoming worn and comfortable over time. Literary Arabic was not a language of infancy, not a tongue heard in the household or the street. One chose to learn it: one had to work to make it one's own. Arabic became *lisānī, my* tongue, as the result of a series of actions—many of them voluntary, the product of deliberation and conscious choice—and at the end of a long period of training, a moral as well as literary education.

It would be useful, as a point of comparison, to study the word for *language* in Christian scripture, in order to gain perspective on the Arabic-Islamic distinction between linguistic singularity and linguistic multiplicity. But in which language ought one to approach the Christian Bible? From the beginning, a kind of linguistic scarification marked the sacred texts of the Christian community. Few Christians could read the Old Testament in the original Hebrew. The New Testament was written in Greek as a cosmopolitan language, and some passages were in accented Greek, showing signs of use by linguistic extracommunitarians. Early Christians could study the Old Testament, too, translated into Greek (in the translation known as the Septuagint, created by and for Greek-speaking Jews and begun in the third century BCE). Perhaps for these reasons, the scripture of the Christians proved much more amenable to translation than the Qur'an. Still today, some Christians see the King James translation as both historically contingent—executed under the patronage of the English monarch in 1611—and inspired: "the pure word of God," to quote a church marquee I often drove past in rural Ohio in the early years of this millennium.

Linguistic contingency is an intrinsic quality of Christian scripture. Each of the languages in which Christians might read the Bible during the first Christian millennium and the opening centuries of the second—Hebrew, Greek, Latin, Arabic, Armenian, Georgian, Coptic, Syriac, Old Church Slavonic, and so on—was a literary lingua franca designed to mediate between speakers of distinct mother tongues. In some cases the mother tongues were close enough to each other that the cosmopolitan register needed no more than a boost above the colloquial to become a shared literary medium. In others, one had to learn a wholly new language in order to become literate: in order to become a reader and a writer, one had to undergo a linguistic conversion. Thus Palestinian Christians, who likely spoke a Semitic language as mother tongue, heard Mass in Greek, although translation made their scripture available to them in a language closer to the one they spoke.

In the Abbasid context, in a similar way, Persian Muslims might learn Arabic in order to contribute to the cultural life of their age. Arabs in the

Abbasid world might claim pride of ownership in their language; but it is the premise of this book that they, too, had to labor to perfect their craft in the language of culture, in order to purge it of any taint of the nursery or the street. The cosmopolitan languages—the linguistic media of premodern literature—were always learned languages, and for that reason they served as indices of the distance that one had traveled from the linguistic and intellectual habits of youth. The reader's or writer's apprenticeship in a language and its literary tradition pushed him ever farther away from the person he had been; his studies initiated him in new linguistic, literary, and moral habits. Yet the acquisition of a cosmopolitan language was not figured as the *loss* of another tongue. One did not turn away from the mother tongue in order to take on the cosmopolitan language. As in quantum physics, the mother tongue/cosmopolitan language dichotomy is not expressed by the formula "either/or" but rather "both/and": the writer possessed both the formal language of literature and the spoken language of daily life. Precisely because of its formal quality—because it is no one's mother tongue—the cosmopolitan languages presupposed an environment of irreducible linguistic complexity. Every writer who set out to compose a work in formal Arabic or Latin was a translator, possibly composing with speed and ease, but still translating from the language (or languages) of her lived experience.

The cosmopolitan languages negotiated between the spoken languages of the street, on the one hand, and between competing literary languages, on the other; and translation from the literatures of neighboring languages played an important role in their literary development. With disarming frankness, both Arabic and Latin depended upon translation to generate a corpus of texts, scaffolding up which swarmed the writers building a new literary tradition in their newly minted (or recently baptized) literary language. The translation movement becomes a familiar motif in the life of the cosmopolitan language. This is the first paradox that defines the languages studied in this book. The cosmopolitan language was self-sufficient and complete, sealed off from the historical winds that buffet lesser languages, and it allowed the writer too to withdraw in splendid isolation from the contingencies and indignities of daily life. At the same time, it depended upon a network of languages: the written languages from which it derived a literary repertoire via translation, and the spoken tongues upon which the writer relied in her daily life.

∴

In illustration of the moral and ethical problems raised by the exclusive quality of the cosmopolitan language, I offer the first of two portraits in the diptych that opens this book: a still life with language, set roughly two centuries after the revelation of Islam, in the middle of the eighth century CE. The Arabic language has accompanied the Muslim armies, merchants, traders, bureaucrats, and legislators riding out from the Arabian Peninsula to conquer territories from the Strait of Gibraltar in the West to the foothills of central Asia in the East. The first wave of Islamic expansion, led by the Umayyad caliphs (661–750 CE), made little effort to Arabize (or, for that matter, to Islamize) the conquered. But this would change under the Abbasids; over time, the political and martial conquest would mature, becoming a linguistic, cultural, and religious expansion as well. The articulation of a new Arabic-Islamic culture generated two diametrically opposed responses in the Abbasid heartland (Baghdad, Basra, and their hinterlands): on the one hand, the Greek-to-Arabic translation movement, and on the other, a resistance movement opposing the Arab conquerors, known as *shuʿūbiyya* (from the word *shuʿūb*, meaning "tribes"). The Abbasid translation movement exploited the linguistic wealth of western Asia. Ruled before the Umayyad conquest by the Sasanians, who elevated translation to a moral virtue, the region was home to Aramaic, Pahlavi, and Greek traditions and neighbored dozens more. It put cosmopolitan languages into conversation with each other, moving the philosophical treasures of Greek antiquity into linguistic and cultural modernity by translating them and their attendant commentary traditions from Greek into Arabic (often by means of Syriac or Pahlavi intermediaries). The *shuʿūbiyya* movement, at its simplest (although it was never a simple phenomenon), gave voice to the discontent that shadowed the triumph of the Abbasids and their language. It used the eloquence of the Arabic language to express the resentment of the conquered peoples: the avant-garde of cultural resistance to Arab domination on the part of Persians and Nabataeans in particular.[8]

The poet Bashshār ibn Burd (ca. 714–83 CE) came of age in this milieu. He began his career under the Umayyads and lived through the Abbasid revolution in 750. Most courtiers do not survive regime change. Bashshār, remarkably, managed to cultivate the patronage first of Umayyad governors and then of their Abbasid successors, establishing a reputation as one of the masters of the Arabic poetic tradition in the process—despite the occasional *shuʿūbī* outburst. In a famous poem, he taunted the Arabs by claiming descent from Sāsān, the ancestor of the Sasanian dynasty, rulers of central Asia before the Islamic expansion. He boastingly attributed the territorial ascendance of Islam to the warrior horsemen of his own people of Ṭukhāristān (the name used by the Arabs to refer to Bactria): "We restored sovereignty to the family of the Arab Prophet."[9] And he scorned the Arabs for their lack of history, ancestry, and culture, deriding them as lizard-eaters, drinkers of goat's milk, and trailers after "scabby camels"[10]—

mocking the lexical niceties of the poetry of the Bedouins, who had perfected the art of living in an exiguous environment. Yet, as was the case for all *shuʿūbī* writers, the medium Bashshār used to slander the Arabs was precisely the linguistic instrument forged by the Bedouin nomads and the merchants of Mecca and Medina. "Even the most fanatical *Shuʿūbī*," as H. T. Norris succinctly explained, "expressed his sentiments in the tongue first spoken by the Arabian lizard-eaters he so despised."[11]

The great compilation of Arabic poetry, the *Kitāb al-Aghānī* (or *Book of Songs*) collected by Abū al-Faraj al-Iṣfahānī (897–972/73 CE), records a meeting between Bashshār and the Abbasid caliph al-Mahdī in about 780 CE. When the caliph questioned Bashshār about his origins, he responded: "My language and dress are Arab, but my origin is non-Arab [*ʿajamī*]."[12] Note the precedence that Bashshār grants to language as a marker of identity: he asserts his linguistic pedigree first, then his Arab customs, and finally acknowledges his non-Arab lineage. Pressed about his ancestry, Bashshār continued: "I am [descended] from the greatest of horsemen, the harshest to our rivals, the people of Ṭukhāristān."[13] The region of Ṭukhāristān (ancient Bactria; now, mostly, northern Afghanistan) had put up fierce resistance to the Umayyad forces of expansion, and Bashshār may be recalling his ancestors' reputation for resilience when he speaks these words. The people of Bactria had another association for the men of Bashshār's time and place. When Bashshār mentions them, another of the men present replies, "Are they the Soghdians?"—as if trying to place Bashshār, to locate him ethnically and linguistically. "No," Bashshār replies dismissively. "The Soghdians are merchants."[14]

Bashshār turned away from the culture and the linguistic affiliations of the mercantile class to embrace a cosmopolitan language, its literary history (quite brief, during Bashshār's life), and its cultural network. This vignette crystallizes the linguistic paradoxes and competitions of the Abbasid age: the tension between the centripetal force of the translation movement and the centrifugal force of *shuʿūbiyya* that animated it. Under the great umbrella of the *shaʿb*, the metatribal unity of humanity, multiple *shuʿūb*, or tribes, might coexist. Their disparate origins and lineage divided them. What they shared, what united them as a people, was in part Islamic practice and customs and in part the Arabic language.[15] The centuries of Abbasid rule saw numerous sectarian conflicts and debates within the Muslim community and between Islam and the older religions practiced by the peoples governed by Muslims: the growing pains of a civilization in its youth. But Arabic literary culture thrived, and much of this culture was produced by men who were themselves converts to the language. Ibn al-Muqaffaʿ (d. ca. 756 CE), writer of the earliest models for Arabic literary prose and himself a translator from the Pahlavi, and Sībawayhi (d. 795 CE), author of the first compendious and authoritative grammar of the Arabic language, were of Persian descent. Al-Jāḥiẓ (ca. 776–868/869), who wrote a prodigious number of works on a prodigious range of topics, seems to have been of humble and quite possibly non-Arab origin (although the details of his lineage are obscure and a topic of heated scholarly debate). Both the Abbasid translation movement and—in a diametrically opposed way—the *shuʿūbiyya* movement proved that the Arabic language might, as the Islamic religion did, win converts beyond the Arabian tribes. *Shuʿūbiyya* demonstrated that the Arabic language was greater than the Arabs.

Bashshār, unfortunately, did not long enjoy the caliph's favor. He died when al-Mahdī had him flogged, on suspicion not of anti-Arab sentiment but rather of heresy; thus, he fell victim to another of the bitter controversies of the first century of Abbasid rule.[16] In the vignette recorded in the *Kitāb al-Aghānī* he parries heroically with the caliph, replying to the caliph's questions with jaunty verses in which he celebrates himself as a great man, a womanizer, descended from the "aristocracy of the rubes"; he is playfully mocked by the men present at the caliph's court and mocks them in return; and he does so in effortless Arabic. But we do well to remember that Bashshār had little choice in the matter. Had he chosen to compose in another language, we would likely know little or nothing about his work, and his conversation with the caliph would not have taken place. His career as a poet, in fact, would occur outside our line of sight, beyond the light of historical memory. If he did not pray for the knot to be loosened from his tongue, we would not hear him sing today.

The *Kitāb al-Aghānī* records his exchanges with the caliph and his court in flawless formal Arabic, and Bashshār's Arabic is a formidable weapon. But this exchange should not be read as documentary realism—or, for that matter, as *linguistic* realism. The *Kitāb al-Aghānī*, written at least a century and a half after Bashshār's encounter with al-Mahdī, is not (and was not intended to function as) a reliable historical witness.[17] It seems extremely unlikely that a poet in the presence of the Commander of the Faithful would express himself so forcefully. A twenty-first-century narrative sensibility sees verve and spirit in the rapid-fire exchange between Bashshār, the caliph, and the other men present in the caliph's court. Perhaps, however, this jumpy narrative rhythm simply demonstrates how the work was made: anecdotes and comments stitched together from a patchwork of written and oral sources, integrating traces of the sensibilities and historical concerns of a multitude of authors, transmitters, compilers, and copyists. In the first place, one must use the *Kitāb al-Aghānī* with probity when mining it for historical information. In the second place, we should think carefully before relying upon it as a linguistic record. The *Kitāb al-Aghānī* collects poems by more than one thousand poets, along with anecdotes that tell us how to read the poems. Compiled from unknown sources, woven together to form a connected and coherent record, transmitted in manuscript versions through the centuries, the *Kitāb al-Aghānī* is a loving tribute to a cosmopolitan language. As such, it is under no obligation to represent with granularity the linguistic realities on the ground in each of the geochronological coordinates in which its songs were sung. It is not the work of the cosmopolitan language to be attentive to microlinguistic detail. Rather, the cosmopolitan language links site to site, *carefully obscuring* linguistic polyphony in order to generate a linguistic web elastic enough to allow communication across the centuries and the continents. The *Kitāb al-Aghānī* gives us vibrant if not factually accurate snapshots of the personalities of singers and their songs. But on every page we find vividly realized depictions of the expressive power of the cosmopolitan language.

The anecdote that al-Iṣfahānī reports—the tale of Bashshār's audience with al-Mahdī—illustrates the intensity with which a language worker may feel the cosmopolitan language to be "my tongue," even as he looks toward the borderlands between "his" tongue and its neighbors and competitors. A glance at the background against which this anecdote is set reveals the complexity of the linguistic environment into which the Arabic language expanded. Bashshār identifies himself boastingly as descendent of the Sasanians, whose empire dominated central Asia before the Arab expansion (and who had been challenged, before the Arabs, by the Greeks). The Sasanians' Pahlavi literary tradition, too, flourished in portions of western and central Asia that would be Arabized (and Bashshār himself contributed to the process of Arabization). A century after Bashshār's interview with the caliph, at the end of the ninth century, the Pahlavi linguistic-literary vein, long suppressed but never extirpated, would re-emerge and in the ensuing centuries would flower as New Persian letters.[18] From this point, a direct line of descent connects medieval Persian authors, like Ferdowsi (d. ca. 1020) and Niẓāmī (1141–1209), to the authors of modern Iran. Bashshār—who, for reasons that we cannot at this distance guess, chose to be a writer of Arabic—gestures toward the vanishing point of linguistic cohesion, the boundary where the center no longer holds, when he refers with haughty pride to the mighty Sasanians.

Bashshār also claims descent from the "horsemen of Ṭukhāristān," an even more tenuous identification (to modern eyes, at least). The Tokharoi, nomads from the north (and literal or figurative ancestors of Bashshār's Ṭukhāristān horsemen), overran Bactria during the second century BCE. Other nomads would invade the region through the centuries. The

Tokharoi, however, survived as the toponym by which the region was known to Hellenistic writers as well as to the Arabs. Medieval Arab geographers used the Arabized form of the name to refer to a region along the banks of the Oxus (a river known today as the Amu Darya). But little was known about the language of Bactria until the discovery in the 1990s of a cache of leather documents bearing Bactrian inscriptions. The documents made a splash in the field of Indo-Iranian studies because they brought to light a language that had survived only in fragments—the only Middle Iranian language, furthermore, written in a script adapted from the Greek alphabet (a remnant of Alexander's adventures in the region).[19] The find provides a glimpse of the front lines of the Arab expansion. In the earliest of the documents, debts are paid in Sasanian coinage; by the end, the currency used is Arab silver dirhams. The cache also includes a small number of documents in Arabic that seem to date, according to internal evidence, to roughly the same time as Bashshār's meeting with the caliph al-Mahdī—about 770 CE.[20]

Bashshār's grandfather, according to the (admittedly sketchy) evidence we possess, had been enslaved and carried out of Bactria by the armies of Arab expansion and had settled in the region that at that moment was in the process of becoming the Arabic-Islamic heartland. Bashshār himself was born in Basra. Did he still speak at home a language that his family had brought with them from Bactria? Did he or his family know the Greek writing system used to record that language? It is surpassingly unlikely that this was the case; Bashshār came from humble stock (his father was a bricklayer), and his bravado is often understood as a symptom of class anxiety. Were the Indo-Iranian language of Bactria and the Pahlavi of the Sasanian heartland mutually comprehensible? Could Soghdian be understood in Bactria? At this distance, particularly for one not trained in the niceties of central Asian history, names and languages blur. Certainly, the unnamed man present at the caliph's court who asked a fishing question about the Soghdian merchants could be excused for his ignorance of a region so far distant from his home and clamoring with such a cacophony of alien tongues.

Bashshār turned to Arabic in part as an alternative to the confusion of tongues that surrounded him: it transcended the welter of tongues in any one place. His chosen language served another, crucial purpose: it moved with him from one location to another. Bashshār's antecedents had been displaced from the valleys and foothills of Bactria to Basra. He himself moved from Basra to the Abbasids' new capital, Baghdad, and his chosen language came with him. Here, too, the cosmopolitan language improves on the mother tongues. Resolutely local, rooted in the soil of a given place, the mother tongue may be carried by émigrés far from home. It may be spoken around the hearth in strange new lands and may serve as a bond linking those who share a point of origin. But Bashshār could not use his mother tongue as a language of literature. For that, he had to look elsewhere: to a language that could be grammatically categorized, quantified, and described, a language that already possessed a literary record. During the eighth century CE—during the lifetime of Bashshār and Ibn al-Muqaffaʿ and Sībawayhi, when al-Jāḥiẓ was born—the Arabic language was a relatively new literary instrument (and Bashshār, Ibn al-Muqaffaʿ, Sībawayhi, and al-Jāḥiẓ contributed to its refinement). Yet it already possessed the power to send a literary text from central Asia to the Strait of Gibraltar. It could propel speaking subjects, too, on these same pathways of connectivity, from places where Indo-Iranian languages were spoken (on the eastern fringe) to the lands of the Berbers and Latins (in the West), with both texts and writers moving through the web generated and sustained by the communicative capacity of the language itself.

This rarefied atmosphere—far above vernacular babble, constantly in motion on the paths of migration—is the natural habitat of cosmopolitan languages. Only the cosmopolitan language can serve the interests of a man who wishes to compose poems that will still be recited more than a millennium after their composition, thousands of miles away from their place of origin. Many of the languages I have mentioned in this chapter at one point served as such a platform for poets and philosophers: ancient Greek, Pahlavi, Arabic, Persian. The sacrifice of the mother tongue as literary record, the need to learn a new language in order to participate in the literary life of the age, seems a small price to pay for the expressive power it provides. And the mother tongue is not really lost, of course. It serves its purpose in the kitchen and on the streets; and, as we will see, it has a way of working through the tensile surface of the cosmopolitan language and into the viscera of the language itself.

[CHAPTER 3]

A Cat May Look at a King

Latin in Paris, 1361; Italian in the Veneto, 1374

Twentieth- and twenty-first-century readers typically associate Francesco Petrarch (1304–1374) with the Italian vernacular and with lyric poetry. In this chapter, I try to capture the strength of Petrarch's feeling for Latin. Petrarch lived much of his itinerant life outside of Italy and directed most of his literary industry to Latin prose. Born in Arezzo in 1304 (his father had recently been exiled from Florence), Petrarch moved with his family to the papal court in Avignon in 1312. He studied at Montpellier and Bologna and traveled in northern Italy, Gascony, France, the Low Countries, and Germany as a young man. He took his first trip to Rome in 1337 and spent some time in Rome and Naples in subsequent years. After a long period divided between residences in Parma, Verona, Padua, and his own property at Vaucluse (near Avignon), along with diplomatic trips to other cities, mainly in northern Italy, he settled in Padua in 1358. He moved to Venice in 1362, intending to end his days there; after a change of heart, he resettled in Arquà (near Padua) in 1369. There he died, in 1374. Latin furnished the linguistic soundtrack for this nomadic life. Petrarch lived in Latin wherever he found himself: from Naples to Liège, from Avignon to Cologne, even (to the dismay of his audience) in Paris.

And yet, Petrarch—who had devoted his youth to the tongue of the fathers—turned in his own old age to the youthful language of the poets: the emergent Italian vernacular, at this point relatively untested as literary medium. He started to write Italian poetry as a young man and continued to tinker with the poetry throughout his life. But Latin was his preferred linguistic medium for much of his life. The late work on the poetry, therefore, is a puzzle: why, in his old age, did Petrarch return to the poetry of his youth, the love poems written for the long-dead Laura? In this chapter, I reflect on the problems and the possibilities of old age, on both the human scale and the linguistic. In its dotage, Latin developed an awareness of competing cosmopolitan language systems, and I discuss emergent Latin vocabulary used to describe the Alexandrian language of cultural life in a generic sense. Finally, I use Theodor Adorno's work on late style to describe the appeal of the vernacular that lured Petrarch away from Latin at the end of his life. The previous chapter focused on the propulsive energy of the Arabic language at the beginning of its career on the world stage. This chapter considers the ongoing vitality of Latin toward the end of its viability as a world actor, and it foreshadows the rise of Latin's vernacular challengers at the end of the Middle Ages.

∴

In January of 1361, Petrarch—who, at the age of 56, had been crowned poet laureate by the King of Naples and had acted as emissary for popes and monarchs—was sent on a diplomatic mission to King John II of France, to congratulate him on his recent release from captivity under the English. John, remembered as Jean le Bon, had been taken prisoner following his defeat in battle at Poitiers in 1356 and held in London. Released in 1360 after his son, Charles, concluded a treaty that promised a ruinous ransom to buy his freedom, John returned to Paris. Petrarch met him there on behalf of his patrons, the Visconti of Milan, to celebrate his safe return to the capital.[1]

The version of the speech that Petrarch made on this occasion, which he himself edited and recorded for posterity, begins with a disclaimer defending his use of Latin, rather than French, in his audience with the king—a systematic statement of Petrarch's attachment to the language. King John's court, it seems, requested that, as a concession to local sensibilities, he address his audience in French. In his opening comments, Petrarch explains his decision not to comply. He recognizes his duty to speak in the language that would be more agreeable and more familiar ("acceptior et notior") to his audience. Even Athenian Themistocles worked up some Persian before his negotiations with the King of Persia, rather than "offend the ears of the king with a foreign tongue [*peregrinum ydioma*]. Indeed," Petrarch continues, "willingly would I myself do the same, if I could. But I am not a man of such wit: I do not know the French language, nor am I able to command it with ease." Though modest about his own linguistic capacity, Petrarch is emboldened by the knowledge that King John as a young man was himself devoted to the study of Latin. He cannot be expected to address so magnificent a personage in a language that no one could expect him to have mastered; he begs the king's condescension and announces his intention to say his piece in their common tongue, Latin.[2]

As is usual with matters relating to Petrarch's biography, we have only his own version of this story. Petrarch edited his papers carefully, with an eye to shaping his reputation and managing his fame. Historians commenting on this episode typically assume that Petrarch received a formal request to speak in French and read these sentences as his refusal to do so—shocking temerity on his part, if this is the case. Indeed, it's difficult to imagine the sequence of events leading up to Petrarch's audience with the king. Did King John (or a member of his retinue) make a preemptive strike against a man known for his fluid Latin, a man who might well have responded to the French court's Latin with haughtiness and superciliousness? Did the French court attempt to dictate the terms of the ceremony, to be rebuked by Petrarch? Or was there a more spontaneous exchange: did Petrarch begin his comments in his fluent, Italian-accented Latin to be interrupted by the king and only then continue (perhaps halting and uncertain) his prepared text, aware that the king was not following his periodic sentences and rhetorical flourishes? Was this exordium part of the speech that the king and the court heard, or was it added later, as self-justification on Petrarch's part?

Perhaps most provocative, the episode compels us to ask: how well did Petrarch know his audience? King John is remembered today, among other things, as the originator of a French vernacularization movement, a movement that would come to fruition under his son and successor, Charles V, also present at Petrarch's address. During John's reign, Jean de Sy created a vernacular translation of the Bible. Jean de Vignay translated Vincent of Beauvais's *Speculum Historiale*.[3] But the first vernacular translation of John's rule and with his patronage was made by another man who was there when Petrarch was presented at court. Pierre Bersuire (also known as Pierre of Poitiers) translated Decades I, III, and IV of Livy's *Ab Urbe Condita* into French.[4] Pierre was an old friend of Petrarch's; they had known each other since Petrarch's days in Avignon, where Petrarch lived until 1353. Indeed, Pierre's vernacular translation of Livy would not have been possible without Petrarch's intervention. It was Petrarch's philological detective work that brought Livy fully into the Middle Ages. Before Petrarch's search for new manuscript versions of the Decades, before his editorial work on the text, Livy was known in countless vernacular variants circulating as independent texts. Petrarch used his knowledge of Latin and his acute sense of Latin style to restore Livy's Latin text, which Pierre in turn reproduced in the French vernacular.[5]

We know that Pierre was there during Petrarch's speech (along with King John and the dauphin) because, once again, we have Petrarch's own account of the event, recorded in a letter written to Pierre. Thanks to this letter, we know that John and his retinue did pay attention to Petrarch's Latin address that day; at least, they took in portions of it. Petrarch reminds Pierre of the events of the day: he noticed, as he spoke, that King John and his son Charles both responded eagerly to Petrarch's mention of Fortune. In fact, Petrarch tells Pierre that he had a visit later that night from a messenger who told him that he would be summoned to the king's presence to discuss and debate the role that Fortune played in human affairs.[6] Given John's recent adventures—his defeat and capture; the hostage exchange negotiated as part of the terms of his release, which required him to send another son, Louis, along with thirty-nine other French nobles to take his place—it seems that the royal family had every reason to be interested in the subtle machinations of Fortune. Yet John's interest in Petrarch's meditations on the twists and turns of fate, it seems, extended only so far. Petrarch informs Pierre that he attended the king and the dauphin, who whiled away the hours in vagaries and self-preening. A cat may look at a king—but he may not, it seems, speak to one. Petrarch left without saying his piece on Fortune.

Perhaps the king simply had little interest in inviting another torrent of voluble Latin from his Italian visitor's mouth. A glance at the text of Petrarch's address to King John allows another, admittedly uncharitable, assessment of the day's events. Petrarch addresses the topic of Fortune in the opening lines of his speech, building to a verse from Virgil on the subject: "Fortuna omnipotens et ineluctabile fatum" (All-powerful Fortune and inevitable fate). One imagines Petrarch intoning the word *Fortuna* sonorously each time it occurs—typically placed, for emphasis, at the end of a phrase—and giving Virgil's verse the fervent emphasis it merits.[7] One also imagines the king's and the dauphin's ears perking to the sound of a word they recognized. The Latin word *fortuna* entered French, as it entered all the Romance languages, virtually unchanged. The French *fortune* is a cognate of the Latin *fortuna*, and hence immediately familiar even to an ear untrained to the niceties of literary Latin. Certainly Petrarch's periodic sentences—larded with subordinate clauses, meandering toward the *ineluctabile fatum* of that final Virgilian verse—must not have gone down easily at the French court. The quickening that Petrarch saw in his audience when he discussed Fortune was perhaps a sign of linguistic as well as moral comprehension and recognition—anagnorisis, as the Greeks would call it, though King John would probably prefer *entendement* or *savoir*: good Latinate words that had, by one path or another, been naturalized by the fourteenth century as French.

It is difficult for twenty-first-century readers to understand the depth of Petrarch's feeling for the Latin language. The Italian poetry presents a strong distraction. Petrarch, for us, is the voice of poetic modernity: the poet who taught Europeans to appreciate the immediacy and urgency of the vernacular (and its bosom companion, inconstancy). But Petrarch himself spurned the vernacular. He placed his trust in Latinity: a language that accompanied the nomad from Rome to Avignon and Avignon to Paris, that allowed the moderns to read and even to address the ancients—as Petrarch himself did in the letters he wrote to his literary models, Cicero, Virgil, even Greek Homer. He derided the vernacular poetry that defines his reputation for us as "trifles"—*nugae*—in a note he wrote (in Latin, of course) on the working draft of one of his vernacular poems.[8] One need only scan the titles of his works to understand Petrarch's sense of the relative value of the two languages. In his vernacular, in Italian, Petrarch wrote two works: the *Canzoniere* and the *Trionfi*, both collections of verse addressed to the love of his youth, Laura. In Latin, he composed the *Africa*, an epic poem; *De remediis utriusque fortunae* (*Remedies for Both Kinds of Fortune*), moral advice to aid the reader in facing fair fortune or foul; *De viris illustribus*, or *Biographies of Exemplary Men*; *Itinerarium ad sepulchrum Domini*, the literary pilgrimage to the Holy Land that Petrarch would never take in person, because of his fear of the sea; the *Letters*—in five distinct collections, not counting the *Invectives* that started as vituperative letters and became so much more; and so on, amounting to some twenty-eight works, from the youthful early letters to the somber finality of the *Testamentum* (*Last Will and Testament*). Petrarch's thoughts made their home in Latin. He spoke Latin even to himself, in the privacy of his own mind: the *Secretum*, an autobiographical meditation that he kept to himself—it did not circulate during his life—was composed in Latin.

The episode with King John obliged Petrarch to tip his hand, to reveal his attachment to Latin. His waspish rejection of John's vernacular was not likely to win him friends at the king's court; but Petrarch himself had no use for the frivolities of court life. He had written elsewhere, long before this journey, that he was scandalized by the French court's ignorance of Latin, and that he could not picture himself as courtier among those who had no feeling for Latin.[9] As for King John, he would last less than four years in France. By the end of 1363 he had slipped back to England, called back either by a sense of honor (his ransom had not been satisfied) or, according to some, by the gaieties of English court life.[10] What language, one wonders, did the king speak with his captors: Norman French, the French of King Jean's court, English, or some combination of these? Perhaps John himself had acquired a taste (as those who travel sometimes do) for living in translation: in the *peregrinum ydioma* of the English court, a linguistic register liberated of regionalisms and unburdened by the idiosyncrasies of hearth and home.

∴

Arabic and Latin are incommensurate languages in so much: the one a Semitic tongue and the other Indo-European, according to the classification system used by modern linguists; the one used (mainly) by Muslims and the other by Christians; the one written from right to left, the other from left to right; the one still used as a language of literature and culture and the other all but defunct, surviving only in faculties of classical languages and as the idiolect of the Roman Catholic Church. Only recently has the English language struck upon a generic term that might be used to describe two languages like Arabic and Latin as parallel linguistic formations and thus as comparanda, languages that might be balanced and contrasted in order to study their behaviors and think about how they work.

Cosmopolitan language is the term now used to designate the acquired tongue of premodern literary life: the singular and unified language used in a context of linguistic complexity; the learned language that displaces the mother tongue, yet makes the speaker more (not less) eloquent.[11] It is curious that premodern grammarians did not have a word to designate the learned language in the generic sense, despite the fact that the literary landscape was littered with cosmopolitan languages during the Middle Ages. There is no word in Arabic or Latin that means "a transregional, transhistorical language of literature" without reference to one or another language in particular. More accurately, under the pressure of the Arabic-to-Latin translation movement that began during the twelfth century (which postdated the Greek-to-Arabic translation movement by roughly two centuries), Latin produced a technical term that might be used to refer to the cosmopolitan languages in general. But the development occurred late in the history of the Latin language, and this lexical range did not long endure.

During the tenth century, in the Abbasid East, the philosopher al-Fārābī (870–950 CE) wrote a treatise known as *Iḥṣā' al-'ulūm*, a *Catalogue* or *Survey of the Sciences*. As the title suggests, the treatise was intended as a prerequisite for the analysis of natural phenomena. It lists and analyzes the logical tools that human reason could use to study and understand the world. Al-Fārābī begins by describing language and logic as the most basic instruments in the philosopher's tool kit. But he identifies one fundamental difference between the two: the laws of logical analysis are the same for all humans, he writes, whereas the science of grammar (*'ilm al-naḥwī*)[12] is valid only for one (linguistically defined) community.

Two centuries later, when al-Fārābī's treatise was translated into Latin in the workshop of Gerard of Cremona (1114–187), the word *gramatica* was used to render al-Fārābī's "'ilm al-naḥwī."[13] The translator's "gramatica"—because it must account for both the Latin that Gerard's community uses and the Arabic that al-Fārābī's community used—must therefore designate "a learned language *in the generic sense*." A sliver of philological evidence suggests that this broader lexical range came to be (or was on the cusp of being) an accepted connotation of the word *gramatica*. A little more than a century after Gerard, in his treatise *On Vernacular Eloquence* (*De vulgari eloquentia*), Dante, too, used the Latin *gramatica* to refer to Latin and, in general, any learned tongue used as an instrument of study and culture (explicitly opposed, in this case, to the vernacular). Dante gave examples of other learned languages that functioned in the same way: Greek "and others."[14]

This, to my knowledge, is the closest that either Arabic or Latin came to producing a term meaning a generic "cosmopolitan language." Both languages possessed words that designated the *spoken tongues* as a class of languages. The Arabic *ʿāmmiyya* and the Latin *vulgaris* referred to vernacular languages in general: those languages that could not be fixed in writing but existed only as ephemeral modulations of sound; languages that were bound by no formal grammar. And the great literary languages had expressions that they used to designate *themselves* as formal, literary tongues, proper names that indicated broadly defined cultural as well as linguistic categories: terms like *lisān al-ʿarab* or *lingua Latina*. But before the late Middle Ages, neither Arabic nor Latin generated a widely used generic term for the cosmopolitan languages. Arabic and Latin, it seems, did not need a word to designate this category of language because each saw these qualities as proper to itself alone. Gerard's and Dante's use of the Latin *gramatica* to refer to the learned tongue as a generic category suggests that during the late Middle Ages, the Latin language had begun to develop self-awareness, learning to see itself as one of *a class* of learned languages, opposed to those tongues that exist only in the mouths of speakers and parallel to other formal languages of culture. But Latin itself would atrophy during the centuries of early modernity. The noun *gramatica* (more familiar to modern eyes in the classical spelling, *grammatica*) and its Romance and Germanic cognates came to refer first to philological study (typically of Latin and Greek literatures) and then to the grammatical rules common to all languages, spoken or written. The Latin *grammatica* lost the meaning that Gerard and Dante sought to attribute to it, and it was no longer used to refer to the transregional and transhistorical megalanguages in general.

The opening gambit of this book is that one can balance Arabic and Latin as comparanda without losing the granularity that can be gained only through detailed reading of individual texts. I am not a linguist, and my aim is not to write a Big History of language. Rather, I study the behaviors of cosmopolitan languages and think in particular about how they differ from that curious linguistic construction, the modern European national language. Compared to the cosmopolitan languages, the national languages of modern Europe are microtongues. They are linguistic singularities, wedded to a sliver of time and space. They come to life in the incubator of the baby's mouth and are mastered, first, outside of the classroom. They are bound to the standard of spoken practice in a specific time and place, so that the regional accent is often perceived as a curiosity, a linguistic impediment, or an aberration.[15] The rise of these languages at the end of the Middle Ages, their acceptance during the centuries of modernity as the appropriate linguistic media of literary and cultural life, is one of the most extraordinary chapters in modern literary history. Petrarch did not know it, but he stood at the brink of the abyss. In fact, his poetic practice—that sliver of lyric poetry he wrote in his ephemeral, unsystematic, slight, errant vernacular, Latin's homely little sister—would serve as a linguistic and literary model that would help to standardize literary practice in the languages of early modern Europe. *Après moi*—as Petrarch most emphatically would *not* have said—*le déluge*.

∴

Petrarch's return to the vernacular poetry at the end of his life seems an extraordinary decision on the part of a man who had himself reshaped Latin to serve as a vibrant and responsive vessel of thought. Petrarch is recognized as the chief architect of the renaissance of Latin that gave rise, during the fifteenth century, to the Italian humanist embrace of Latin as consummate literary vehicle. Yet at the end of his life, with the great Latin works behind him, Petrarch set his hired copyist to work on the fair copy of the *Rerum vulgarium fragmenta* (the *Vernacular Fragments*, as he called it; we know it as the *Canzoniere*). After the demanding work schedule ran the copyist ragged and he left Petrarch's employ, the poet himself took up the work of writing out the manuscript. We possess that partial autograph copy of the *Canzoniere*, and we know that it was among the last things that Petrarch worked on. Why, given his heavy investment in Latinity, did he come back to the Italian poetry for the long-dead Laura at the end of his own life? It's hard to know how to read Petrarch's late work, given the contours of his career and given in particular what we know about his devotion to Latin. Perhaps the late turn to vernacular poetry marks a crisis of faith in Latinity, Petrarch's anxiety that the future belonged to the vernacular clamor that had emerged in recent years in the works of men like Dante and his dear friend Boccaccio.

Or perhaps the *late* poetry is precisely that: *late style*, expressed not only in the urgent voice and fragmentary quality of the poetry but also in its linguistic tissue. I am thinking of Theodor Adorno's understanding of late style, which Adorno analyzed in particular in the late works of Beethoven.

In a brief, provocative essay, Adorno characterized Beethoven's late works as "ravaged. Devoid of sweetness, bitter and spiny, they do not surrender themselves to mere delectation."[16] The late works lack the harmony and elegance of the works of youth and middle age. Rather than float free of formula and convention, they pile up conventionalisms, as if shoring up a seawall against the approach of storms gathering just beyond the horizon. Nor does Adorno see any grandeur of spirit in this urgent repetition of slogans and half-remembered phrases:

> The power of subjectivity in the late works of art is the irascible gesture with which it takes leave of the works themselves. It breaks their bonds, not in order to express itself, but in order, expressionless, to cast off the appearance of art. Of the works themselves it leaves only fragments behind, and communicates itself, like a cipher, only through the blank spaces from which it has disengaged itself.[17]

Rather than show us a sweet, sweeping landscape—as the works of youth and maturity do—late works illuminate glimpses of a flinty terrain that are harsh, startling, at times flaring into beauty, but without the measured harmony and balance of the early and mature works. "In the history of art," Adorno's essay concludes, "late works are the catastrophes."[18]

Petrarch let go of Latin at the end of his life and turned toward Italian, treating it at once as an old, familiar plaything—a tool balanced perfectly to the shape of his hand—and as a new, untried instrument. In the certain knowledge that these would be the last works he wrote, Petrarch *played*. The spirit of his late inventions has proved all but impossible for subsequent generations of readers to resist. Fluent and lyrical, obsessive yet delicately calibrated, the late lyric is the Petrarch we know—not the balanced periodic sentences of the early and middle work, written in the language in which the nomad writer invested the energy and vision of his youth and maturity, Latin.

What are these late poems, after all, but catastrophes? The flinty crags upon which the rock of Petrarch's thought crashes, splinters, and swirls; compulsive and repetitive, fixedly addressing all that Petrarch has lost and no longer regrets, the late lyric is nothing more (or less) than the *late work* of Latin. In Latin, Petrarch composed (roughly) 720,000 words of prose and poetry. In Italian, he wrote approximately 68,700 words. Of Petrarch's total literary production, 91.3 percent was written in Latin and some 8.7 percent in Italian.[19] Once Petrarch's Latin exhausted itself—after he exhumed and renewed the Latin works of his distant masters, once he said what he needed to say—his Latin circled and recircled in order to tramp itself a bed, curled in upon itself, and went to sleep. Then Petrarch's Italian lyric began to sing: in Adorno's words, "like a cipher," "through the blank spaces" left by the retreat of Latinity. Adorno's adjectives don't describe Petrarch's late style perfectly; the Italian lyric is not "bitter and spiny." Yet neither is it written for "mere delectation." The Italian lyric—written after the monument of Latin has collapsed under its own weight—devotes itself with hypnotic intensity to forgetting Latinity. Petrarch's *Canzoniere*, viewed as an event in the linguistic biography of its author, is catastrophe.

In this book, I aim to rewind the newsreel. I look past the seductive Italian lyric, to capture the allure of the language that Petrarch used to win the poet's laurel and the power of the language that allowed Bashshār ibn Burd to secure the patronage of both an Umayyad caliph and his Abbasid successor. This story may seem on the surface counterintuitive. The attraction of Petrarch's Italian is all but impossible to dispel, and Bashshār's classical Arabic has already spun into entropy. Yet it bears repeating that the linguistic choices that these men made—Petrarch's elevation of Latin, Bashshār's cultivation of Arabic—incommensurate though they are in so much, are identical in certain fundamental features. Both Petrarch as Latin stylist and Bashshār as Arabic poet chose languages other than their mother tongues as literary medium. But in so doing, they did not destabilize themselves as authors; rather, the cosmopolitan language became the stage on which they performed. The vernacular will do in the intimacy of the bedroom, for murmured exchanges between two who share a mother tongue. In the vernacular Petrarch wooed his Laura, and (we can presume) Bashshār communicated with his family (to his beloved, ʿAbda, he wrote in polished if somewhat randy Arabic). For a literary conversation capable of spanning centuries and continents, however, one needs a language with heft and reach: a language with a communicative power that lifts it above the register of chatter and scuttlebutt, above the cacophony of the quotidian. The poet uses the cosmopolitan language to entice, to defend, to assault. With his superior knowledge of the imperial language, a poet may stare down the haughty court of France or the awesome caliph: a cat may, after all, look at a king. The refusal and erasure of the mother tongue becomes (to paraphrase Ernest Renan's oft-quoted line[20]) a scar at first accepted, then forgotten by the man of letters.

[PART TWO]

∵

Space, Place, and the Cosmopolitan Language

[CHAPTER 4]

Territory / Frontiers / Routes

> Of the thousand millions of human beings that are said to constitute the population of the entire globe, there are—socially, morally, and perhaps even physically considered—but two distinct and broadly marked races, viz., the wanderers and the settlers—the vagabond and the citizen—the nomadic and the civilized tribes. . . . To each civilized tribe there is generally a wandering horde attached; such wandering hordes have frequently a different language from the more civilized portion of the community, and that adopted with the intent of concealing their designs and exploits from them.
>
> HENRY MAYHEW, *London Labour and the London Poor*[1]

What is the place of the cosmopolitan language? Under the influence of the national language model, moderns find it difficult to resist the association of language with territory. In this chapter, I propose a different strategy for locating language, drawing on a range of models used to analyze space, place, territory, and the pathways of human migration. I move from a wholly abstract, theoretical discussion of the interactions between space and sovereignty into more concrete treatments of territoriality in the work of political scientists and geographers. From there, I return to the medieval Mediterranean and the circuits of Mediterranean trade, as described in the classic scholarship on premodern Mediterranean history. Finally, I discuss a figure with both contemporary relevance and an ancient pedigree: the nomad. In the present context, the nomad stands in for the writer not situated territorially, who traveled—or whose writings traveled—from place to place, thanks to the superterritorial reach of the cosmopolitan language. The model that can account for the territorial situation of the cosmopolitan language in the Mediterranean basin and beyond must describe the complex and shifting investments that linked language to territory even before the emergence of vernacular cultures. But it must give precedence to the networks traced by the literary languages that gave voice to writers and linked speakers to each other on the paths followed by travelers and texts in the premodern Mediterranean.

We start with the most abstract term of analysis in the geographer's tool kit: *space*. In *A Thousand Plateaus*, Gilles Deleuze and Félix Guattari describe two distinct modes of organization that characterize space: actors may experience it and interact with it as either "smooth" or "striated." In smooth space, one negotiates a series of ephemeral networked relations with other actors or with the landscape itself. Striation functions by demarcating space and, inevitably, hierarchizing it: the image is one of vertical pillars, symmetrical and regular, receding to the horizon and calibrating the actor's understanding and use of space.[2] Here, I am using territorial metaphors to describe the distinction between smooth and striated. However, it is difficult to visualize Deleuze and Guattari's two categories embodied in an actual landscape. Smoothness and striation are abstractions, rather than topographic descriptors; even in the abstract, they do not exist in isolation but rather in degrees. Yet the categories are suggestive of distinct qualities of interaction between human beings and their environment, or between the built environment and the landscape, or between language and territory. Striated space might be rendered using the columns of a fascist post office, an architecture that projects sovereignty over territory and over networks of communication, throughout the fascist nation and empire. A warren of city slums (a rookery, as they were called in nineteenth-century London) might provide an example of smooth space, devoid of the monumental landmarks that help to orient passage through and out of cacophonous, labyrinthine urban dystopia.

I literalize Deleuze and Guattari's analytic categories in order to give force to my topic: the physical location of language.[3] The ideology of the nation-state created bold swaths of striation across the map of Europe. It territorialized language, proposing that the place of one's birth should dictate the language one uses for both daily life and literature. Here, the image is clear. Territory is saturated with language, like the brightly colored political maps of the primary-school classroom: red for French, stretching from border to border of the hexagon; green for German and Germany; and so on. In some cases, a change of address might bring with it a change of language: Assia Djebar and Amin Maalouf write in French, Pap Khouma and Amara Lakhous in Italian, Emine Sevgi Özdamar and Feridun Zaimoglu in German because of their place of residence. The decision to write in the language of one's adopted home may be presented as *prise de position*. Yet in modern Europe, language choice is dictated in the first instance by territory, which acts as sorting mechanism, determining what language one uses as an instrument of culture. Language shares territorial sovereignty with the state itself, possessing dominion throughout the territory of the nation.

Before territory is understood as territory—before it becomes a *place* invested with human meaning—it is inert and abstract: it is mere *space*. Geographers use these two homely English words, *place* and *space*, as terms of art. For geographers, generally, space is an abstract term. Space is a blank canvas: the precondition of what geographers study, terrain not invested with human meaning. Place is constituted by the coordinates of human affection, human understanding, human reason, and social behaviors, a location that has meaning for a human community.[4] At the end of this chapter, I will return to the distinction between place and space and argue that—while the vernacular is the obvious language of *place*—the cosmopolitan language alone can articulate *space*. An author is able to conceive of and address a global human community only thanks to the range and the discipline of the Alexandrian languages, which make it their objective to convert the space of the planet as a whole to place.

In recent years, the English language has learned to use the word *world* as verb. Scholars speak of *worlding* the local, that is, understanding the global context in which local histories unfold. On the one hand, my discussion in this chapter attempts to *world* the cosmopolitan language by creating a conceptual tool kit for understanding the ambit of individual cosmopolitan languages from a comparative and global perspective. On the other, I aim to point out how Arabic or Latin might *language* the world: how a mere language, the communicative instrument of a discrete human community, acquires the ambition, the range, and the chutzpah to write a world into being.

∴

Modern states propose a robust relationship between territorial space and political sovereignty: they grant territorial sovereignty to the authorities of the state. But geographers and political scientists have identified a new and contrary relation between territory and sovereignty emerging in the late twentieth and the twenty-first century. A variety of factors—weak or failed modernization; a radical increase in the mobility of human beings, information, diseases, physical artifacts, and commodities; and more—blur the brightly colored boundaries of the familiar map linking sovereignty to territory. This process generates a net increase in articulations of (competing or cooperating) zones of sovereignty, such that terrain comes to be inhabited by multiple expressions of sovereignty. Rather than a world without borders, we inhabit a world in which discrete jurisdictions proliferate in any given space. Thinking of the crowded megacities of the developing world, never successfully reached by the social services of a strong, centralized state, and of underdeveloped rural regions in Afghanistan, postwar Iraq, or even the American heartland, scholars identify a multitude of sovereign entities capable of supplying the goods and services upon which human society depends. The image is one of territory so hyperstriated as to approach what Deleuze and Guattari termed *smooth space*, in which nomadic actors with no sentimental or legal attachment to a single patch of ground interact selectively with multiple competitive or cooperating networks of sovereignty. Images like the "Twitter Tongues" map of London, which represents the languages of tweets posted in London during the course of a single summer, give vivid image to the complexity of *linguistic* pluralism in particular in a given territory.[5]

The phrase *new medievalism* has come to be used in recent years by both political scientists and geographers to describe this configuration of weak, multiple, networked sovereignty. The term was coined in the 1970s, when political scientist Hedley Bull used it to describe the "overlapping authority and multiple loyalty" that characterize a terrain in which weak central state institutions allow nonstate actors to emerge, in order to provide the services once associated with governmental agencies.[6] Defining the "new medievalism" of the political scientists, Susan Strange writes, "The state is coming to share authority in economy and society with other entities."[7] Political geographers in turn adopted the term in order to characterize the networked sovereign actors operating in any given territory in the contemporary world. Transnational migration, globalization, and the global movement of information in particular have trivialized the boundaries between states. "Given the changing meaning of territorial boundaries," writes Mathias Albert, "reference is frequently made to a 'new medievalism,' an overlapping of various authorities on the same territory."[8] Stuart Elden uses "new medievalism" to characterize a world "where boundaries are overrun and sovereignty plural and overlapping."[9] Multiple configurations of sovereignty might operate in any given territory. It is tempting to describe the relation between them as competitive, but that's only part of the picture. Frequently, plural sovereign actors work in formal or informal collaboration, supplementing each other by delivering goods and services that a centralized state is no longer (or never was) able to supply.

The new medievalism of the political scientists and the political geographers picks out commonalities between the Middle Ages and the twenty-first century in order to isolate what was distinct about the architecture of modern Western state formations, and, in the case of the geographers in particular, to show how the aims and ideologies of the nation-state were reflected in their notion of territoriality. The modern nation-states projected clearly delineated territorial boundaries—an explicit, fully articulated example of striated space instantiated in territory.[10] The bureaucratic paraphernalia of the modern border—the military checkpoints, the customs and immigration forms, the bilingual signage—may be understood as the solemn (at times pompous) anointment of a territorial articulation of sovereignty. The apparatus of the border implies that within these boundaries, only one sovereign authority is recognized: the government of the nation-state itself. In contrast, if we look at the new medievalism or the old—at the twenty-first-century metropolis or the premodern empire—we find much more granularity and much less cohesion. Scholarship on articulations of sovereignty in the premodern world argues that "one of the essential features of the medieval European landscape was its lack of cohesion and unity; its discontinuity and disordered character. . . . The quest for homogeneous realms in the medieval world is an attempt doomed to fail, due to the lack of internal coherence in medieval polities."[11] In the premodern world, political sovereignty was geographically discontinuous, with respect to both the internal discontinuity of structures of political authority and the soft delineation of external boundaries.

To illustrate the *internal* complexity of the premodern terrain, one could point to the merchant colonies in cities like Venice, Tunis, Constantinople, or Tana, occupied by representatives of foreign trading partners.[12] At sea, ships were manned by multiethnic and multilingual crews, plagued by pirates from all the ports of the Mediterranean, and legislated by multiple jurisdictional codes.[13] In medieval Islamic cities, the presence of sizeable Jewish and Christian populations gave rise to legal pluralism and legal forum-shopping, as litigants sought the jurisdiction most favorable to their case.[14] The porous internal boundaries of *linguistic* sovereignty in particular were generated and sustained by bureaucrats, merchants, and the military—the agents of empire—along with the circulation of traveling scholars, poets and musicians, and texts, and they cut through the cosmopolitan metropolis itself: the heart of empire, recognized by literary historians as an engine of premodern literary production. Linguistic "frontiers" might divide one neighborhood from another and one street from another within the cities that functioned as hubs of empire. Distinct communities used distinct textual languages, and one presumes (although medieval records say little about microlinguistic actualities) had their own spoken tongue too, the jargon of their quarter, the register of the market and of neighborhood gossip.[15] Rising above the fractal fray, cosmopolitan languages compensated for linguistic discontinuities, negotiated between vernaculars, and mapped the discontinuous terrain—including the linguistic ruptures—of empire.[16]

The *external* frontiers of empire were zonal rather than linear, and they functioned as zones of conflict and convergence in variable degrees.[17] Premodern frontiers were not necessarily no-man's-land between states like the border zones and green lines of the modern world. Rather, they were often busy thoroughfares marked by heavy traffic. We might think of them not as boundaries but more accurately as transit zones. Indeed, some of the key vocabulary used to designate the frontiers between distinct zones of political sovereignty originally signified not boundaries but a cleavage that ruptured a boundary. *Limes* in Latin, *thaghr* in Arabic, and *kleisoûra* in Byzantine Greek each first meant a narrow opening that breached a dividing line of one kind or another, and then acquired a broader lexical range referring to the frontier or boundary itself. The Latin word *limes* referred first to the access path between fields known in English as a *balk*; then "*a boundary, limit* between two fields or estates, consisting of a stone or a balk" or in general "*a boundary, limit*." *Kleisoûra*, in Byzantine Greek, meant "*gorge*; *pass* between two mountains"; then, like the Latin *clausura*, it came to refer to the fortifications that secured access points, like gorges or mountain passes. Arabic *thaghr* referred first to the front teeth; then to "any gap, opening, interstice, or open intervening space, in a mountain, or in the bottom of a valley, or in a road along which people pass." Finally, it signified a "frontier-way of access to a country . . . the part of a country from which the invasion of the enemy is feared; so that it is like a gap in a wall . . . a place from, or through, which one fears the enemy's coming, in a mountain or fortress; the frontier of a hostile country."[18] In the popular imagination, we think of the Great Wall of China as an enduring symbol of the territorial boundaries between nations. Thomas Barfield showed that the wall functioned as a dividing line between polities but also as a zone of intensified contact between polities, acting as both a barrier and a magnet for the nomadic tribes to the north.[19] The widespread urban myth that the Great Wall is visible even from the moon seems to date to an English work written in 1754: long before the age of space travel, but at the dawn of the era of modern nationalisms.[20]

Of course, empires—although they were fractured by internal frontiers, although their external frontiers were sometimes ill defined—did manage to sustain sophisticated networks of material, intellectual, and literary culture. What held empires together, enabling the communication of details of state across great distances, was the roads and the sea-lanes that allowed merchants and intellectuals (as well as corsairs, highwaymen, and slavers) to pass from one metropolitan center to another. In the scholarship, these routes emerge as the defining characteristic of the premodern Mediterranean in particular. Braudel follows Lucien Febvre in asserting that "the Mediterranean is the sum of its routes"; and a footnote to the English translation of *The Mediterranean and the Mediterranean World* tells us that Braudel took the French name of the chapter in which this comment appears—"Routes et villes, villes et routes"—from Febvre's response, when Braudel first showed him these pages in draft.[21] John Wansbrough's *Lingua Franca in the Mediterranean* uses the term *orbits* to refer to the constant circulation of ships, sailors, commodities, and linguistic matter through the Mediterranean basin. Following Peregrine Horden and Nicholas Purcell, whose synthetic work has breathed new life into Mediterranean studies, the noun *connectivity*—referring in the first instance to the mercantile networks that linked port to port and shore to shore—has become the single most important term of art in scholarship on the premodern Mediterranean.[22]

Of this short bookshelf of Mediterranean scholarship, Wansbrough's *Lingua Franca in the Mediterranean* is the least accessible, thanks both to Wansbrough's challenging rhetorical style and to the fact that, in this book in particular, he regularly ranges through millennia of linguistic history in a single paragraph. Yet the work is a crucial point of reference for the history of language (and hence of literature and literary transmission in particular) in the Mediterranean. Wansbrough's first, decisive intervention is to repurpose the term *lingua franca*: for him it refers not only to the contact language of trade in the early modern Mediterranean but more broadly to the portfolio of linguistic and proto- or pseudolinguistic strategies used in order to move people and products through the Mediterranean basin.[23] He posits the existence of a *typological continuum* in chancery practice in particular, of a sort that might support the circular orbits of Mediterranean trade and travel through the centuries.[24] The word *orbit* describes the format of Mediterranean trade: people, ships, commodities, resources leave a port; ideally, people and ships return with new commodities in stowage.[25] The voyage inevitably transforms them. Value is added (or subtracted) as people, goods, and resources move from one shore to the other. Artifacts may take on new significance in a new market; resources (wheat, cotton, lapis lazuli, ivory) remain unchanged but may be differently purposed and differently priced. People, the languages they speak, the stories they tell, and the songs they sing suffer a sea change.[26] Wansbrough's *orbits* designate at once movement; the circular nature of that movement, from one shore to another and back again; and the duration of the circular movement of trade over millennia of human history.

Although he does not draw the connection explicitly, Wansbrough's *lingua franca* supplies the linguistic dimension of Braudel's *longue durée*: he conceptualizes a linguistic register that might support trans-Mediterranean trade for as long as humans have possessed the technology to cross the Mediterranean. Furthermore, although he does not use the terminology himself, his formulation of the concept of orbits seems indebted to complex systems theory. In this passage, he addresses the complexity of Mediterranean orbits of trade. But the metaphor he uses to elucidate this point, in true Wansbroughian style, may only add to the difficulty: his talk of variable conductors and voltage gaps evokes imprecise yet urgent memories of the moldering science fair projects of youth, an electromagnetic madeleine.

> The question is thus *location of orbits,* in the sense both of geographical route and channel of cultural dominance. Like their electrical paradigm, these circuits would be susceptible to variable conductors (resistance), voltage gaps (collapse), and inconsistent amperage (motivation). The model is one in which feedback, both positive and negative, is the norm, and fresh input always liable to adjustment, diminution or oblivion. A version of the imagery was employed by Braudel who, in his description of the "greater Mediterranean," wrote of the configurations of a "magnetic field" fluctuating with the ebb and flow of forces seasonal, mechanical, and spiritual.[27]

Here Wansbrough prepares the ground for a history of the cycles of human migration and trade "in which all the evidence combines across time and space, to give us a history in slow motion from which permanent values can be detected."[28]

Perhaps if he had used the less visceral but (today) more familiar vocabulary of complex systems theory, his ideas would be more readily accessible. For his topic is, in essence, the systems of Mediterranean circulation: the *entanglement* of Italian and Arabic accounting practices, for instance (Wansbrough published brilliant essays on the contracts drawn up between Italians and Arabs, drawing on archival research conducted in Italy); the *recursion,* or feedback loops, that may vitiate circuits of trade or linguistic practice—or, in ideal conditions, may lead to stylistic breakthroughs; the *entropy* that results when a system relies upon flawed practices or products; the balance between *competition* and *cooperation* that Wansbrough characterizes, in the passage just quoted, as "motivation." Wansbrough brought the linguistic turn to bear on the circulation of people and objects through the Mediterranean. Like Ludwig Bertalanffy, the father of systems theory, Wansbrough proposed that the scholar must view entities (the term of art for the phenomena and objects studied by systems theory scientists) not in isolation but rather *holistically*:

> In the past centuries, science tried to explain phenomena by reducing them to an interplay of elementary units which could be investigated independently of each other. In contemporary modern science, we find in all fields conceptions of what is rather vaguely termed "wholeness."[29]

It is difficult to imagine a more valid model for creating a holistic account of the strategies used to support Mediterranean circulation than complex systems theory. But Wansbrough had no interest in popularizing his material or in watering down his erudition in order to reach a wide audience. *Lingua Franca in the Mediterranean* remains an underutilized source for scholars of the premodern Mediterranean.

The circulation of people, texts, and ideas on the routes that led between the far-flung cities of empire played a generative role in the constitution of the megalanguages of the Mediterranean—from Arabic and Latin to the homely lingua franca (see chapter 12). Sea-lanes and roads brought these languages into being and sustained them through the long centuries; and the transregional cosmopolitan languages, not the regionally specific mother tongues, were the lifeblood of literary life in the premodern Mediterranean.[30] It's hard to overemphasize this point, in part because it feels so awkward to a modern European sensibility. Cosmopolitan languages are not the linguistic register of hearth and home. They are, rather, koines honed by communicative negotiations between speakers whose mother tongues are mutually incomprehensible. Languages like Latin, Greek, and Persian were transregional and transhistorical megalanguages, and they got that way thanks to the travelers and the traveling texts that carried them between metropolitan centers (and between linguistically incommensurate quarters within metropolitan centers). Recent scholarship suggests that even the Arabic language was formed in contact between travelers and sedentary populations. Sentiment teaches that Arabic was the proud possession of the nomadic tribes, spoken around the fire, carried from one encampment to the next but not adulterated by contact with the languages of sedentary peoples. It seems more likely, however, on the basis of recent comparative linguistic studies, that the language took shape on the ancient trade routes that threaded through the Arabian Peninsula, to start upon its career as a world language following its apotheosis in the Qur'an.[31]

The cosmopolitan language was not instantiated in territory. Rather, it lived in the mouths of individual speakers, language workers who were as a rule multilingual—they used the local tongues of daily life in the home and the marketplace—and moved nomad-like through territory. And it lived in the texts that moved physically with people between regions and metaphorically between languages via translation. Or, more precisely, the subject of the cosmopolitan language (be it the speaker or the text) negotiates a contingent, constantly changing relationship with territory: he or it, the writer or the text, is defined by motion. "The life of the nomad," Deleuze and Guattari write, "is the intermezzo."[32] Each territorial point that the nomad crosses (each *place*, as the geographers would term it) exists only as point of departure for the next, a resting place where he pauses—if only for the caesura between footfalls—to remember (the textual or lived past; the abandoned encampment of the beloved) and prepare for departure toward the next goal. He experiences territory as a constantly recalibrated progress toward a constantly renegotiated destination. Territory is not elided in the literary history of the cosmopolitan languages. It remains potentially present; it can be (and frequently is) deployed as literary image. But the nomad does not have a necessary, primary relationship with a delineated territory. He understands affiliation first in other terms: with a tribe—perhaps a confessional community, perhaps a cultural public, but certainly a community identified first and foremost with language and constituted first and foremost in language.

The nomad's journey (in and with language) points relentlessly forward. Or, perhaps, it noodles in circles. Maybe it's simplest to say that the nomad's journey is nonlinear. As a result, the literary text—the language worker's *work*—is not collocated in territory. It creates a platform elevated above terrain upon which the nomad as writer can perform. In recent scholarship that addresses the impact of increasing human mobility on our sense of territory, geographers place judicious emphasis on *routes*, not *roots*. They do so in order to underscore the importance of connectivity between discrete places and in order to push back against the nostalgia for an imagined authenticity of place.[33] In a moving passage from her book *For Space*, Doreen Massey reflects on her regular journeys home—she traveled several times a year from London, the metropole where she lived, to the North, where she grew up. In the book, she recalls the landmarks visible from the train, gradual changes in the landscape, the familiar homely foods that her mother prepared for her on her return. She concludes this vignette by countering the notion of *place*—caught in the aspic of memory, in the amber glow of nostalgia—with the reality that geography moves: it is articulated by agents that traverse space: the people, animals, vegetation and objects whose perceptions, actions, and memories generate geography. Even the looks, sounds, and smells of Massey's south Lancashire intersect with global trends, thanks to the steep increase in human mobility in late twentieth-century Europe.

> You can't hold places still. What you *can* do is meet up with others, catch up with where another's history has got to "now," but where that "now" (more rigorously, that "here and now," that *hic et nunc*) is itself constituted by nothing more than—precisely—that meeting-up (again).[34]

Massey's definition of "place" acknowledges the network of connections that bind it to other places, relying on the mobility of people, things, information, ideas, and so on.

> Instead then, of thinking of places as areas with boundaries around, they can be imagined as articulated moments in networks of social relations and understandings, but where a large proportion of those relations, experiences and understandings are constructed on a far larger scale than what we happen to define for that moment as the place itself, whether that be a street, or a region or even a continent. And this in turn allows a sense of place which is extroverted, which includes a consciousness of its links with the wider world, which integrates in a positive way the global and the local.[35]

I am arguing that the cosmopolitan language of literary life is the tongue in which Massey's "meeting-up (again)" occurs. It is the dialect of extroversion. We feel a sentimental attachment to the bounded territorial languages of memory, of perceived authenticity, of *home*. Yet—as Marcel Proust and Thomas Wolfe told us, each in his own mother tongue—"home" is a place that we can't visit. The cosmopolitan language is artificially constructed, bound by its rules and paradigms, in order to create wormholes between the moments, far-flung in space and time, when language workers "meet up." It is the conveyance that allows us to travel to distant lands (and to the country of the past). This is the promiscuity that makes the *cosmopolitan* language alluring, that grants the mistress tongue her appeal.

The Alexandrian language of literary life is a language of mobility, one that holds itself at a remove from "place" in order to colonize "space." While Massey's "extroverted sense of place" aims (mostly) to celebrate the networks that link places to each other, she also acknowledges the position of those on whom mobility is imposed—by strife at home (no sepia-toned nostalgia for the places left behind for these travelers) or by economic necessity. The movement of capital isolates others, born to less desirable locales, in backwater places.[36] In a similar way, the cosmopolitan languages of premodern literary life demanded a significant investment on the part of language workers: the intellectual discipline required to acquire a new dialect in which to express their thoughts. They punished those who failed to make the grade, those who could not achieve proficiency and eloquence by the standards set by literary history. Some language workers, inevitably, policed the boundaries of their beloved language and trolled those who they believed did not belong. The would-be writer who could not perform was sentenced to irrelevance, or perhaps left to tell vernacular tales after dark to the women of the household. In late medieval Europe, the vernacular revolution promised to loosen the tongues of those who preferred not to spend the precious hours of their youth memorizing paradigms: it promised to put the instrument of literacy into the hands of all. If the mother tongue is the language of literature, then any man jack may be a writer! Over time, the familiarization of this paradigm encouraged distrust of those who used a learned language in order, presumably, to hide their work from others: in the quote that stands as epigraph to this chapter, the wandering hordes who used a cant "adopted with the intent of concealing their designs and exploits" from more honest segments of society.

I do not disavow the shadow cast by the cosmopolitan language, its disenfranchisement of a large swath of the population. In the two chapters that follow, I will tell the stories of two men whose relationship with language was fraught, complicated in particular by the rupture of exile. Cast out of *place*—the homeland to which they were bound by a dense network of affiliation, the bonds of family and intimacy, the smells and tastes of home, and the familiar melody of the mother tongue—they struggled to take language with them. On the road, they negotiated a new relationship with language. The stories told about these two men are stories of the road, redolent with the creak and lurch of the wagons and the smell and snort of the beasts that carried them out of town. Both Dante and Sībawayhi were nomads (in the sense that I use the word in this book) who negotiated a relationship with language in movement between places. Both of them created a literary language that made its home in *space*.

While I do not aim to idealize the cosmopolitan language in this book or to deny that it is a harsh taskmistress, I do wish to honor the labors of the nomads who took it on and used it as literary instrument. Rather than write from (a single) *place*, rather than write in the tongue of place, the nomad writes *space*. *Routes* web out from his text; and *roots* feather into the ground—only to be dislodged as he moves on. The Alexandrian language may talk about "place," in the sense in which the geographers use the word, but with a crooked grin, knowing that *place* is ephemeral but language is not. Language sheltered both Dante and Sībawayhi. It put a starry sky above their books and a tapestry of cultivated soil beneath them, and it furnished a tent to shelter them from wind and rain. Perhaps most important in political terms, the Alexandrian language does not limit its sphere of influence to imperial capitals. It traverses territory and expands through the provinces, allowing provincial elites to speak back to the metropole. In one of the most elegant formulations of the geographers' definition of *space* and *place*, Yi-Fu Tuan writes: "If we think of space as that which allows movement, then place is pause; each pause in movement makes it possible for location to be transformed into place."[37] The cosmopolitan language is the lingua franca of space, the language in which networked places may speak to each other. It wins the nomad's affection by liberating her from the narrow confines of home.

[CHAPTER 5]

Tracks

Latin and Italian in Italy, early fourteenth century

> Inter alias ergo scientias gramatica potest dici semita vel viculus sive kiasso tum quia stricta est cum a nullius alterius scientie ingressu in eam latitudinem aliquam habeat tum quia ducit ad viam idest ad logicam.[1]
>
> Among the other sciences, *gramatica* can be called a *path* or *lane* or *alleyway*—because it is narrow, receiving breadth from no other science that opens onto it; and because it leads to the high road, which is logic.

The Italian Peninsula displays the classic Mediterranean geography. The Alps divide the peninsula from the continent and the Apennines run down its center like a jagged backbone. Seas wash its shores: the Ligurian to the northwest, the Tyrrhenian to the west, the Ionian to the southeast, and the Adriatic to the east. In this geography, cities isolated from each other by rugged terrain may easily come to see themselves as independent, linked by frequently traveled roadways but culturally and linguistically distinct. During the lifetime of Dante (1265–1321), inhabitants of the cities of the northern half of the peninsula—where he spent his life—spoke mutually incomprehensible dialects. Medievalists know little about how premodern people communicated, in a quotidian and casual context, before the spread of standardized and formalized languages. Medieval witnesses themselves don't tell us how they bartered for bread, or negotiated passage on a ship, or shared gossip with people from other towns. In Italy, premodern linguistic divisions were particularly stark and particularly enduring. Even at the time of national unification, in 1861, only 12 to 59 percent of the male population and 3 to 44 percent of the female population understood the national language, standard Italian (there were substantial regional differences in literacy rates).[2] Most knew only the dialect of their own locale.

But Italians did have a linguistic instrument that compensated for the confusion of the vernacular tongues. Latin, they felt, was their peculiar possession. The Italian language preserved more of the ruins of Latinity, lexically and grammatically speaking, than did other Romance languages: more than Spanish, for instance, which had absorbed lexical matter from the Arabs who occupied the Iberian Peninsula during the Middle Ages; more than French, which had acquired Germanic etymons from the Franks and Celtic ones from the Gauls. Because of the special relationship between Latin and Italian, competition between the Alexandrian language and the vernacular was a particularly drawn-out affair in Italy. I have chosen to focus on this period of rivalry in my discussion of Latinity in part because in broad outlines it is familiar, even to nonspecialists. The age of the great late medieval writers—Petrarch, the lyric poet and ardent lover of Latin; Boccaccio, the writer of narratives; and Dante, the author of the great epic, whom I will discuss in this chapter—cast a long shadow on the literary history of western Europe in general. Each wrote in both languages, Latin and Italian. The battle between Latin and its particular friend, Italian, is an important episode in the internecine competition of vernacular and cosmopolitan language in Europe: Jacob wrestling with the angel, Romulus battling Remus, or the ouroboros consuming itself, the story has much to teach us about linguistic succession.

The topic of this chapter is Dante's language choice—or, more precisely, what he *wrote* about language choice, which (as we will see) differed from his actual practice. Dante lived at a watershed moment. In the northern part of the Italian Peninsula, during the late thirteenth and the early fourteenth century, Italian men of letters who chose not to write in Latin had vernacular options. They might use Occitan or Franco-Italian, languages with some literary pedigree. If they wrote in Italian, a new literary language without panregional norms, it would inevitably take on a local coloring. In order to think through the vernacular landscape of Italy, Dante first wrote a sober, sturdily Aristotelian treatise (in Latin, of course) on the dialects of the Italians. Then—when he set out to write the epic for which the Latin treatise was a preamble—he chose a third path. He elected to write neither in Latin nor in the idealized Italian that he had imagined in the treatise but in a vernacular based on his own native Tuscan. Why did Dante dream one language, only to write in another? What inspired him finally to accept a register based on his mother tongue as the linguistic model for the masterpiece? In this chapter I aim to understand how Dante's language of *place* came to function for him as a language of *space*.

∴

Dante is a key figure in any account of the fates of Latin on the Italian Peninsula for two reasons. First, he wrote the epic that showed what an Italian vernacular could do as literary medium. Second, Dante wrote a treatise debating and defending his choice of the vernacular over his *gramatica*. In 1301, due to his outspoken political commitments and against the backdrop of the complex and ruthless political struggles of the age, Dante was exiled from his native city, Florence. During the early years of his exile, he began a work that studied the difficulties posed by the linguistic complexity of the Italian Peninsula: *De vulgari eloquentia*, or *On Vernacular Eloquence*. At this time—Dante composed the treatise probably in late 1304—Italy was still centuries away from linguistic unification. It seems likely that he already had a plan for the epic that he would undertake to write in the final decade of his life. He tells us in the closing words of his previous vernacular work—the *Vita nova*, or *New Life*, a songbook collecting his lyric poetry with explanatory autobiographical prose—that he will "write no more about this blessed lady [Beatrice, to whom the lyric poetry is dedicated] until I am able to speak of her in a manner more worthy."[3] Perhaps he had another work in mind, or perhaps he already envisioned the *Commedia*. He may have intended to write the sequel in Latin, or he may have known from the beginning that he would write it in the vernacular. Whatever his initial intentions, the *Commedia* was the tribute he wrote.[4] Dante wrote *De vulgari eloquentia* in the years immediately following his exile in search of the language that could do justice to Beatrice. Because it was a scientific work, Dante wrote it in Latin.

The problem that Dante studies in *De vulgari eloquentia* can be simply stated: How should the poet find or forge a language that can serve as a literary medium, one that is as close to the skin as the mother tongue, yet that a public might understand throughout Italy? He recognizes that other literary languages have emerged already on the model he imagines: the *langue d'oc*, or Occitan, and the *langue d'oïl*, or French (the use of the affirmative particle to identify Romance languages seems to be Dante's innovation).[5] But he, of course, is interested only in the fates of the *lingua di sì*, Italian. What he seeks is a variety of the vernacular, or *vulgaris*—a language that infants learn from the first voices they hear, as he defines it in the opening lines of the treatise[6]—that might have the geographical and historical scope of the formal languages of literature, a linguistic category that he calls *gramatica*. He seeks this eloquent vernacular throughout the Italian Peninsula—examining and rejecting the Italian dialects, in their near-infinite variety—and in the end is obliged to admit that it does not exist in any one place but rather is immanent in the disparate voices of the Italians, leaving traces of itself throughout all of Italy. In the closing lines of book I of *De vulgari eloquentia*, Dante tells us that this language has yet to be discovered (or invented; the verb he uses, *invenire*, can convey either meaning). This, he declares, is the topic of his study in the present treatise.[7]

De vulgari eloquentia is a rich and original discussion of language theory, and this brief synopsis cannot do it justice. My aim is not to work through the intricacies of Dante's argument but rather to identify in it a series of provocations relevant to my topic: the intersection between territory and literary language. The treatise is straightforward, yet it poses two difficulties for the literary scholar. In the first place, Dante left it unfinished. He completed book I and started a second book, on Italian poetry, which ends mid-thought. He intended, apparently, a third book on Italian prose and (in his most capacious vision of the treatise) additional books on more popular forms of literary Italian and even on the vanishing point of linguistic complexity: the microlanguages and subdialects spoken in individual households.[8] But he put the treatise aside, presumably because the portion he had completed already served his purpose. It did not circulate during his lifetime and was little read during the two centuries that followed his death (the modern editor of *De vulgari eloquentia*, Pier Vincenzo Mengaldo, calls the manuscript tradition *poverissima*, "extremely poor").[9] Only three fourteenth-century manuscripts of the treatise are known to scholars. The work dropped out of sight during the fifteenth century: no manuscripts or printed editions were made at all during the quattrocento and the treatise was not discussed. Thanks to the humanists' elevation of Latin as literary language, the questions surrounding the constitution of literary Italian posed by Dante seemed uninteresting and were sidelined during the fifteenth century. *De vulgari eloquentia* attracted a flurry of interest at the beginning of the sixteenth century—Machiavelli was among the (small) number of scholars who studied and discussed it[10]—when Italian intellectuals engaged in a heated debate regarding the questions that Dante had addressed in his treatise two centuries earlier: the ideal form of literary Italian. Scholars came to recognize the treatise as a crucial component of Dante's oeuvre only during the twentieth century.

The flimsy reception history of the treatise illustrates the difficulty of assessing its importance to the development of Dante's thought. But *De vulgari eloquentia* poses a second, thornier problem for the literary historian. In this treatise, Dante circumambulates the problems of language that faced Italian poets at the turn of the fourteenth century. The years following his exile in 1301 were extraordinarily tumultuous for Dante. He wandered restlessly and incessantly. He described himself, during these years, as "a boat without sail and without rudder."[11] Early in this period, likely in 1304, he worked on both *De vulgari eloquentia* and the *Convivio*.[12] In both treatises, Dante makes a number of arguments concerning the language of literature. In the *Convivio*, writing in the vernacular, he asserts the "nobility, power, and beauty" of Latin (although he ultimately champions the vernacular as literary medium).[13] In *De vulgari eloquentia* (as we will see), writing in Latin, he attributes the same qualities to the vernacular. The language debates commenced in these unfinished treatises would be superseded by the *Commedia*, the crowning glory of his literary career, one that consumed all his attention during the later years of his life—a work that he wrote not in the superregional vernacular he dreamed of inventing (or discovering) in *De vulgari eloquentia* but rather in Tuscan Italian.

Language is his topic in *De vulgari eloquentia*. But Dante does not study the language problem as a grammarian would. He is a poet, and he observes and studies language like a poet: he quotes poetry; he transcribes strange phrases he has overheard in different parts of Italy; he mocks unbeautiful Italian and appreciates the gracious Italian of the poets. Modern scholars have used the medieval grammatical tradition to explicate Dante's argument in *De vulgari eloquentia*, and it seems evident that Dante knows this philosophical tradition, although he is not motivated by the same concerns as the philosophers. He uses the tools of Aristotelian logic to argue for the possibility of inventing a perfect form of Italian, a koine that might be distilled by studying and combining the achievements of the poets of Italy. It seems that Dante abandons this language and turns back to an elevated version of Tuscan Italian—a literary riff on the language of hearth and home—only once it is no longer the language of his daily life, when it has become for him something like a cosmopolitan language. The sublime language that Dante would forge in the *Commedia* speaks with its own authority and deflects attention from the statements on language in the unfinished treatise. Yet this elevated Tuscan would be brought into being by rupture and shaped by the contingency of exile. Only when Dante became a nomad, living in an uprooted vernacular, which he invested with the gravitas of a *gramatica*; only then did he have the tongue he needed to write the great work.

In *De vulgari eloquentia*, Dante makes his affection for his native tongue palpably evident, despite his disparaging comments about the Tuscan dialect.[14] Early in the treatise he drops the bombshell that has justly attracted the attention of readers through the centuries when he defines first the vernacular, next the *gramatica* (or Latin), then states that "the nobler of the two is the vernacular." The statement—made in Dante's elegant, flowing Latin—startles the reader:

> Harum quoque duarum nobilior est vulgaris: tum quia prima fuit humano generi usitata; tum quia totus orbis ipsa perfruitur, licet in diversas

> prolationes et vocabula sit divisa; tum quia naturalis est nobis, cum illa potius artificialis existat.[15]

> The nobler of the two is the vernacular: because it was the first used by human kind; because it is used by everyone throughout the whole globe of the world, though it is divided into distinct forms of speech and vocabulary; and because it is natural to us, while the other [i.e., *gramatica*] is, rather, artificial.

Dante makes no secret of his attachment to his vernacular, and he challenges us to recognize its superiority. Yet at the same time, he acknowledges the instability of the vernacular. The urgency of *De vulgari eloquentia* arises from his search—and then the failure of his search—for a form of Italian that possesses the immediacy and the beauty of the vernacular but also the scope and the stability of the *gramatica*. He specifies in the same opening passage of the treatise that the use of the *gramatica* is out of reach of most speakers: "Few acquire the language as habitus [*ad habitum . . . perveniunt*], since we are trained in it and taught it only through long and assiduous pursuit."[16] Here, he uses the technical term *habitus*—the Latin equivalent of the Greek *hexis*—to refer to a habitual behavior that is acquired through study and sustained through practice.

Later in the treatise, Dante acknowledges the admirable qualities of the *gramatica*, qualities that his perfected vernacular should emulate: it is "a certain inalterable [language], of identical locution in diverse times and locations."[17] This language, Dante tells us, was created to battle the instability and variance of the spoken tongues, to erect a lasting home for thought.[18] Throughout the treatise (as Justin Steinberg has shown in a persuasive reading of the text) Dante scorns the merely *municipal* reach of the spoken tongues, each used as the literary medium for an individual city, none with the pan-Italian scope he desires.[19] He envies the *gramatica* for its ability to transcend the local, despite his impatience with its formality and artificiality, and he frames a theory of the vernacular that possesses both the easy familiarity of the local languages and the range and stability of the *gramatica*.

The fact of formality is crucial to Dante's understanding of the *gramatica* and is constitutive of the ideal vernacular he seeks, which must have a grammatical exoskeleton that can be abstracted, analytically described, and taught. More central to my concerns here, however, is Dante's representation of the ideal vernacular as (returning to the theoretical framework outlined in the previous chapter) not a language of *place* but rather of *space*. Dante has fun at the expense of the regional dialects of the Italian Peninsula, which he depicts as idiosyncratic and risible, a mockery of what language could and should be. At the heart of his description of the linguistic usage of the Italians, Dante divides the peninsula into sections and then, one by one, describes and derides their manner of speaking.[20] The Romans speak "not a vernacular, but a squalid jargon," and Dante quotes an example: "Messure, quanto dici?" ("Sir, what do you say?").[21] Those of Aquila don't speak so much as blurt; the Pugliesi are "base babblers" ("turpiter barbarizant"); and as for Tuscany, Dante satisfies himself by repeating phrases that one might hear from the mouths of the locals, which he seems to feel are sufficient to damn them.[22] He is, as Justin Steinberg points out, exasperated with languages "confined to and by place."[23] His ideal Italian vernacular, the one he yearns for but does not find, would not be located in the mountains or the valleys or along the coastlines of Italy. It would have the appearance of a language that belongs "to every city of Italy and yet to none."[24] It would be the Italian dialect of space, not place.

The image that Dante coins in order to characterize this linguistic ideal is the most famous in the treatise: the eloquent vernacular is like the panther, which "leaves its scent everywhere yet is sighted nowhere."[25] In a tidy piece of rhetoric that leaves a fair few questions unanswered, Dante argues that each and every thing that can be measured is measured (and, implicitly, judged) against that which is the simplest thing of its sort.[26] The common law is used to judge the actions of people. And "we, when we act as Italians, have certain very simple standards of manners and behavior *and speech* [*simplicissima signa et morum et habituum et locutionis*] by which we are weighed and measured as Italians": standards "proper to no one Italian city, but common to all."[27] Of course, the language alluded to in this sentence does not yet exist as such. It is the register of a literary culture just coming into being: as Marianne Shapiro explains, "the new language is to generate public consciousness, which will exist through it just as society can be said to exist through language."[28] More precisely, Dante suggests that it is to be sought in the poetry of Cino da Pistoia, Dante himself, and the illustrious poets of Italy in general.[29] He intends to expound the language in some detail in book II—which would be left unfinished. It seems fair to say that the language exists *in potentia*, not yet codified (as the *gramatica* has been and must be), but able to be extrapolated from the writings that Dante holds up as embodying the best that could be achieved in the lofty vernacular.

Dante's nomad vernacular is engineered to remove or reduce the striation generated by the territorial variations in the Italian dialects (to return to Deleuze and Guattari's metaphor; see chapter 4), to create a smooth linguistic medium that poets from any part of the peninsula can use effectively. Is his ideal vernacular simply a micro-*gramatica*, that is, a language whose rules might be abstracted and formalized; a megalanguage in microcosm that, once codified, might acquire transregional and transhistorical valence? Would his project, if carried through, result simply in the scaling down of Latin through carving up the territory of Latinity into Romance subregions: the *pays d'oc*, the *país d'oïl*, the *terra di sì*, and so on? We can't know the answer to these questions, since the world we live in is not Dante's—or rather, is not the world of *De vulgari eloquentia*. The Italian vernacular that emerged in the early modern centuries (like most European vernaculars; German is the obvious exception) would privilege one regional variety, promoting the Florentine dialect (with inevitable adjustments and additions) as standard for literary composition.[30] Dante's *Commedia* made a crucial contribution to the elevation of Florentine Italian as a model for Italian poets. Despite what he argued in his treatise on language, in the *Commedia*, Dante—as Boccaccio did in the *Decameron* and as Petrarch did in the *Rerum vulgarium fragmenta*—spoke in the voice of a Florentine. Between them, the *Tre corone* (or Three Crowns) of Italian literature, with the serene authority of genius, granted transregional sovereignty to a language of place. Imitated by authors throughout the peninsula, their Tuscan Italian would form the model for the national language as it emerged after Italian unification five centuries later.

In a memorable passage from *De vulgari eloquentia*, Dante hints at the linguistic direction he would follow, despite the conclusion to which his argument builds in the treatise itself. The lines soar from vituperation to exilic sobriety and are instantly recognizable as Dantean in their grandeur and somber beauty. He is discussing the Edenic ur-language; he mentions an Italian village that has the temerity and ludicrous self-regard to propose its own dialect as identical to that spoken by the first man. He then shifts into autobiographical mode, describing his own status as (linguistic) exile:

> Nos autem, cui mundus est patria velut piscibus equor, quanquam Sarnum biberimus ante dentes et Florentiam adeo diligamus ut, quia dileximus, exilium patiamur iniuste, rationi magis quam sensui spatulas nostri iudicii podiamus. Et quamvis ad voluptatem nostram sive nostre sensualitatis quietem in terris amenior locus quam Florentia non existat, revolventes et poetarum et aliorum scriptorum volumina quibus mundus universaliter et membratim describitur, ratiocinantesque in nobis situationes varias mundi locorum et eorum habitudinem ad utrunque polum et circulum equatorem, multas esse perpendimus firmiterque censemus et magis nobiles et magis delitiosas et regiones et urbes quam Tusciam et Florentiam, unde sumus oriundus et civis, et plerasque nationes et gentes delectabiliori atque utiliori sermone uti quam Latinos.[31]

> To me, however, the whole world is a homeland, like the sea to fish—though I drank from the Arno before cutting my teeth, and love Florence so much that, because I loved her, I suffer exile unjustly—and I will weight the balance of my judgment more with reason than with sentiment. And although for my own enjoyment (or rather for the satisfaction of my own desire), there is no more agreeable place on earth than Florence, yet when I turn the pages of the volumes of poets and other writers, by whom the world is described as a whole and in its constituent parts, and when I reflect inwardly on the various locations of places in the world, and their relations to the two poles and the circle at the equator, I am convinced, and firmly maintain, that there are many regions and cities more noble and more delightful than Tuscany and Florence, where I was born and of which I am a citizen, and many nations and peoples who speak a more elegant and practical language than do the Italians.[32]

Dante is an exile, like the other poets whom he champions in *De vulgari eloquentia*: in Justin Steinberg's wonderful phrase, "postmunicipal poets and recent exiles."[33] In these lines, Dante uses a familiar expression to refer to his exile: "the wide world is my fatherland [*patria*]." But he makes it clear that his first loyalty and his deepest attachment are to Florence, on whose waters he was weaned. Here, and in the measured, magnificent Italian verses on exile from the *Commedia* (*Paradiso* 17:43–93), we find in its most potent, beautiful and alluring form the image of language as birthright—and the loss of the language of childhood as a form of exile, a rupture that time cannot heal. *De vulgari eloquentia* (which Marianne Shapiro termed Dante's "book of exile"[34]) tracks Dante as he moves restlessly along the routes that link valley to coast as they wind through mountains along the Italian Peninsula, in a failed search for a language that might serve him as poet. But the arc of Dante's lifework (the end of which is revealed only in the great book of his exile, the *Commedia*) tells another, contradictory story: a return to the language of youth and the exaltation of that primordial tongue as the medium of sublime poetry. Here, in this passage from Dante's abandoned linguistic manifesto, is both a blueprint for the construction of the placeless language of the poets—the nomadic cosmopolitan language—and a key to understanding the passionate attachment to the language that bears an intimate link to place and to time, the language of childhood and of home, that grants the national language system of Europe its lasting power.

In the lines quoted as epigraph to this chapter, taken from a Florentine manuscript containing sermons by Remigio dei Girolami, an anonymous author describes the *gramatica*—the formal language of literary life; for Remigio and his contemporaries, Latin—as a footpath or winding alleyway that leads away from the language of youth and of home, toward the broad avenues of learning and thence to the wide open spaces of the life of the mind. Remigio's is not a household name, even for medievalists. For forty years, he served as lector at Santa Maria Novella (best known to students of Italian literature as the place where the young men and women of Giovanni Boccaccio's *brigata* encountered each other in the introduction to the *Decameron*). He was a man of considerable erudition; his time as lector coincided with Dante's years in Florence, and it's possible that he introduced Dante to Aristotelian thought.[35] It is chiefly because of his association with Dante that Remigio has been remembered at all by scholars. In the passage cited above, the scribe who collected Remigio's sermons begins a lecture on the *trivium* by defining the *gramatica* as a path that leads the student away from the here and now and into the wide world of letters.[36] The metaphor conveys clearly the expressive power of the cosmopolitan language—while acknowledging its distance from the language of youth, of hearth and home.

Any written language acts as an estranging filter that both alienates and clarifies thought. Information science has given us new vocabulary to describe the dream of a common language: we aim for a register that allows *lossless transmission*, that we can use to represent emotional and intellectual truths with accuracy while remaining comprehensible to a wide public. It was the genius of Europe's national language system to connect the language of literature to the mother tongue, and hence to youth. In cosmopolitan language systems, the poet typically learns the language of literature as an adult. More precisely, the acquisition of the formal language marks the passage from childhood to maturity. The national language system, in contrast, locates the first steps toward literary training in childhood. No process of refinement (some would call it alienation) distances the writer from her or his childhood; no new language must be learned in order to reach the threshold of literacy. The adoption of the mother tongue as language of literature guarantees cultural literacy to all and allows cultural phenomena that use nonstandard or informal linguistic registers, like children's literature and rap music, to flourish alongside formal literature.

The dream of a gapless language—a tongue that gives full expression to our thoughts, that conveys image and emotion with the urgency they merit—doubtless inspires poets. In the *Vita nova*, his compilation of his youthful love poetry for Beatrice, Dante explains that "the first who began to write Italian as vernacular poet was moved [to do so] because he wanted to make his words understood by his lady, who was not comfortable understanding Latin verses."[37] Who would deny the pleasures of this register? What language possesses the attractions to lure us away from the mother tongue? When do the virtual companions of literary history become more important to the writer than the visceral companionship of the lady who can understand him only when he talks plain?

In the twenty-first century, it is no longer reasonable to conceptualize an aspiration language that denies access to women. But the broad appeal of the vernacular register transcends the historically specific terms in which Dante celebrated it. Dante turned back to his own Florentine Italian, presumably, for practical reasons (because he needed to write the masterpiece, and he realized that one life was too short to create first the language and then the epic), but only after abandoning his dream of another kind of literary invention, a formal language common to all Italians. Both *De vulgari eloquentia* and the *Convivio* were pushed aside when Dante found the voice he sought in a polished and refined form of the Tuscan Italian he had learned as a boy, peppered with the occasional Latinism or regionalism from other parts of northern Italy. Is it coincidence that he discovered (or settled for) this language only when he came to accept that Tuscan Italian would never again be the linguistic register of his daily life? Only when he lost access to his own language as spoken tongue of daily life—when it became idiolect, the possession of the solitary exile—did he accept it as a literary instrument worthy of the epic. It seems that the rupture of exile allowed (or compelled) him to embrace the language: only when Dante lived in his language, when it sheltered him like the tent of the tribal nomad, did it become a viable literary instrument.

We have become so used to the notion of the mother tongue as ideal cultural medium (and to the idea of Tuscan Italian as foundation for the literary language of the modern Italian nation) that it takes an effort to reconstruct the literary terrain of Dante's era. Dante presumed a primary plurilingualism. Indeed, medieval men and women would have found it impossible to be monolingual in the modern sense, to use a single language in all times and places and for all purposes. The linguistic register of everyday life differed from the register used as record for affairs of moment: literacy, in many instances, meant literacy *in Latin*, the language that was able to preserve and pass on thought from one age to the next and from one town to the next.[38] *De vulgari eloquentia* is, among other things, the record of an innovative, daring, and failed attempt to imagine the perfect vernacular, one that would have the requisite beauty to create the epic and that (like the *gramatica*) might function as a "form of speech inalterable and self-identical in diverse times and places."[39] This pumped-up vernacular would be able to push aside the vernacular competitors—Occitan and Franco-Italian, the Romance weeds in Italian soil—as well as local dialects, in order to establish itself as *inalterable and self-identical* language of literature across mountain ranges and from coast to coast of the peninsula.

A generation after Dante, Francesco Petrarch (1304–1374) undertook a diametrically opposed project: the resuscitation of Latin. He absorbed the structures of classical Latin. He studied ancient textual traditions and restored works thought lost. In so doing, he created a new, pristine Latin on the ruins of the old. Neither Dante nor Petrarch, of course, could have known that Latinity's moment in the sun had passed. Dante, who advocated the use of the vernacular for literary composition, used Latin until the end of his life in more formal settings (in letters and treatises). Petrarch was a vernacular dabbler: he used Latin for almost all of his works; yet he returned at the very end of his life to the vernacular poetry (see chapter 3). Boccaccio (1313–1375), like Dante and Petrarch, wrote in both Italian and Latin and found a use for both languages as distinct, equally necessary literary media. The three men lived through a moment of transition in the linguistic life of Italy. Indeed, as literary craftsmen and as scholars they had a profound influence on the direction that the literary life of Italy would follow. But only Dante produced an extended account of his reasons for the linguistic choices he made. It seems flippant but not entirely inaccurate to call *De vulgari eloquentia* a journaling exercise: the immortal poet, pen in hand and *almost* ready to write the masterpiece, thinking out loud about his craft. In the treatise, he describes a vision of an Italian *language of space*, a variety of Italian capable of speaking on a grand geographical scale, throughout the peninsula. But in the *Commedia* the poet speaks in a *language of place*: a Tuscan Italian that compels Italians throughout the peninsula to come to it, to become Tuscan in order to be Italian poets (in this quality it emulates the cosmopolitan language). Dante, as craftsman of a national language dispensation that he could scarcely imagine, realized that the mother tongue was itself plastic enough to be refashioned as sublimely expressive literary medium and capacious enough to live in.

In this book, I compare Latin to Arabic, but I have chosen two specific phases in the lives of the great languages as comparanda. In general, I focus on the moment in late medieval and early modern Italy when Latin and the Italian vernaculars entered the last stage of a zero-sum struggle for the hearts and souls of the Italians. I have chosen a much earlier moment in the history of Arabic to compare to this: the period of Abbasid consolidation, when Arab poets and grammarians formulated the rules and structure and created the canon of what is sometimes called today (with no great precision) *classical* Arabic. This choice—like the decision to focus on late medieval Italy—is inspired by the manifest interest of the Abbasid period. We seldom have the opportunity to watch the birth of a premodern literary language. But the Arabic language performs a number of maneuvers on the public stage early in its life. It appears in the Qur'an fully formed—indeed, miraculously expressive—yet larded with lexical and grammatical enigmas. Following the Arabic-Islamic expansion, Arabic must learn to articulate the mysteries of the Qur'an. It must explain itself to new populations, who use different textual and spoken languages. It must acquire new behaviors in order to function in its new roles as a bureaucratic language and to record the history of the Arabs. It must import a philosophical system as well as literary models from adjacent languages. Such concerns informed the work of self-study and explication undertaken by the Arab grammarians and translators during the Abbasid era.

But there are other motives as well behind my choice of chronotope. I focus on the Mediterranean because it is a place where cosmopolitan languages converge. But the Abbasid East, in a literary sense, behaves at moments like another Mediterranean. It brings together linguistic and literary communities separated into linguistic ghettos yet in constant communication with each other—like the communities of the Mediterranean described in the previous chapter. The languages at play include but are not limited to ancient Greek, Pahlavi (or old Persian), and Sanskrit (these three being the languages most frequently translated into Arabic in the Abbasid translation movement), Middle Persian, Syriac (a vehicular language called into play by Abbasid-era translators as well as a lingua sacra in the Abbasid East), and demotic Greek. In addition to this dynamic of linguistic complexity drawn into intense conversation, the Abbasid example gives balance to the family portrait I aim to create in this book. If in late medieval Italy we see a language nearing the end of its useful life, in the Abbasid East we find an Alexandrian language in its youth: curious, dynamic, and ready to step onto the global stage.

[CHAPTER 6]

Tribal Rugs

Arabic in Basra, eighth century

وَاللَّهُ جَعَلَ لَكُم مِّن بُيُوتِكُمْ سَكَنًا وَجَعَلَ لَكُم مِّن جُلُودِ الْأَنْعَامِ
بُيُوتًا تَسْتَخِفُّونَهَا يَوْمَ ظَعْنِكُمْ وَيَوْمَ إِقَامَتِكُمْ وَمِنْ أَصْوَافِهَا
وَأَوْبَارِهَا وَأَشْعَارِهَا أَثَاثًا وَمَتَاعًا إِلَىٰ حِينٍ

> And God has made for you, in your homes, a place of rest [or pause] and has made for you, from the hides of beasts, homes that you find light [to carry] on your day of travel and your day of encampment; and from their wool, fur, and hair, furnishing and enjoyment for a time.
>
> QUR'AN 16:80

Sometimes, screenwriters call it "burning down the house." In the first act, we meet the protagonist and learn about her world. In the second act, the protagonist turns a page and starts a new chapter of her life. She is pushed to try something new; she learns something about herself and understands that she is capable of more than she knew. To create a compelling first plot point—the beat that ends the first act and propels the audience into the second—the screenwriter might "burn down the house." When Luke Skywalker discovers that Imperial Stormtroopers have killed his family in *Star Wars* (1977), any disincentive he might have had to reinvent himself and fight the Galactic Empire is gone. Luke becomes the warrior-hero the moment requires because there is no way for him to move but forward, into his destiny.[1]

In the previous chapter and in this one, the house burns down more than once. Dante's exile gave him the exilic Tuscan Italian that became the linguistic register of the *Commedia*. In 1306, Dante humbled himself in a letter to the priors of Florence, hoping to win amnesty and the ability to return to the city. The Florentines were unmoved by his performance.[2] The Florentine government offered amnesty to some exiles in 1311, but Dante wasn't included among them because he had continued to criticize the politics of those in power in Florence and northern Italy in general.[3] Finally, in May 1315, the Florentines offered a mass amnesty, which made it possible for Dante to return to Florence. He refused the offer, saying that the conditions it set were humiliating to his conscience. Because of his refusal, the Florentines reaffirmed his death sentence and expanded it to include his sons.[4] If the screenwriter or the hand of God had burned down the house the first time—with the exile that sent Dante out of Florence—Dante himself set the second fire, the one that ensured that he would die an exile. Maybe, like King John II, he had grown accustomed to living in the languages of others (see chapter 3). As we will see in this chapter, the biography of another nomad, Sībawayhi—in the telegraphic details that have come down to us—is bookended by two cataclysmic scenes. The first brought an end to the first act of his life and made Sībawayhi into the hero that his age required. The purpose of the second crisis, as we will learn, is open to interpretation.

I have chosen to focus on Sībawayhi and Dante in this section because—despite the many differences between their lives and careers and the languages they served—both men, at a critical moment, were cast out of a charmed circle in which they lived and that supported their work. This expulsion turned each into a nomad (as I use the term in this book): a man who lives in his cosmopolitan language. Sībawayhi's and Dante's lives were separated by half a millennium and by around 4,000 kilometers. Sībawayhi was a grammarian; Dante was a poet. There are stark differences as well between the languages they loved. Sībawayhi's mistress tongue was a language in its youth, one that still had scant written resources on which he might draw as reference to analyze its behaviors. Dante served two mistresses: although he wrote the masterpiece in the vernacular, Dante also knew and used and, in his own way, loved the Alexandrian language of his people, Latin. As we saw in the last chapter, Dante was able to imagine the great epic in the vernacular only when he left behind Tuscany, the region where his vernacular was spoken. Yet despite the many differences between their lives and careers, Sībawayhi's and Dante's experiences illustrate the rupture that separates old self from new, for the writer who chooses to live in the cosmopolitan language. It is a language in which the nomad can make a home. But for some, possibly for most, this happens only when other linguistic options have been removed.

∴

Sībawayhi was a Persian and a convert both to Islam and to the Arabic language. As a young man (the date and place of his birth are not known) he moved to Basra, probably in about 145 AH[5]/762 CE, to pursue his studies.

He may have intended to study law, or he may have planned to study one of the corpora on which the law is based, *āthār*.[6] This noun comes from a lexical root that connotes movement and, more precisely, the traces that movement leaves behind: "footsteps" or "tracks." The noun *athar* denotes first vestiges, a track or trace or remnant: a footprint, for instance; the ruins of a house, or the ruined monuments of antiquity. In the plural, *āthār*, it can refer to signposts set up to designate a route. In the study of the era of revelation, scholars used this noun to name the hadith, the sayings and tales of the Prophet, which they analyzed in order to understand virtuous and upright behavior.

One of the few stories preserved about Sībawayhi's life—undoubtedly largely apocryphal, yet probably containing an element of truth—relates an anecdote about how the father of Arabic grammar, the author of the monumental study that brought the grammatical science of the Arabs into being, chose his field of research. Historians know little about the beginnings of Sībawayhi's career because it was interrupted early and abruptly. Whatever the object of his studies, they were cut short when during a lesson he was asked to read aloud a sentence in Arabic, and he misconstrued a noun. His teacher chose to make an example of him. Following his public humiliation, according to the tales told about him, he chose to seek a field of study in which he would not be accused of making mistakes.[7] He made the decision to study Arabic grammar—like the study of law and the traditions of the Prophet, a nascent field at this time, a scant century and a half after the death of Muhammad. He would devote the rest of his life to grammatical research and would leave behind the first grammatical analysis of the Arabic language: once gathered and organized by his companion al-Akhfash, the text became a massive volume (almost a thousand pages in modern editions) known simply as *al-Kitāb* (*The Book*) of Sībawayhi.

Already, this sketchy biography is rich with interpretive possibility. The young Persian student is humiliated by the Brahmins of the language, the trolls who guard the citadel of Arabic from outsiders: this story will become a familiar scene in the life of the Alexandrian language. Sībawayhi leaves behind the first schoolroom, the pale faces of teacher and students gathered around paler manuscript pages. The screenwriter has burned down the house. Looking back at the smoking embers, the vestiges of the plans that brought him to Basra, the young protagonist makes a vow that propels him into act 2. But why does he make this promise to himself in particular: to seek a field of knowledge in which he can be confident that he will not place a foot wrong? Grammar, language, human speech is a field that all but guarantees mistakes. It's virtually impossible to avoid error in language. If this were a screenplay, the director might send it back to the screenwriter.

The protagonist's oath is a transparent setup. Surely, the audience sees already where this story is going.

Thus, Sībawayhi—with no sense of foreshadowing, and with a renewed sense of purpose—sets out on the path that will occupy him for the rest of his career. At this point, Islamic culture is in its infancy. Revelation was delivered to the Arabs in the form of a book that had no linguistic antecedents. Although poetry and poetry competitions existed in pre-Islamic Arabia, no written literary tradition in the Arabic language predates the Qur'an. The only surviving written texts in Arabic recorded earlier than the Qur'an are inscriptions. The poetry of the pre-Islamic pagan Arabs remained a fluid corpus of oral poetry during Sībawayhi's life. It was not anthologized in its final, written form until the end of the second Islamic century, around the same time that Sībawayhi died. Islamic doctrine holds that the Prophet Muhammad did not perform miracles. The Qur'an offers only its own linguistic substance as miraculous. The eloquence of the book spoken through the mouth of the illiterate Prophet is the sole proof of the legitimacy of its message. Indeed, the linguistic tissue of the book is a marvel: at times dense, knotted, demanding assiduous study to unveil its meanings; at others flowing and clear; and, at moments, soaring and poetic (surah Yāsīn and the verse known as *āyatul-Kursī*, the "Throne Verse" [2:255], are two of the classic examples). But Sībawayhi lived before the doctrine of *i'jāz*—the inimitable linguistic miracle of the Qur'an—had been formulated and clearly articulated.[8] For him, the Qur'an represented revelation, but also the largest and most eloquent archive of Arabic available in written form. Most important for our story, during Sībawayhi's life, at the dawn of the Abbasid era, no one had yet undertaken to systematize the behaviors of the Arabic language. No grammar of Arabic existed to explain the linguistic revelation. Given the unique dynamic of early Islamic history—the rapid expansion of the Islamic polity, its incorporation of a large, linguistically diverse population—and given the centrality of the Qur'an to Islamic doctrine and ritual, this oversight had to be addressed earlier rather than later. Sībawayhi was the hero the moment demanded.

In the circumstances, Sībawayhi was forced to invent. He had neither a substantial corpus of written literary texts that he might study, in order to understand the behavior of the language, nor a set of technical terms and standards that he could use to analyze it. Sībawayhi drew chiefly on three sources for examples of Arabic usage: the Qur'an; the pagan poets, whose work circulated in oral form and likely in early written texts that did not survive; and the speech of the Bedouins. According to then-emergent Arabic language ideology, the language existed in its purest form in the mouths of the nomads. For this reason, Sībawayhi sought out and consulted those who spoke a form of the language not adulterated by sedentary life. Rooted life, civilization, urbanism: according to early Arabic language ideology, these are the enemies of linguistic purity. In order to understand the nature of the language in the wild, Sībawayhi—who lived in the city, Basra—had to track the language to the natural habitat of the nomads, or the closest he could come to it. He frequented the urban markets where the Bedouins came to hawk their wares. In conversation with them, he studied the behavior of the language. Often, in his grammar, he uses verbs of hearing to report his sources: "I heard a Bedouin say" or "We heard them say" or "A trusted source heard them say. . . ."[9] Thus, Sībawayhi supplemented a scanty written archive with the spoken words of the original Arabs, the Bedouins.

At this point, to be honest, the screenwriter has pushed aside the scholar. In truth, we know little about Sībawayhi's sources. This account—in which the first grammarian of Arabic studies the behavior of the language in conversation with "the nomadic Arabs," *al-ʿarab*, in their natural habitat—derives from Sībawayhi's book. Recently, however, scholars have pushed back against the ideological constructs inherent in this interpretation of the book. Kristen Brustad, in particular, has proposed that the consolidation of the grammatical data and the crystallization of Sībawayhi's book in the form in which we have it occurred during a subsequent generation. She suggests that non-Arab urban grammarians systematized Arabic in an effort to understand the language of emergent Islamic culture and wield it themselves. These same grammarians created the beats of Sībawayhi's biography in order to lend credence to the grammar. The confabs with the Bedouins at the urban markets of Basra, in this case, would be fictions, invented in keeping with the ideology that the grammarian must seek the purest form of the Arabic language on the tracks followed by nomads.[10] In the last analysis, we have no way of knowing the truth, given the absence of reliable contemporary records. Either version—whether the authorities on the behavior of the language are Bedouins or scholars, Arab or non-Arab—is a fiction. It may be either a beautiful fiction or an ugly one, depending on the screenwriter's decisions.

In part, too, the ambiguities of Sībawayhi's story have to do with the curious texture of the grammar he produced. Consider, for instance, the technical terminology that he formulated to describe the Arabic language. What tools does the grammarian use to analyze the behavior of language? In creating a grammar de novo, he may derive terminology from adjacent sciences, and scholars have sought the origins of Sībawayhi's grammatical terminology in the grammar or the logic of the Greeks or in late-antique grammatical works in Syriac, themselves derived from Greek grammar.[11]

However, Sībawayhi's terminology is not only original but somewhat perversely original. His grammatical categories, at times, draw upon metaphors of mysterious origin. The opening sentence of his grammar, for instance, divides words into three categories: *ism, fiʿl,* and *ḥarf.* The first word, *ism,* loosely correlates to the English *noun.* It means "name" and is frequently used with that meaning in the Qurʾan. In a grammatical context, as the lexicographers define it, it signifies a word that has meaning "outside of time": "unconnected with any of the three times [past, present and future]," as Lane's dictionary explains.[12] The semantic origin of the word is difficult to trace. Most Arabic words derive from a three-letter root, and generally it's easy to spot the definitional connection between the words derived from that root. The semantic root from which the lexicographers derive *ism* (s-m-w) means "to be high, elevated"; the connection between the root and the noun, in this case, is not self-evident. But that, as we will see, is a trifling complaint. *Fiʿl* comes from a root meaning "to do" or "to act." *Fiʿl* correlates well with the English word *verb,* or more broadly, again according to the lexicographers, "what denotes a meaning in itself together with any one of the three times [past, present, and future]."[13] But *ḥarf* is more mysterious. The noun signifies "the extremity, verge, border, margin, brink, brow, side, or edge" and might be used to name (quoting Lane's examples) the (sharp or abrupt) edge of a river, a ship, or a mountain.[14] From there it has a transferred meaning: it designates the *edge* of a word, that is, the letters of the alphabet. Already, the lexical range of the word has stretched far enough to demand a leap of faith, or at least of the imagination, from the nonnative speaker. Furthermore, because Sībawayhi's terminology is recursive—it may be used to discuss the attributes or behaviors of language at multiple scales—the word *ḥarf* may signify a single letter or a particle of speech. Particles, by this logic, derive their meaning neither outside of time nor together with time. They spring into meaning at the (sharp or abrupt) precipice of syntax.[15]

If this metaphor seems queasy, tottering at the brink of meaning, it is in good company. Although much of the grammatical terminology that Sībawayhi uses has been naturalized over the centuries, some of the words he adopts to talk about Arabic grammar have basic meanings that are difficult to connect with the specialized meanings he gives them. The noun used to designate vocalization of consonants, *ḥaraka,* means "motion, commotion, agitation." It is opposed to a word meaning "stillness, calm, peace," which denotes a consonant that lacks a following vowel: *sukūn.* A word from the same root appears in the Qurʾanic epigraph to this chapter; it means "a resting place" or "a place to pause." Agitation and inertia, the quick and the still, vocalized and unvocalized consonants: the metaphor, thus far, is busy but straightforward. But the words that Sībawayhi uses to name the vowels that might be attached to a consonant introduce an element of mystery. For the /a/ sound, "opening up," "conquering" (*fatḥ*), or "raising up, erecting" (*naṣb*). For /i/, "breaking, shattering" (*kasr*); "breaking, dragging" (*jarr*). For /u/, "embracing, joining together" (*ḍamm*) or—like the /a/, once again—"raising aloft" (*rafʿ*).[16] One gets the sense of a jostling crowd of vowels, lifting and breaking, embracing or dragging off their consonants, striving or subdued: a rabble more than an alphabet, phonology in riot.

Sībawayhi's *Kitāb* has puzzled Western scholars, who expect different metaphors—or, perhaps, just fewer of them—from technical descriptions of linguistic behaviors. Gérard Troupeau, who wrote a guide to the lexicon of the *Kitāb*, calls Sībawayhi's terminology "primitive." Another historian of the early Arabic grammatical tradition, Henri Fleisch, writes that the *Kitāb* has "poor style; the phrasing lacks the desired rigor and clarity."[17] More recently, Michael Carter has defended Sībawayhi's seminal work in Arabic linguistics as a bold and ambitious act of creation. As Carter points out, "It is in the nature of technical terms to be metaphors, and the *Kitab* abounds with them."[18] Carter argues that Sībawayhi saw the Arabic language as "a society of words," and he points out that much of Sībawayhi's terminology anthropomorphizes language. Lexical roots, for Sībawayhi, have "daughters" (the words derived from those roots). Particles have "sisters" (words that look similar and have a similar grammatical influence on adjacent phrases). Words may belong to a "community" or to a "tribe" of grammatically or morphologically similar words. Carter contends that Sībawayhi used the same cognitive structures as the jurists to describe and adjudicate the behaviors of this society of language. He drew upon legal categories to analyze linguistic behaviors and, especially, linguistic propriety.[19] Sībawayhi saw the science of grammar as an extension of ethics: like the jurists, he refers to correct (linguistic) behavior as virtuous—the word that Sībawayhi often uses is *ḥasan*, "good" or "beautiful." Incorrect language is "ugly" or "vicious," *qabīḥ*.[20]

From the teeming lexical chaos of the *Kitāb*, a simple story emerges. Grammar is ethics is aesthetics: language works or it doesn't; it may be virtuous or vicious, beautiful or ugly. In the opening articles of *al-Kitāb* (also known as *al-Risāla*, the *Report* or *Treatise*) Sībawayhi reviews some of the basic functions of Arabic grammar. In addition to the technical terminology described above, he rolls out sample nouns and verbs in relative abundance to illustrate the concepts he describes. The nouns are *man, horse, wall.* The simple verbs, denoting an action that has taken place: *he went*; *he heard*; *he stayed*; *he was praised*. The verbs describing actions not yet completed:

Go! Kill! Strike! Or: *he kills*; *he goes*; *he strikes*; *he is killed*; *he is beaten* (or *stricken*).[21] A muscular assortment of vocabulary—the sort that one would expect from Bedouins and their horses, who go or stay, kill or strike, praise and are praised. In article 3 of the *Risāla*, simple phrases are introduced: *Abdallah departs*; *I saw Abdallah depart*; *I passed Abdallah as he was departing*.[22] These grammatical examples are simple and straightforward, illustrating language at its most decorous. As the *Book* advances, the sample language becomes more abstruse and the descriptions more granular. Complex sentences and logically impossible statements appear, in order to put the language through its paces and to find the point where Arabic stops meaning. The Arabic language is a magnificent horse whose maneuvers Sībawayhi watches, admires, and describes. The correct is also the good is also the beautiful. When the language attempts something counterfactual, the horse rears, pixilates, and vanishes. This is an arena in which Sībawayhi cannot make a mistake.

Until the screenwriter chooses to burn the house down *again*. According to the stories told about Sībawayhi's life, after years of study and work on the *Kitāb*, another public humiliation brought his time in Basra to an end. In a formal debate regarding a fine point of grammar, Sībawayhi made a pronouncement concerning appropriate and correct Arabic usage. His opponent disputed his judgment, supporting his opinion by calling in a group of Bedouins—clearly enlisted ahead of time and possibly bribed as well—as witnesses. The Bedouins agreed with the opponent, and this tribunal found Sībawayhi guilty of grammatical wrongdoing. Shamed and discredited, Sībawayhi left Basra following this episode. The date and place of his death are unknown. It may be that he took his papers out of Basra with him and continued work on the *Kitāb*; some say that he died, heartbroken, soon after leaving Basra. In either case, after his death, Sībawayhi's notes were gathered, preserved, and taught as the authoritative resource on the Arabic language by another grammarian of his circle, al-Akhfash. Thus the *Kitāb Sībawayhi*—Sībawayhi's Book—was born.[23]

It is difficult for nonspecialists to understand how few resources were available to a student of the Arabic language at this point in its history. In the mid-eighth century, less than a century and a half after the death of the Prophet, the written sources regarding early Islamic history were still emergent. The pre-Islamic poetry, hadith (the traditions of the Prophet), the legal and exegetical traditions, all were in various stages of being systematized in robust oral traditions and recorded as written texts during these early centuries. Sībawayhi's work is known simply as the *Book* because it was the first extended prose work—other than the Qur᾿an—that circulated as book in Arabic. Curiously, the *Book* begins in the same way as that other book.

The Qur'an begins with the Bismillah, "*in the name* of God" (Qur'an 1:1). In its first article, Sībawayhi's *Book* too begins with the *name*—the *ism*, the noun: that which, like God, has meaning without reference to time. The *Kitāb Sībawayhi* begins *in the name* of the Arabic language:

بِسْمِ اللَّهِ الرَّحْمَٰنِ الرَّحِيمِ

In the **name** [***ism***] of God, the Compassionate the Merciful

فَالْكَلِمُ: اسْمٌ وَفِعْلٌ وَحَرْفٌ[24]

Words [i.e., the words of the Arabic language] are the **noun** [***ism***] and the verb [*fi'l*] and the particle [*ḥarf*]

Sībawayhi's departure from Basra—that second rejection and humiliation, cruel as it was—seems, from the perspective of the biography of the Arabic language, a narrative necessity. The cosmopolitan language had already moved out of the Arabian Peninsula with the Islamic expansions. It had been elevated to the status of an Alexandrian language—one that must be studied and learned—by non-Arab client populations, of which Sībawayhi himself was a representative. Sībawayhi sought out and consulted the Bedouins who were his native informants (again, according to narrative convention) in order to learn about its behaviors. Now, once the spark was nurtured in the urban center, Basra, the language had to set forth again, because Arabic (in its "purest" form: what is known to modern Arabs as *fuṣḥā* Arabic) is not a *settled* language. It is the linguistic register of travel between urban centers and metropoles, at home only on the road.

The success of the Arabic language during this early chapter of its history has fascinated scholars. In the course of a mere century or two, Arabic became a cosmopolitan language throughout an extensive empire. Data mining provides a strategy for visualizing the dazzlingly swift growth of Arabic, the geographic spread achieved in the blink of a historical eye. Arabist Maxim Romanov has culled the geographical markers from the *Ta'rīkh al-Islām* of al-Dhahabī, a history of Muslims from the earliest generations (ca. 660 CE) through 1300. The names of prominent Arabs from this period typically include a place-marker, or *nisba*, which indicates the place of origin or adopted home of a prominent man. Romanov used coding to extract and map the occurrence of these geographical markers. He produced an animation—six and a half centuries in forty-five seconds—that visualizes early Islamic history: the spread and growth of urban centers throughout the first Islamic centuries.[25] The prominence of the Arabian Peninsula in the earliest period is soon eclipsed by urban centers in the Levant, then in Syria and Iraq. Smaller regional centers emerge. Dots indicating new metropoles flicker and disappear. Soon an arc stretches from the Strait of Gibraltar in the west—al-Andalus to the north and the Maghrib to the south—to Iran and central Asia in the east: the capacious "home" of the Arabic language, encompassing big cities and small market towns and implicitly (they are invisible on Romanov's maps, but they must exist) the tracks that connect them.

In a book published in 1972, linguist Giovanni Garbini tells a similar story about the origins of Arabic. Garbini studies the emergence of Arabic by describing its entanglements with other Semitic languages, focusing precisely on the paths between urban settlements followed by merchants and transhumant nomads. In Garbini's account, Arabic emerged not from the Bedouin encampments of Arabia but rather on the trade routes used by merchants speaking dialects of Arabic and other Semitic languages. Traveling between various parts of the Arabian Peninsula and Syro-Palestine, these populations pooled in the urban centers. The business they transacted together obliged them to communicate with each other.[26] The result was a kind of convergent evolution, as originally disparate languages acquired vocabulary and grammatical habits from each other, learning to be mutually comprehensible. Garbini's argument shares a dynamic with John Wansbrough's account of lingua franca (and with Mediterranean studies in general; see chapter 4). The heroes of this tale are the common merchants, pilgrims, scholars, and nomads and the tracks that connect them, the constant movement that brings human beings into intermittent communion with each other over a period of centuries. The friction of repeated contact between languages generates a koine. A language is not *born* Semitic, with three-letter lexical roots, two temporal tenses or aspects, and *iʿrāb*, declensional endings that are not written because they take the form of short vowels. Rather, language *becomes* Semitic, acquiring structural and lexical habits in negotiation with other languages. Both shared lexica and linguistic behaviors, like two-aspect verbs or the derivation of semantic material from three-letter roots, are emergent, learned simultaneously by languages that intermittently share physical space. Garbini does not discuss Sībawayhi in his book on early Arabic and its relation to other Semitic languages, *Le lingue semitiche*. But his version of the story puts Sībawayhi in the cross hairs, precisely where he needs to be to study the language: in Basra, a market town, where merchants gather and words are traded like any other merchandise.

Because he sees language change as convergent rather than divergent, Garbini argues against the genealogical metaphor to represent language change over time.[27] In this chapter, I am describing not how languages change through time but rather how they exist in space. But I am, like Garbini (and like Sībawayhi), interested in curating metaphors. For that reason, here—to replace the family portrait so intimately connected with representations of language in the modern imagination—I offer a metaphor intended to capture how the cosmopolitan language interacts with territory: *The cosmopolitan language is a tribal rug.*

The rugs woven by nomads serve a number of functions.[28] They are aesthetic objects. Their vivid colors and repeated intricate designs make them a balm for the eye. Natural light brings them to life, and the colors change slightly as the observer moves and light strikes the fibers from different angles. The carpets also functioned, in the nomadic economy, as currency. Women wove them and lay them up as dowry. They advertised a woman's domestic competence and would play a utilitarian role, keeping her family warm and dry, once she married. They have meaning as well as linguistic objects—or, more precisely, as artifacts that communicate using a symbolic alphabet with only a notional connection to a spoken mother tongue. The patterns woven into them tell a story about tribe and family. The tribal rug serves a number of purposes at once: both functional and beautiful, it provides both meaning and shelter.

In American and European households these rugs are familiar objects—even homely ones, although we know that they come from far away. The nomadic tribes of central Asia wove the earliest known knotted carpets. The oldest surviving tribal carpet, known as the Pazyryk carpet, has been dated to the fifth century BCE. A number of characteristics distinguish the tribal carpet: the technique of knotting sheep's wool (or, in some cases, camel hair fibers) into a woolen or cotton warp and weft; the use of specific vegetable dyes to color the wool; and, of course, the designs. But their domestication in European households dates at least to the Renaissance. We know about their presence in Europe because they appear as backdrops in Renaissance paintings: by Antonello da Messina, by Lorenzo Lotto, especially by Hans Holbein.[29] Holbein in particular recreated tribal rugs in such voluptuous detail that it is possible to discern the motifs and patterns of the originals and even to guess at the knot count. Yet although the tribal rug is a familiar aesthetic object to a European and North American public, it is not legible to us. It speaks a language that was instantly recognizable to those who lived with it; what it talks about is home.

Or, rather, the tribal rug doesn't talk about home: it *is* home. This was its primary function: though the carpets were also made by sedentary urban dwellers (and marketed to the sedentary elite), those most closely associated with tribal rugs were nomads who had no fixed, permanent dwelling.

The nomads of central Asia moved between pasturelands that were productive at different times of the year, and where they stopped in the path of migration, they erected the tents that we call yurts. They lined the insides of their tents with carpets and kilims (woven rather than knotted carpets). They slept between carpets: on beds made of piled carpets, under rugs that kept them warm. They used carpets as doors and as dividers to create rooms within the tents. They stored their belongings in woven saddlebags that were essentially hanging kilims. The rugs filled the interior of the tents with color and with meaning. Those who understood the language of the rugs would see their identity and their history in the repeated colors and motifs beneath their feet, lining the walls, under their heads as they slept. The Christian polyglot, wanderer, and saint Cyril (whom we will meet in the next chapter), in the modern novelist Milorad Pavić's vivid portrait of him, said, "My home is where my rug is."[30]

This is the shape of a language one can covet: a language that one can hear and feel in one's mouth, that one can see and touch on the page, that one can even smell (if only virtually, as Dante "smelled" the path of the panther in *De vulgari eloquentia*; see chapter 5). Like the animal hides and rugs evoked in the Qur'anic verse quoted as epigraph to this chapter, the Alexandrian language serves as both shelter and aesthetic object. This language is not fixed territorially but rather provides a virtual location or situation for the subject, by virtue of the durable structure of its grammar and by virtue of its deep literary history. It is fluid and flexible, yet at the same time it provides a structure for thought: the warp and woof of grammar; the lexicon of symbolic representation. It creates a stage for those who speak, read, and write the language, but also for inanimate actors: the texts that carry the language through the wide world. Most delicate metaphorical displacement of all, it stands in the place of the mother tongue; in its haptic and mobile fiber, it substitutes for that place that we in English call, in the most homely word in our language, home.

The geographers (again) give us vocabulary that helps to describe the relationship between mobile subject and stationary terrain, and the role played by the cosmopolitan language in articulating that relationship. Yi-Fu Tuan writes that both space and time may be colonized by the nomadic subject. In either case, boundless space or time is interrupted by a *pause*:

> If we think of space as that which allows movement, then place is pause; each pause in movement makes it possible for location to be transformed into place.
>
> If time is conceived as flow or movement then place is pause.[31]

Pause, for Tuan, describes the interruption in a flow (either temporal or spatial) that allows for the creation of meaning: *pause* sculpts the undifferentiated mass of space or time into a form that communicates a meaning to the human mind. I am arguing that language is the technology that allows this operation to occur. Language articulates the transformation of "location" (or "time") into "place." The *cosmopolitan* language allows this to happen on a magnificent scale: the nomad writer pauses, transforms abstract space into place, then sends his text out on the tracks of human transience, creating a network of linked places that may span and connect continents. Tuan's pause—to connect the dots between Tuan and Sībawayhi and the Qurʾanic epigraph to this chapter, and to complete the metaphor—is the Arabic *sakan*: pause, and also a place of rest or comfort; home; the nomad's encampment; the site where meaning and beauty are made.

The cosmopolitan language domesticates the world. ("When space feels thoroughly familiar to us," Tuan writes, "it has become place."[32]) But, of course, it demands from its acolytes sacrifices in return. This is our reward for internalizing the paradigms, declensions, and sequences of tenses recorded and studied by grammarians like Sībawayhi. The language boosts the nomad writer out of the local and the quotidian, giving her an elevated stage on which to perform, connecting the local and the global. The cosmopolitan language is itself the nomad's home: a cognitive architecture that is logical, beautiful, and good, a structure that *means* in both an aesthetic and an ethical sense.

All the more cruel, for Sībawayhi, to have the rug pulled out from under him (pun intended): to realize that he had not, after all, found a field of study in which he could avoid error. Sībawayhi's idea that he could speak without putting a foot wrong suggests the placid faith he has in grammar. His use of logical strategies and legal terminology may reduplicate some of that desire for certainty. The biography was almost certainly constructed at a historical remove, as a teaching tale that illustrates an old truth. But what truth was it intended to teach? Perhaps the bland *mathos pathos*, "learning is suffering." In a darker mode, the biography might be seen as the language trolls' revenge, the moment when the Arab patriarchs of the language take it back from the non-Arab paramour. Like the autobiographical pilgrim whose travels in the next world we follow in Dante's *Commedia*, the Sībawayhi we encounter in the biographical stories told about him is both true and invented—and is all the more powerful for that. Indeed, that same biography may be (although it generally is not) read in a triumphal mode. Sībawayhi's second castigation precipitated his apotheosis. It sent him out from the metropolis to live with the nomads, to live in the language (and in the *Book* that captures the arcane and beautiful behaviors of the language). In this screenplay, in the last act of his life, Sībawayhi sets out to track Dante's panther: the Arabic language is the beast that is smelled but not glimpsed, that leaves its scent on the paths followed by the nomads.

Sībawayhi's movement to and from Basra is an inevitable pilgrimage, dictated by narrative logic. It is perhaps best to call the transits of his biography a psychogeography, the peripatetic progress of a man in search of a language that is itself generated by movement through territory.[33] It's a mercy that he did not need to change language as he moved. Granted, at that early stage in the history of Arab expansion, the cosmopolitan language would have been largely unknown in the countryside—except, of course, by those passing through it: men like Sībawayhi himself, linguistic aristocrats who had made a study of the tongue. With this elect company, however, Sībawayhi could relax and converse in his mistress tongue, the one he never ceased to covet and always sought to win.

How dreary and yet wonderful Sībawayhi's journey out of Basra must have been: the author—his cases filled with volume upon volume of compendious, detailed notes on Arabic usage; recall that the modern editions of *al-Kitāb* run to nearly a thousand pages—crooking his ear to hear the chatter from the farthest reaches of the Arab-Islamic world; the banter, bouncing off the swaying textile walls of the nomad's tent. If Sībawayhi's grammar created a foundation for all subsequent study of the Arabic language, his biography provides a powerful ethical model for the philologist. Rebuked and rebuffed, he still trained his attention on the elusive object of his study: Arabic, the best and purest Arabic, the language of the Qur'an, the scholars, and the Bedouins. Sībawayhi inspires a fiercer affection than most grammarians, a measure in part of the respect of the Arabic-speaking and writing public for his inventive genius and his diligence.[34] In part, I suspect, the attachment to Sībawayhi is also due to his witness to an era when the best Arabic usage was not to be sought in dusty books but to be listened for in the voices of the Bedouins at urban markets and around the fire. If this book is a ballad for a language that is dead, Sībawayhi opens a window to the period before its demise. Language workers like Sībawayhi—who devoted themselves with singular affection to the language that was the object of their desire—worked to keep the sound and texture of that language alive: a living mesh of meaning.

The dream of the lossless language—the perfect poetic register, one that puts up no resistance but conveys our thoughts and ideas with seamless accuracy and vivid intensity—is precisely that: a dream. In truth, as poets and singers know, it's the resistance to harmony that produces the most irresistible image and the most unforgettable music. The appoggiatura note that falls aslant of the melody, the poetic image that startles: dissonance, tension, and surprise catch at the heart as circuitry without resistance never can. This, too, is part of the power of the cosmopolitan language model. The struggle to acquire it (Jacob wrestling with an angel of verb paradigms and vocabulary lists) grants the cosmopolitan language some of its allure and its signifying muscle. And disconnection from the mother tongue—from languages of place—is the symbolic first step that separates the cosmopolitan register from those languages "which we acquire without rule, by imitating our nurse" (as Dante described it).[35] When Dante's mother tongue became the scar of exile—when he was able to work it like soft metal, in the workshop of his craft, without hearing it as the language of everyday life—he was able to see it as the literary medium he sought. And when Sībawayhi was humiliated and forced out of Basra, the language that traveled with him was both proud possession and sign of his dispossession.

In the epigraph to chapter 5, an anonymous copyist called the *gramatica* a "path or lane or alleyway." For Sībawayhi, too, the grammar of the cosmopolitan language was a road, a path out of the tangled linguistic warren of the spoken languages. The word that Sībawayhi uses most often to refer to the study of language and its behaviors, *naḥw*—like many, but not all, of the technical terms Sībawayhi used—has become naturalized in the technical meaning he gave it. One of the meanings assigned to the word in modern dictionaries is "grammar, syntax." But it's not clear that the word had those connotations before Sībawayhi adopted it to name the work that he and his colleagues did as grammarians. *Naḥw* comes from a lexical root that generates words meaning "a way, road, or path" (in nominal forms) or "to go, direct oneself, take to the road" (in verbal forms). The first meaning of *naḥw* in modern dictionaries is still "direction, way, road." A number of other words meaning "way" or "path" were used as well, in the early Arabic grammatical tradition, to refer to grammar and grammarians.[36] The cosmopolitan language makes exacting demands on its practitioners. In exchange, it opens a path that leads to a new world: capacious lands, unknown but discoverable. In this section, I have used Dante's and Sībawayhi's lives and works to illustrate the promise extended by the cosmopolitan language, but also the sacrifices made by the nomad writers who adopt a learned language as literary medium. The screenwriters call it "burning down the house," and they—with the wisdom of the experienced storyteller—see in it the potential for both tragedy and liberation.

[PART THREE]

∵

Translation and Time

[CHAPTER 7]

The Soul of a New Language

Old Church Slavonic in Moravia and Venice, ninth century

> Jesus spoke in Aramaic, but His sayings were transcribed in Greek, a generation after His time on earth. Aramaic and Greek are different languages. Very different. The differences are profound. This fact cannot be emphasized enough.
>
> But none of Jesus's teachings were written down in Aramaic.
>
> JOY WILLIAMS, "TRANSITION"[1]

The definition of the sacred language—or, to use the term of art, *lingua sacra*—is notoriously slippery.[2] The sacred language might be identified as the language or linguistic register used in ritual, prayer, or scripture. In some cases, it also serves as the lingua franca of religious bureaucracy. It may be a tongue no longer spoken in the community—the textual shadow of a formerly "living" language—or a register of a spoken language that demarcates itself as distinct from the vernacular by virtue of its archaic vocabulary, grammar, or syntax. In medieval Sicily, for example, Hebrew served Jews as a sacred language but was not a spoken tongue. Jews used Aramaic as textual language and as language of ritual even though (or, more precisely, because) it had not been a daily language of the community for centuries.[3] Jews—like Muslims and Christians—spoke Arabic throughout the medieval Mediterranean as a language of daily commerce. But for one community, Muslims, one strain of Arabic was marked off as different, specifically and uniquely *sacred*: a register of Arabic distinct in vocabulary, syntax, and usage, namely, Qur'anic Arabic.

The situation for Christians was, of course, murkier. I discussed above (in chapter 2) the complex relationship between revelation and language in the Christian context. Jesus was born into a world of linguistic contingency. The language in which the scriptural accounts of Jesus's life were recorded, Greek, was a bureaucratic language of convenience in the eastern Mediterranean during late antiquity. New Testament Greek is different from the literary Greek of antiquity. Syntax and vocabulary are simplified, streamlined, and used to point to a reality external to the text: the irruption of the divine into human history. More relevant to my topic, Christian scripture seemed from the first to invite translation. The descent of tongues, a gift borne by the Holy Spirit to the celebrants at the first Pentecost (the seventh Sunday after Jesus's resurrection), was understood by medieval Christians to abrogate the confusion of tongues at Babel, God's punishment for human hubris (see Acts 2:1–13). Christians generally recognized the utility of using a multiplicity of languages to communicate the Christian message—although, as we will see in this chapter, at times they tried to police the boundaries of translation.

After the translation of the Hebrew and Greek Bibles into Latin by Jerome (ca. 347–420), a text known as the Vulgate Bible, the language of scripture and liturgy distinguished Roman Christians (who used the Latin Vulgate) from Orthodox Christians (who used the Greek translation of the Old Testament known as the Septuagint). Both Latin and Greek might use their service to their spiritual community to lay claim to status as lingua sacra, which heals the rupture created by the confusion of tongues. Any lingua franca creates linguistic unity and unity of message where linguistic plurality has given rise to discord. But the sacred language possesses a quality of transcendence that grants it access (in its most soaring moments) to the divine. At its most elevated, it stands outside of time and place: it is a time-based key to eternity and a territorially instantiated key to the cosmos. In the Christian context, Greek (the Greek written by those who recorded the deeds of the Aramaic-speaking Messiah, and used in the Orthodox service) and Latin (the medieval Latin of the Vulgate Bible and of liturgy) smell of frankincense and taste like consecrated host. They hoist the congregant outside the reach of time and dangle her in the presence of God.

In this section, I will study the temporal dimension of the distinction between vernacular and cosmopolitan language. I will admire in particular two strategies used by the cosmopolitan language to maintain its authority through the linguistic *longue durée*. First, it uses its deep textual history to slow its rate of change. The cosmopolitan language burrows into its own lexical history. It collates meanings that emerge over time, so that a word may mean one thing and another at the same time. Its grammar, too, resists change—although a quick comparison of the Vulgate Bible to the *Aeneid* or to Cicero's letters will show that its rules evolve, though at a glacial pace. Second, the cosmopolitan language at times exploits the presence of adjacent language systems. It uses translation to import the knowledge embedded in competing cosmopolitan tongues, in order to keep current with scientific and aesthetic trends. On occasion, too, it delegates authority to subsidiary languages.

The lingua sacra is an exceptional register of an exceptional language. Any cosmopolitan language stands apart from history and from those vernaculars that get the grime of day-to-day commerce and industry under their fingernails. But the lingua sacra claims for itself a status altogether outside of time. It is the tongue of divine mysteries, serene and unchanging. The dynamic is relatively straightforward in the case of Arabic. There, revelation is embedded in language. For this reason, only Arabic can plausibly claim the high ground for Muslims. But for Christians, the situation is more complex. The Christian Messiah spoke Aramaic, but none of his words or deeds were recorded in Aramaic. He lived and died in the eastern Mediterranean, where multiple language systems converged. The religion initiated in his name spread into the central Mediterranean, the precinct of another cosmopolitan language system. And so in Christian communities east and west, an exceptional understanding of the lingua sacra evolved, one that viewed linguistic complexity as a virtue—until it didn't anymore, and it moved to restrict and legislate the clamor of tongues.

The episode I describe in this chapter—the Venetian disputation, in which saints and clergymen brawl over translations and the status of language(s)—is an exceptional episode in the life of the lingua sacra, even by the standards of Christianity, which was born in a borrowed language.[4] In the story of Cyril, Apostle of the Slavs, a vernacular spoken in a geographically delimited place (although its location is, as we will see, contested), newly trained to the page, is anointed as lingua sacra. A translation movement brings ancient texts into the new language. Teachers and trolls bicker over the use and legitimacy of the language. In this chapter, I examine the demands made upon the unified and unifying sacred language in the Christian context. In a sacred text economy—a religious environment where deity uses the written word as instrument of revelation—Christianity is unique in its ability to assert the authority of texts despite their evident linguistic contingency. In the fullness of time, and in a secular dimension, the Christian West would learn to present the failure of its lingua sacra as a positive historical development. This chapter provides context for the vernacular revolution by describing the emergence of a vernacular, located in a precise place at a precise time, first written in order to serve as lingua sacra for its community.

∴

The story begins in 862 CE, when Rastislav, Prince of the Moravians, writes to the Byzantine Emperor Michael.[5] The Moravians have been converted to Christianity, but they are rough and backsliding Christians. Rastislav asks the emperor to send a missionary to teach them the right way to worship and believe. Emperor Michael has just the man for the job: a rising star in the Byzantine capital, a young man known to modern historians as Cyril—or, as his biographers regularly call him, the Philosopher.[6] The most important thing to know about Cyril, a quality stressed in particular in the Slavonic redaction of Cyril's biography, is that he possessed a facility for languages. Immediately following his conversion as a young man—when he was still living in Thessalonica, where he was born—Cyril sought out (as the Slavonic *Vita* puts it) "a certain foreigner who knew grammar" and "begged that he teach him thoroughly the art of grammar."[7] The foreign instructor refused Cyril's request for reasons that are not explained in the text, and we learn nothing more about him. He has served his purpose in the narrative, however. The unnamed foreign teacher personifies the learned tongue of culture, which is no one's mother tongue but always a foreign language. Any ambitious young man, like Cyril, must apprentice himself in an Alexandrian language in order to take possession of his literary heritage and take part in the cultural life of his age. This process might be arduous: even one who petitions for access to the language might be denied. Trolls might turn the suitor away. The mistress language might withhold her favors, no matter how ardent the petitioner's pleas.

But she may also, with time, relent. Soon after this episode (and this first, failed linguistic conversion scene), Cyril undertook the journey from Thessalonica to the Byzantine metropolis, Constantinople, and there he commenced his studies and presumably (though the *Vita* does not tell us this) studied and learned Greek. Perhaps propelled by the first rejection, Cyril became a linguistic Don Juan, seducer of numerous (and difficult) languages. From the beginning his knowledge of languages was represented as miraculous. He undertook a mission to the Khazars of central Asia—a Turkic people who observed a number of religions, including Judaism and Islam—in preparation for which he learned Hebrew.[8] A Samaritan visiting Constantinople showed him the Christian scriptures in his language; Cyril proved miraculously able to read Samaritan letters without error.[9] Presented with the Gospels written "in Russian letters," Cyril immediately acquired the ability to read and speak the language.[10] This episode predates the invention of the Cyrillic alphabet and the conversion of the Russians to Christianity, and scholars have not agreed on the significance of the passage.[11] The most plausible explanation is that the gospel in question was Syriac, not Russian; the Old Church Slavonic words for "Syriac" and "Russian" are quite close and have been confused in other texts.[12] Thus, at the time he was approached to undertake the mission to Moravia—when Cyril was about thirty-six years old—according to the *Vitas*, he had already learned Greek, Hebrew, Samaritan, and (possibly) Syriac. Both the Slavonic and the Latin *Vitas* regularly refer to Cyril as "the Philosopher." They present him as a man of learning, but the *Vitas* celebrate not his knowledge of philosophy in the modern sense; not even natural philosophy, or science, which is what the word *philosophy* generally connotes in premodern texts, but, rather, languages. Cyril is a polyglot.[13]

Scholarship on the linguistic actualities of the eastern Mediterranean during this period—the ninth century CE—demonstrates the extent to which Cyril's peculiar skill set answered the exigencies of his age.[14] During the life of Jesus, Latin served as a language of bureaucracy, Greek served as a language of culture, and Aramaic, the superseded cosmopolitan language of western Asia, maintained a respected status as textual language; the spoken languages of the region were legion. With the collapse of the Roman Empire, Hellenism filled the void left by the contraction of Latin. But the expansion of Islam brought a new linguistic player onto the stage. Under the Abbasids, Arabic literacy would grow swiftly in the eastern Mediterranean. Thus, during the first millennium of the Common Era, a succession of learned languages served as linguistic media for cultural and bureaucratic life. But even these languages—Aramaic, Latin, Greek, and Arabic—authoritative and commanding though they were, had to negotiate complex power-sharing arrangements with a host of other tongues. In the eastern Mediterranean, including the Byzantine East and the Levantine territories under Abbasid rule, Christians might have celebrated Mass in Greek or in Armenian, Syriac or Georgian.[15] No one language had territorial sovereignty in the eastern Mediterranean. Rather, a network of languages interacted in order to serve the linguistic needs—bureaucratic, literary, liturgical, and commercial—of the populace.

Cyril was, like Sībawayhi before him, the hero his age required: in Cyril's case, a man with a miraculous ability to absorb languages who embodied the linguistic pluralism of the Byzantine East. In the Slavonic *Vita*, when Emperor Michael approaches him regarding the Moravian mission, Cyril has just finished his mission to the Khazars. Despite his fatigue, he is willing to go to Moravia—"if," he says, "the Moravians have a script for their tongue." The emperor's reply gives him pause. Their language has never been written; a script has been sought, but none has been found. Cyril falters; he is on the verge of despair; he prays, and his prayers are answered with an alphabet. He immediately begins to write out the Gospel in Slavonic translation, using the alphabet revealed to him—beginning, of course, with the Gospel of John: "In the beginning was the Word."[16]

At least, so the Old Slavonic version of the *Life of St. Cyril* has it. A number of redactions of the *Vita* survive: the Old Slavonic text—the longest and most detailed source on Cyril—as well as several Latin versions. As is typical of premodern textual traditions, they agree on some points and differ on others; and at this critical moment, they diverge. The Slavonic *Vita* represents the alphabet as divinely inspired. Most of the Latin *Vita*s, however, don't mention the alphabet. They simply tell us that the philosopher Cyril "translated" scripture and liturgy from Greek *and Latin* into the Slavonic tongue and used this text to convert the Slavs of Moravia to right belief and practice.[17]

Armed with his new alphabet, Cyril set out from the metropolis for Moravia. Only at this point do the *Vita*s mention his brother, Methodius, who must have been at his side on the earlier missions as well. Together, Methodius and Cyril were in the field for four and a half years. Cyril taught the alphabet to princes and priests in the region and worked to spread the Slavonic Gospel and liturgy. Then, in 867 CE, the two brothers turned back toward Constantinople. The route that they traveled on the return trip brought them through Pannonia, northeast of the northern end of the Adriatic. In order to return to Constantinople, the sensible thing to do was to travel to Venice and there to book passage by boat. In Venice, the most fascinating episode in this drama took place, one that reveals most clearly what is at stake in discussions of language in the Christian Mediterranean at this moment.

At that moment, Venice was linked by close economic, cultural, and religious ties both to Byzantium and to Rome and the Latin West. The Italian Peninsula as a whole was on the verge of the technological revolution that would make the Italians the mercantile masters of the Mediterranean, and Venice would lead that revolution. Venetian sailors and merchants would exploit their historical connections to the eastern Mediterranean, developing close trade relations with Byzantine Greeks and the Arabs of the eastern Mediterranean and Egypt. Thus, Venice—perched between Rome and Byzantium, between Latinity and Hellenism—provides the ideal stage for the scene that unfolds when Cyril disembarks in Venice and is beset by a mob of Latins:

> Bishops, priests and monks gathered against him like ravens against a falcon. And they advanced the trilingual heresy, saying: Tell us, O man, how is it that you now teach and have created letters for the Slavs, which none else have found before, neither the Apostle, nor the pope of Rome, nor Gregory the Theologian, nor Jerome, nor Augustine? We know of only three tongues worthy of praising God in the Scriptures, Hebrew, Greek and Latin.[18]

Undaunted, Cyril takes the matter in hand. He lists those peoples who "possess writing and render glory unto God, each in his own tongue: Armenians, Persians, Abkhazians, Iberians, Soghdians, Goths, Avars, Turks, Khazars, Arabs, Egyptians, and many others."[19] He then recites a series of biblical topoi in defense of his audacious act of translation, beginning with the Psalms and working his way through the Gospels. It is striking that he concludes not with the Pentecost—understood by modern scholars and by some medieval thinkers as well as the abrogation of the scandal of Babel and the confusion of tongues[20]—but rather with Paul's admonition to the Christian community to use the full breadth of their linguistic capacity to reach the widest possible audience.[21] "And with these words and many more," the episode concludes, "he shamed them and went away."[22]

The Venetian disputation is a dramatic scene—cinematic in its economy and its picturesque backdrop—and I am sorry to say that it is almost certainly an invention of Cyril's Slavonic biographer. The episode does not appear in the Latin *Vitas*; nor do the Venetian chronicles of the era mention Cyril's visit to the city.[23] The chronicles do, however, give us a clearer sense why Venice serves as the perfect setting for this scene—why a location scout might choose the city as an ideal place to set the encounter between the Byzantine missionary to the Slavs and the representatives of the Roman Church. Around the time that this episode is supposed to take place, 867 CE, the Venetians are defending the Adriatic against the "Saracens"—moving up from the southern end of the sea, they have reached the Croatian coast, perilously close to Venice—and against the Slavs, who have come marauding through Dalmatia and into Istria (just south of Trieste).[24] The term "Slav" is quite imprecise at this moment—the Slavs pillaging the coast and preying on Venetian ships were certainly not Moravians—yet that very ethnic imprecision makes the scene that much more powerful, if one views it as a production designer or a location scout would. Cyril arrives with the dust of Moravia on his knees and the tongues of the Slavs in his mouth. Any Venetian would regard him as suspect.

Reading as a literary historian, I can give another argument against the historical veracity of this scene, another reason to see it as a set piece marked off from the core of the *Vita*, which is more clearly documentary in nature. The passage begins with a simile: "Bishops, priests and monks gathered against him *like ravens against a falcon*."[25] Given the economy of language typical of this *Vita*—and typical of medieval Christian hagiographic writings in general—that simple simile sends up a flare: it tells us that we are entering the allegory zone. Cyril's conversion at the beginning of his *Vita* is marked by the appearance of a falcon as well. When his hunting falcon is carried off by a sudden gust of wind, its loss teaches Cyril to scorn the material trappings of an aristocratic life and to love a greater good.[26] Now, at another turning point of Cyril's life, a second falcon represents our hero himself, beset by the cawing crows who represent the Roman Church. As far as I am aware, the image has no scriptural precedents. It seems, rather, to be a naturalistic rendering of crows mobbing a hawk. The bird is a common metaphor for the soul in the literature of the Christians, regularly used to represent the Holy Spirit. Although the author of the Slavonic *Vita* is not likely to have known this, birds also appear in literary depictions of the Mediterranean to represent the linguistic plurality of the port cities and the ships that cross the sea.

Though the scene in Venice may not represent historical actuality, there is an element of historical truth in it. The leader of the Roman Church accused Cyril of crimes against language and in particular of violating the monopoly held by the three sacred languages of Christianity. A series of popes undertook a long negotiation with Cyril—and his almost-forgotten brother Methodius, who outlived Cyril and would participate in the language debates over a longer term—about the appropriate language of worship in the new churches of Moravia. Initially they celebrated Cyril's linguistic innovations, although they tried to preserve a place of privilege for Latin in the liturgy. Over time, however, the Roman Church would become increasingly hostile to the vernacularization of liturgy and would insist on setting up Latin as first among equals of the Christian languages.[27] The scene in Venice serves one clear narrative function in the Slavonic *Vita*: it allows Cyril, as the representative and in a sense the author of a new lingua sacra, to rehearse what would become the chief scriptural arguments against a linguistic position adopted by the Roman Church, referred to in the Slavonic *Vita* as "the trilingual heresy." Cyril addresses the Venetians who oppose him as "trilinguists" and "Pilatians," since they defend their position by pointing to the three languages inscribed by Pontius Pilate on the cross on which Jesus was crucified.[28] The Venetian disputation uses the "trilingual heresy" of the Latins to frame Cyril's responses in defense of translation. Small wonder that the Latin *Vita*s omitted this episode.

The standoff between Byzantium and Rome on the topic of the sacred language would continue for some centuries to come. The "trilingual heresy" counts among the "errors of the Latins" listed by Constantine Stilbes, a Byzantine clergyman writing against the Roman Church in the wake of the Fourth Crusade:

> Νομοθετοῦσι μόναις τρισὶ γλώσσαις τὸ θεῖον δοξολογεῖν, λατινικῇ, ἑλλενικῇ και ἑβραϊκῇ, ἑτέρᾳ δέ μηδεμίᾳ τῶν πιστευσάντων ἐθνῶν.[29]

> They have made it law to recognize the divinity of three languages only—Latin, Greek and Hebrew—and no other language of those that have received the faith.

The "trilingual heresy," however, was but one of a great multitude of errors committed by the Romans (in the eyes of the Byzantines). Byzantine scholars did not dwell upon it, particularly given the fact that the Orthodox Church felt it necessary to assert the primacy and the unique authority of the Greek language in the centuries following this event. By the end of the first millennium of the Common Era, though the Orthodox Church continued to prop up the Greek language as (again) first among equals, it found itself obliged to recognize the de facto validity of other liturgical languages used by Christians in the eastern Mediterranean.[30] Both Greek on the eastern edge of the Mediterranean and Latin in the middle of the Mediterranean had to negotiate a peace treaty with local languages in order to promote and serve the interests of their community. In the circumstances, one must admire the theological innovation of the Roman Church, its willingness to recognize the sanctity of a constellation of languages—an ancient scriptural language, a historical demotic tongue, and a contemporary bureaucratic language—rather than elevate a single, centralized language as the one truly *sacred language* or *lingua sacra* of the church.

Modern historians often read the episode of Cyril in Moravia in the context of a political struggle. Great tracts of land to the north and east of the Adriatic, in the marches between Byzantine and Roman territories, remained imperfectly Christianized, and the church that succeeded in converting the countryside might more successfully assert its political authority in this territory. This is undeniably an important narrative thread, and one that captures many of the essential truths about Cyril's mission to Moravia.[31] However, a literary historian might see a different message in this episode. Political history typically understands historical change in the light of agonistic power struggles between states. The most powerful secular ruler, the most effective military strategist, or the craftiest tactician on the battlefield wins the day. In the field of linguistic and literary history, however, historical change is seldom so straightforward. Languages function not like armies on a battlefield but rather like complex systems or like networks. They thrive not by defeating opponents but rather by creating connections that link them to a network of parallel languages—competitors or allies, as the case may be. Languages translate each other's texts; they borrow words or semantic habits from each other; they borrow, adapt, or steal alphabets from each other. The three languages inscribed by Pontius Pilate on the cross were there for three different reasons, each using its own alphabet and speaking a distinct code to the local population. The Orthodox Church viewed the attempt on the part of the Roman Church to grant the status of lingua sacra to that constellation of tongues as an arbitrary or mercenary move. But a philologist of the twenty-first century might, with equal justice, recognize the brilliance of the Romans' stance. With the "trilingual heresy," the Roman Church proposed a strategy that both recognized and contained linguistic pluralism within its congregation, acknowledging the presence of Hebrew and Greek alongside Latin, while at the same time working quietly to push Latin ahead of its competitors.[32]

The Glagolitic alphabet invented by Cyril to write the Slavic language now known as Old Church Slavonic would have a complicated history following its invention.[33] Cyril initiated a translation movement that brought a number of texts crucial for the religious life of the community into the language, at the same time importing vocabulary from the Greek to express concepts that a mere vernacular need not treat. Glagolitic looks eccentric to an eye accustomed to the streamlined alphabets of the print era. Some of the Glagolitic letters appear bizarre and rococo—sinuous, sprouting antler-like appendages, made up of multiple components so that they seem almost like fractal minialphabets. Over time the Glagolitic alphabet would fall out of use, replaced by the Cyrillic alphabet (which has a contentious relationship to Glagolitic, as well as to the man whose name it bears), which was more clearly modeled on the Greek alphabet. During the first millennium of the Common Era, a number of tongues came to be written in the eastern Mediterranean that had no previous life as literary languages. When new textual languages were born in the Islamicate world—New Persian, Chagatai and Anatolian Turkish, and Urdu, for instance—the Arabic alphabet was used to write them. These realphabetization movements made no concession beyond the addition of diacritical dots above or below the Arabic letters to record phonemes not used in the Arabic. In the Christian West, too, the Latin alphabet was used to write new literary languages during the vernacular revolution of the late Middle Ages. In the Christian East, however, new languages approached the Greek alphabet with trepidation. Coptic, Gothic, Armenian, and Georgian all adapted their alphabets from the Greek, but each transformed the Greek letters in order to forge an alphabet visibly distinct from the Greek models.[34] During the first millennium, at least, the Greek alphabet seemed to be the special property of the Greek language; it might provide raw materials for new invention, but it could not simply be occupied by a new language, like a disused building taken over by squatters.

The Glagolitic alphabet illustrates the haptic quality of alphabets in general. Alphabet may seem to exist purely as visual register. But as the history of Old Church Slavonic makes clear, alphabet revolutions are always complex phenomena. Languages are never simply shunted onto a new alphabet, like crates moved from a cargo ship onto trucks or trains. When a language takes on a new alphabet it often undertakes a wholesale transformation of lexicon and literary history. At times the imposition of a new writing system is part of a larger political program, as in the case of the Turkish alphabet revolution under Ataturk during the early twentieth century and the alphabet wars that shaped the Maltese language during the nineteenth.[35] At others, as in the case of Old Church Slavonic, the process seems more organic—or perhaps the historical distance between the present moment and the revolutionary era simply blurs our perception. Certainly, the integration of abundant borrowings from the Greek both allowed the Slavonic-speaking public to express religious truths that they could not access in the vernacular and drew them closer to the orthodoxies of the Greek Church—thus achieving the goals of God and Realpolitik at the same time. As Milorad Pavić writes in his novelized life of Cyril, "languages can learn other languages."[36]

Pavić's account of Cyril's adventures in Moravia culminates in the Venetian disputation. In his version of the tale, when the "Trilinguists" confront Cyril, they challenge him with a single question: "Did all of Judas kill Christ, or not quite all?"[37] No one language can account for the whole of human consciousness and the possible range of human passions, it seems. Our experiences, actions, and emotions are parceled out into distinct linguistic containers. Pavić's Cyril learns languages, but they do not coexist easily in his mind. Rather, they contend and dispute—like the Khazars, whom Cyril debated at the beginning of his career, and like the missionaries and the Trilinguists bickering on a dock in Venice. Even the alphabet that Cyril creates has a pugilistic relationship with the language it must write: Cyril makes an alphabet "of barred letters and cage[s] the unruly language in them like a bird," Pavić writes.[38] Like a pagan hero, Pavić's Cyril battles linguistic foes; and in Cyril's moments of weakness, languages recede. "Only illness provided some sort of island of peace in his life," Pavić writes. "As soon as he fell ill, he would forget every other language save his own."[39] Pavić does not, however, tell us what lucky language Cyril considers "his own." Perhaps he imagines an idiolect that (following Dante's description of microlanguages to its *reductio ad absurdum*) is understood only by a single soul.

The lingua sacra, at its simplest, is a cosmopolitan language with religious credentials. Like the cosmopolitan language, it functions as a workaround for the confusion of tongues. But its association with the sacred gives it gravitas and something more: the lingua sacra pushes aside linguistic complexity and replaces it with a sublunary vision of linguistic transcendence and unity. By identifying the language with divinity, its proponents claim for it a kind of serenity that few of us associate with life on earth. Pavić's account of Cyril captures the competition between languages and the violence—implicit or explicit, physical or psychological—of alphabet wars (Pavić himself was born in Serbia, which has two official alphabets: Serbian Latin and Serbian Cyrillic). In fact, the placid vision proposed by the lingua sacra is difficult for all but the mystics to achieve in this life. The cosmopolitan language system—whether or not it yokes language to revelation and claims the status of lingua sacra—represents itself as the one tongue needed to account for all of creation. Those parts of human consciousness that remain outside the one language, it seems, are excluded from this story. They, I can only conclude, are the parts of Judas that didn't kill Christ.

[CHAPTER 8]

On First Looking into Mattā's Aristotle

Arabic in Baghdad, tenth to eleventh century

> Mimicry is a very bad concept, since it relies on binary logic to describe phenomena of an entirely different nature.
>
> DELEUZE AND GUATTARI, *A Thousand Plateaus*[1]

Some four thousand kilometers to the east of the Venetian pier where the men of the cloth beset Cyril, and roughly fifty years later, another scholar and translator—like Cyril—drew the ire of his contemporaries for meddling with languages. We parted ways with Cyril in the mid-ninth century and in the central Mediterranean. The story I turn to now begins in Abbasid Baghdad in about 930 CE. But this is no longer Bashshār ibn Burd's Baghdad (see chapter 2). When Bashshār had his conversation with the Abbasid caliph al-Mahdī, in about 780 CE, Baghdad was a new city; it had been established as the Abbasid capital less than two decades earlier. Now, roughly a century and a half later, the bickering associated with *shu'ūbiyya* is in the past, although ethnic and linguistic tensions remain part of the background noise of Arabic-language culture throughout the abode of Islam. Persians (and other ethnic minorities) still travel to the Abbasid capital, and Persian writers continue to make crucial contributions to the evolution of literary life. In this chapter, the focus shifts to another area of linguistic crosshatching: the translation movement that brought the most important works of Greek philosophy through Syriac and into Arabic. I will discuss the oldest extant Arabic translation of Aristotle's *Poetics*, made by Syriac Christian Abū Bishr Mattā ibn Yūnus in the early tenth century, and the ripples it created in the Arabic language—some of them directly related to the transmission history of Mattā's translation, others more indirect and less predictable.

In the previous chapter, I described the emergence of a textual language, Old Church Slavonic, which mediated between the human and the divine and used translation as one strategy to achieve this goal. Here, I begin a two-chapter arc focusing on an aggregate of translations—in this case, scientific translations, rather than religious—which brought a corpus of texts from one cultural sphere into another. I will look at subsequent translation movements as connected histories, watching Aristotle's *Poetics* move between Greek, Syriac, Arabic, Latin, Hebrew, and the Romance vernaculars. The *Poetics*, a philosophical treatise that studies the mechanics and the ethics of literature, is uniquely well suited for an inquiry into the strategies used by the cosmopolitan languages that are the focus of this book, Arabic and Latin, to respond to the pressures imposed on them by translation movements. Scientific translations introduced new concepts into the Arabic-Islamic and Latin-Christian cultural spheres, and Arabic and Latin found themselves obliged to adapt in order to accommodate new systems of thought. In this chapter and the next, my methods will be, more than in previous chapters, philological. In order to show how words learn new behaviors, I will quote and analyze passages. Readers who are interested in the details of this history—who wish to watch Arabic and Latin mulling the mysteries of Aristotle's *Poetics*—are invited to turn the page and follow the story. But those without a taste for philology can safely skip to chapter 10, which (like chapter 7) talks about intersections between language and history without extended textual analysis. My readers are mortal, unlike the semidivine languages I treat, and do not measure their lives in millennia.

∴

The Abbasid translation movement gifted to Arab philosophers and writers a corpus of scholarly works that served as the foundation of a new science and a new literature. The majority of these works were translated from the Greek. More precisely, they had been written in Greek more than a millennium earlier and had been studied, commented upon, and transmitted in the languages of science in the Near East (Greek and Syriac in particular) throughout those intervening centuries. The Arabic translations of these treatises that appeared between the eighth and tenth centuries of the Christian era had the names of the great Greek philosophers attached to them: Galen, Euclid, Pythagoras, Plotinus, Proclus, and especially Aristotle. But in fact the works that the translation workshops produced, in many cases, could more accurately be described as digests of the originals, elaborated with the notes, addenda, corrections, amendments, and, inevitably, the omissions, elisions, misinterpretations, and errors of translation and transmission introduced by generations of readers.

Translators and scholars devoted a great deal of attention to the Aristotelian corpus during the translation movement, testament to the high esteem with which Aristotle's thought was regarded during antiquity and the Middle Ages. Among the last of Aristotle's works to be translated were those so intimately linked to the Greek literary tradition that the transferal of their content into another linguistic medium posed a peculiar challenge. Aristotle's *Rhetoric* and *Poetics* might have been overlooked by the translation movement; what relevance could Greek strategies of debate, Greek tragic theater, or Greek comedies have for the Arabs? But the Arabs valued public oratory and debate as much as the ancient Greeks had done. Furthermore, both the *Rhetoric* and the *Poetics* were considered—in the late-antique Greek tradition as well as the medieval Arabic tradition—to constitute part of the Aristotelian Organon. The word *organon* means "tool" in Greek. This core of treatises formed the essential logical tool kit for the philosopher: the building blocks of deductive reasoning and argumentation. The treatises in the Organon describe the strategies the philosopher uses to discover and analyze the truth (*Categories*, *On Interpretation*, *Prior Analytics*, and *Posterior Analytics*) and to debate, demonstrate, and teach the truth (*Topics*, *On Sophistical Refutations*, *Rhetoric*, and *Poetics*). For that reason, despite the difficulties they posed, they had to be translated into Arabic and commented upon in Arabic.

The translation tradition is impossible to reconstruct in detail.[2] What seems likely is that by the mid-ninth century CE, the *Poetics* had been translated from Greek into Syriac;[3] and before ca. 935 CE, Abū Bishr Mattā ibn Yūnus (d. 940) translated the Syriac text into Arabic.[4] This translation appears to have been revised during the ninety or so years that passed between its writing and the time the single known manuscript of the work was copied.[5] The *Poetics* was also summarized and discussed by the first great philosophical polymath of the Arabic-Islamic tradition, al-Fārābī (d. 950), and Ibn Sīnā (or Avicenna, 980–1037) would paraphrase it. This flurry of tenth-century scholarship on the treatise—translations of translations and commentaries on translations of translations—is quite typical of the attention lavished on philosophical works imported into the Arabic language, which were massaged through successive translations and commentaries intended to extract the last morsel of philosophical content from each treatise.[6] Indeed, the *Poetics* might have seen more action but for the fact that it appeared in Arabic only toward the end of the era of Arabic-Islamic fascination with Aristotelian philosophy.

For a scholar of literary history, it is hard to imagine a more fascinating transaction between literary languages. On the one hand is an ancient pagan language that derives its literary tradition from the theater, and on the other a modern language, the voice of a rigorously monotheistic tradition whose first literary works were (pagan) poetic odes: what could the first tradition possibly teach the second? How much of Aristotle's thought survived the transfer through languages—through a multiplicity of Greek versions, each one written a step further away from the dramatic tradition that Aristotle knew; into Syriac; and thence into Arabic? The Arabic translations of the *Poetics* have inspired responses ranging from sober debate to bemusement to outspoken contempt, both from their target audience (learned Muslims of the Middle Ages) and from readers whom the Arabic litterateurs of the tenth century could not in their wildest fancies have imagined (modern philologists and historians of philosophy).[7]

At a first glance the tradition is bewildering indeed. Read alongside a modern edition of Aristotle's *Poetics*, the extant old Arabic translation—the version written by Mattā during the early tenth century, extracted from a lost Syriac translation—is recognizably a direct, in some cases quite literal, Arabic rendering of the Greek. Yet what a strange refraction of the Greek literary tradition we find in Mattā's version! In many cases, confusion is generated by the choice of Arabic words used to render Aristotle's Greek (or, more precisely, used to translate the Syriac translation of Aristotle's Greek).[8] In the opening lines, for instance, we find Aristotle's *mythos*—here referring to the plot of narrative-based poetic works—translated with the Arabic *al-asmār*, a word that refers to fantastic tales told at night. We read a short list of technical Greek terms used in literary analysis transliterated and inserted, in all their strangeness, into Mattā's Arabic text: *dīthurambū* (from *dithurambikós*); *awlīṭīqis* (from *aulētikḕ*); even the Greek word *poíēsis*, which, because the Arabic language does not use the /p/ sound, is transliterated into Arabic as *al-fuwāsis*. We find too the most noteworthy and most commented-upon reinterpretation of Aristotle's *Poetics* in the Arabic transmission tradition: already on the opening page of the treatise, tragedy and comedy have disappeared, replaced by praise (*madīḥ*) and satire (*hijā'*).[9] This transformation of the genres of Greek theater was not unique to Mattā's translation. It seems to predate the Syriac-to-Arabic translation of Aristotle's treatise. Mattā's contemporary al-Fārābī (d. 950), too, thought of tragedy as a celebration of the lives of praiseworthy men and comedy as a form of lampooning the weak or vicious, although his wording makes it clear that he didn't derive this description from Mattā.[10] Two centuries later, Ibn Rushd (1126–1198) would accept and repeat Mattā's taxonomy, in a commentary that used the Arabic literary tradition as a proving ground for debating Aristotelian literary theory (as discussed in chapter 9).[11] Finally, Aristotle's theory of mimesis, understandably enough, has been thoroughly reconceived in Mattā's translation. The Arabic lexical repertoire used to designate mimesis appears multiple times in the opening paragraph: one cluster of words drawn from the verb *tushabbih*, meaning "to be made to resemble or be likened to something"; and a second derived from the verb *ḥakā*, which means "to relate, recite, repeat, or imitate."[12] Throughout Mattā's translation, we find lexica derived from these two roots, in various verbal and nominal forms, used to translate the concept regularly designated in Aristotle's treatise with the Greek noun *mímēsis* and the verb *miméomai*: to imitate, represent, or portray.

On first looking into Mattā's *Poetics*, the reader might be excused for feeling confused and even dismayed by any of these transformations.[13] Of course, the modern reader who expects a premodern translation to look like a mimetic representation of the original text is bound to be disappointed by most premodern works described by modern historians as "translations." What Mattā left behind—like the original Greek versions of some of Aristotle's own texts—is closer to lecture notes than a translation. That is, what we call a "translation" is, in this case, a record of a scholar's engagement with the text.[14] Yet some early scholars, too, responded to Mattā's work with dismay. One early response to Mattā's translation is recorded in an account written by Abū Ḥayyān al-Tawḥīdī (d. 1023).[15] Al-Tawḥīdī recounts an episode in which Mattā is cross-examined by Abū Saʿīd al-Ḥasan al-Sīrāfī, a grammarian who himself wrote a commentary on Sībawayhi's *Book* (see chapter 6).[16] Al-Sīrāfī and the other men present at this encounter harangue Mattā at length. He is mocked as a Christian and a native speaker of Syriac. His linguistic limitations, according to his tormentors, make him equally incapable of understanding Aristotle's Greek and of being eloquent in Arabic. Mattā's interlocutors insist that all sense must evaporate from a treatise translated from Greek into Syriac and from Syriac into Arabic. "What do you say," they challenge him, "of ideas that are travestied by transference from Greek to another language, Syriac; and then from that language to another, Arabic?"[17] They accuse Mattā of believing that true philosophy is possible only in Greek, and that logic—the proud invention and most powerful tool of the Greek philosophers—is the universal language of truth, prior even to language (to be understood, in this context, as a language capable of being written: *gramatica*, in the generic sense). But how can the philosopher express truths if he does not have a masterful command of the language he uses to express his thoughts? Trying to answer the chicken-and-egg problem that al-Sīrāfī poses, Mattā finds himself incapable of response, in large part (according to this account) because his Arabic is not equal to the challenge of debating men whose linguistic facility and literary knowledge far outmatch his own.

Like Cyril (chapter 7), Mattā is the falcon mobbed by crows—the trolls and guardians of the coveted language—who plays the coquette, turning her back on the suitor who courts her.[18] Yet despite Abū Ḥayyān al-Tawḥīdī's critical portrayal of Mattā, his translation did find a readership among the philosophers, and, apparently, it had influence beyond philosophical circles. I mentioned above, and will discuss in the next chapter, Ibn Rushd's commentary on the *Poetics*; it was based largely upon Mattā's version. For a more vivid illustration of the immediate impact of the Abū Bishr Mattā ibn Yūnus translation on Arabic letters, consider the tale of two words used by Mattā to translate Aristotle's theory of mimesis. The first, *ḥikāya*—a verbal noun derived from a root that means (among other things) "to tell (a story)"—in modern Arabic means "a narrative, story, or tale." The second, *khurāfa*—according to the Arabic lexical tradition, derived from the name of an inveterate teller of tall tales—came to refer to fantastic stories.

Two clusters of lexica associated with these words are central to the story that Mattā tells in his translation of Aristotle's *Poetics*. On the opening page of the modern edition of Mattā's translation that sits in front of me, I count six words derived from the root *ḥ-k-y* (the lexical root that gives us *ḥikāya*), a figure that is not atypical of the work as a whole and that is indicative of Mattā's methods as a translator. Mattā strafes Aristotle's Greek with Arabic lexica. He responds to the implacably enigmatic key word of the *Poetics*—*mímēsis*—by trying out a range of words that may or may not answer. Consider, for instance, Aristotle's programmatic statement regarding the construction of tragedy: "ἔστιν δὲ τῆς μὲν πράξεως ὁ μῦθος ἡ μίμησις" (*Poetics* 1450a 3–4).

> Since tragedy is mimesis of an action, and the action is conducted by agents who should have certain qualities in both character and thought (as it is these factors which allow us to ascribe qualities to their actions too, and it is in their actions that all men find success or failure), *the plot is the mimesis of action.*[19]

A fluent, modern English translation might render this statement thus: "Plot is the representation of action." Yet a well-educated English-reading audience would be able to recite the sentence—and, in some circles, would find it easier to understand—in a macaronic version, because of our own cultural accommodation of ancient Greek literary concepts: "Plot (*mythos*) is the *mimesis* of action (*praxis*)."

Without this backstory of convergent evolution—a repertoire of cognate words and learned vocabulary adapted from the Greek philosophical tradition—Mattā is obliged to innovate. To render this passage, he writes:

> وعلل الأحاديث والقصص اثنتان، وهما العادات والآراء. وإن بحسب
> (هاتين) توجد اللأحاديث والقصص، من حيث تستقيم كلها بهاذين وتزلّ
> بهما. وخرافة الحاديث والقصص هى تشبيه ومحاكاة. . .[20]

> The causes for the narratives and tales are two: habits and views. Indeed, because of these two things narratives and tales exist, for which reason all of them [i.e., narratives and tales] succeed through [their depiction of] the two [i.e., habits and views], or fail by [failing to depict] the two of them. For *the tale of events and the narrative is imitation and mimicry*. . . .

The clutch of words that Mattā moots to render the Greek *mythos*, *mímēsis*, and *praxis* responds to the challenge posed by the Aristotelian text—a challenge that, admittedly, generates some weirdness in the Arabic. Doublets expand the taut sequential phrase from Aristotle's text: *narratives* and *tales* render the Greek *mythos*; *imitation* and *mimicry* translate the Greek *mímēsis*. The notion of *action* (the Greek *praxis*) seems to have vanished, or been displaced into the following phrase.[21] In this case a macaronic rendering of Mattā's definition of plot would leave a speaker of modern English unenlightened: "The narrative (*khurāfa*) of events and the tale (*qaṣaṣ*) is imitation (*tashbīh*) and mimicry (*muḥāka*)." Here, Aristotle discusses concepts and literary practices that have no parallel in the Arabic-language tradition. Arabs did not derive their literary tradition from dramatic narrative, and indeed the very category of imaginative narrative held a contentious place in early Arabic literature. More important to imaginative literature in Arabic were poetic odes and the poetic prose style known as *maqāma* (discussed below, chapter 13). The task of rendering Aristotle's discussion of narrative in general and dramatic narrative in particular in Arabic creates a webwork that requires these words—*qaṣaṣ*, "tale"; *khurāfa*, "fantastic tale"; *ḥikāya*, "mimicry" or "story"—to articulate a new relation to each other.

At the same time, Mattā must do his best to hoist the Arabic theatrical tradition above the gutter; for contemporary Arabic drama was largely associated with what the Greeks would recognize as satire. It is seldom recognized, in discussions of the Arabic transmission of the *Poetics*, that the Abbasid Arabs did indeed have a dramatic tradition. The word used to describe theatrical performance was the same chosen by Mattā to render Aristotle's *mímēsis: ḥikāya*. The *ḥikāya* known to Arabs in Abbasid Baghdad was a politicized and robustly satirical form of theater. The word *ḥikāya* entered Arabic literary circles to name a form of mimetic performance that was not narrative in structure and in some cases was nonverbal. In a well-known and oft-cited passage, the early Arabic litterateur Jāḥiẓ (ca. 776–868/9) describes *ḥikāya* as a form of pantomime or mimicry in which a performer imitates the actions of a human type (for instance, the halting progress of a blind man), or mimics the sounds of an animal, or performs an impression of the Arabic accent of one from Yemen, from China, from the Maghrib or Khurasan. *Ḥikāya*, by the mid-ninth century (when Jāḥiẓ wrote this description of it), had become a generic term for a range of pantomimes and performances—from lampooning mummery to simple sketch comedy to verbal performances that relied upon a written script. Abū Ḥayyān al-Tawḥīdī's account of the roasting of Syriac translator Abū Bishr Mattā by the grammarians, for instance, might have counted as one of these satirical performances, if it were punchier and more amusing. The *ḥikāya* of Abbasid Baghdad seems to have relied upon ingenious physical and aural mimicry for its dramatic energy, rather than on narrative. Often, such performances imitated and mocked the nonhuman or the foreigner, whose accent in the cosmopolitan language identified him as outsider.[22]

The Abbasid era, as I have stressed, was a period of explosive literary growth. As the Arabic literary tradition was consolidated, new genres emerged and existing genres were transformed; and the Arabic language itself morphed to meet the new demands imposed on it by this emergent literary tradition. One work in particular is central to both understanding the literary experimentalism of the age and assessing the shifting meaning of *ḥikāya* in tenth- and eleventh-century Baghdad: the *Ḥikāyat Abī al-Qāsim* (the *Tale* or *Sketch* [*ḥikāya*] *of Abū al-Qāsim*) by Abū al-Muṭahhar al-Azdī (eleventh century).[23] The book is set on a single night. Full of obscenities and scurrilous jokes, it centers on a vividly imagined character: the boisterous antihero, Abū al-Qāsim, who introduces himself at the beginning of the book as an exile from Baghdad (like Dante and Sībawayhi, he has been cast out of his hometown; see chapters 5 and 6). He crashes a dinner party in Isfahan. Once inside, he mocks, torments, and entertains the gathered guests, and al-Azdī follows the proceedings with barely concealed delight. In his introduction, the author quotes Jāḥiẓ's discussion of mimicry at length, clearly intending his audience to understand his book as a form of *ḥikāya* as described by Jāḥiẓ.[24] Does this mean that the episodes he describes, featuring his antihero Abū al-Qāsim, were intended to be performed as dramatic sketches—the tics and accents of the dinner-party guests acted out for the pleasure of a live audience? Jāḥiẓ, after all, evidently understood *ḥikāya* to refer to a live performance that provided delight thanks to its vivid recreation of verbal, aural, or physical phenomena. Some scholars believe that al-Azdī's vignettes were conceived with performance in mind.[25] Others see the work as cousin to the *maqāmāt*, brief narratives larded with rhetorical and lexical play and intended to be read either silently, for personal enjoyment, or out loud for an audience capable of appreciating such verbal sophistication.[26] Whatever al-Azdī's understanding of the word *ḥikāya*, his work is closest to what moderns would call a picaresque, focusing on a small band of heroes: the salacious, endlessly entertaining Abū al-Qāsim; his plastic and salty language; and two flourishing cosmopolitan metropolises, Baghdad and Isfahan, around the year 1000 CE.

The *Ḥikāyat Abī al-Qāsim* captures a transitional moment in the evolution of the word *ḥikāya*. In early Arabic usage (the word appears in hadith, but not in the Qur'an), the word meant "mimicry"; in modern Arabic, it has come to mean "a narrative, a story." Abū Bishr Mattā's use of the word as part of a portfolio of Arabic lexica translating Aristotle's technical terms seems either to have provided impetus for its reconfiguration or to respond to its shifting semantic range. It is easy for us to translate Mattā's *ḥikāya* with the English *story* or even *narrative* and assume that Mattā meant by it what we mean by those words. Yet even those works that seem to possess the qualities that we associate with literary narrative—extended imaginative prose works, like Abū al-Muṭahhar al-Azdī's *Ḥikāyat Abī al-Qāsim*—were not designed to function like narratives on the Aristotelian model.[27] Certainly, the series of narrative revelations that build to create the fundamentals of drama in Aristotelian terms—the crises and turning points of classical Greek tragedy—have no bearing on al-Azdī's portraits of typical characters of contemporary Baghdad or Isfahan. These portraits, rather, are episodic and essentially about linguistic texture: they capture the spirit of character types familiar to contemporary Baghdadis, without making any effort to represent what P. G. Wodehouse's Jeeves would call "the psychology of the individual." Under the pressure of the Abbasid translation movement, under the strain of rendering Aristotle's *Poetics* in particular, the word *ḥikāya* began a long process of metamorphosis. By the eleventh century, it has come to mean not (only) "mimicry," not (yet) "narrative," but rather a literary performance that captures the verbal spirit of the subject in an episodic mode.

Here is some of the work done by Mattā's translation—admittedly, not the happiest moment in the Abbasid translation movement, yet not an unequivocal catastrophe: his use of *ḥikāya* to render the Greek *mythos* (plot) either responded to contemporary trends or had a hand in initiating the debates that might generate new trends. Adding a crucial dimension to the lexical range of the word, Mattā's *Poetics* allowed *ḥikāya* to move from mimicry toward narrative representation. His use of the term *khurāfa*, in contrast, seems to have done little to draw that word into play as a literary term of art. It meant "fable, fantastic tale, tall tale" before his translation, and its lexical range changed little afterward. Indeed, Mattā's sober discussion of ludicrous stories—the fantastic tales told to children, like *khurāfāt*; the *asmār*, or "night tales," that appeared in the opening passage of his translation—may have made it easier for the upstanding citizens of Abū Ḥayyān al-Tawḥīdī's *majlis* (or gathering) to make sport of him. But al-Azdī's reappropriation of the word that Mattā mobilized to translate Aristotle—his use of *ḥikāya* to name his bawdy literary performances, celebrations of the raucous energy and ethnic complexity of the cosmopolitan metropolis—suggest that the word opened a world of new possibilities to the literary writer. Al-Azdī's *ḥikāya* incorporates elements of realistic representation (the pragmatic details of day-to-day life in contemporary Baghdad) but understands itself first and foremost to connote an episodic literary performance, not primarily realistic but rather referential. It is in continuity not with life (it is not psychological realism) but with language. It proposes that the literary text is a verbal performance capturing the spirit and the verbal identity (rather than a psychological snapshot) of the subject. *Ḥikāya* now occupies a position neither of mimicry nor of narrative but a point between them, where an invented character's verbal brio celebrates the inventive powers of the language itself. It may be overly simplistic—a reduction of the rich literary life of the Abbasid capital—to attribute the new lexical range of the word to Abū Bishr Mattā's translation of Aristotle's *Poetics*, one of the more obscure and ambivalent achievements of the Abbasid translation movement. Yet it does no disservice to more sober and scientific translators and their treatises on logic, mechanics, physiology, and the cosmos to describe Mattā's response to the *Poetics* as generative in its own way. That is the story I have outlined in this chapter. My aim has not been to produce a scientific account of the Arabic translation movement; others have done that work. Rather, I have traced some of the ripples that spread when a translator dropped a pebble into a rather large pond: when Mattā's translation submerged Aristotle's *Poetics* in the sea of the Arabic language. I have not asked what is lost or gained in translation but rather have sketched the web created through the agency of translation: the catchment of translation, which implicates multiple languages and multiple textual traditions.

Arabs of the tenth century—men like Abū Bishr Mattā and Abū Saʿīd al-Ḥasan al-Sīrāfī, the grammarian with whom Mattā disputed the precedence of logic over grammar—understood the Greek of the ancients and the tongue of contemporary Byzantines to be two different languages.[28] Arabs knew contemporary Byzantines and their language by the name that they used for themselves: *al-rūmī*, or "Roman," heirs to the eastern portion of the empire that split when Charlemagne was crowned king of the western half. To the Arabs, ancient Greek was a *dead language*—although they would not have used that metaphorical expression to describe it. A language neither lives nor dies; it is not an organic entity.[29] Rather, in his challenge to Mattā, al-Sīrāfī uses a verb that suggests that Aristotle's ancient Greek, which Mattā claims to translate, has abstained from communion with those who spoke it, as one abstains from actions that are inappropriate or unlawful:

قد عَفَتْ منذ زمان طويل، وباد أهلُها، وأُنقرض القومُ الذين كانوا يتفاوضون بها، ويتفاهمون أغراضهم بتصاريفها. . . .[30]

> It has *withdrawn* long ago, and its people have died, and those who were joined in conversation in the language have perished, along with those who understood each other's intentions through its grammatical distinctions. . . .

Here, al-Sīrāfī uses flowery prose intended to put Mattā (as a non-Arab) in his place. The repetitions of meaning (and of sixth-form verbs) in the two final clauses are not necessary to make his point. But the rhetorical flourishes drive home al-Sīrāfī's point that Mattā is incapable both of understanding Aristotle's Greek and of writing powerful Arabic prose. As the adumbrations of the two final clauses of this put-down mirror each other, so too the first two clauses echo each other with terse efficiency. The language has retreated; its people are long dead. It is fascinating to note that, for al-Sīrāfī, the people belong to the language rather than the other way around; and people die, whereas language does not. The metaphor that al-Sīrāfī reaches for does not draw upon the representation of language as a living thing. Rather, he instantiates life in the community predicated of the language. Like Sībawayhi (chapter 6), he embeds the language in the *legal* network that sustained the community while it lived. Language, like law, is used to articulate relations between human beings. Al-Sīrāfī might be quite happy with the neologism that Philip of Harveng would coin two centuries later to refer to his Alexandrian language, Latin: *legittera*, the language (*littera*) governed by laws (*leges*).[31]

I insist on metaphorical precision in part in order to resist the effort to attribute a specific set of qualities to language: organic vitality, senescence, death, a genealogy similar to the family tree that generates a human being, and so on. Languages do come into being where they did not exist before. But human genetics may prove a less useful metaphor to describe that process than sedimentation, for instance, or deposition—geological terms of art used to describe the formation of rock. Such a metaphor calls attention to the accumulation of multiple, tiny bits of information from diverse sources: like the silt that metamorphoses into rock, lexical and semantic input—over time and in the linguistic practice of generations of speakers and writers—produces a new language. Or again: languages change through time. However, their transformation might have more in common with the growth of crystals—formed following the introduction of an irritant, through nucleation; growing through agglomeration rather than evolution—than with the parenting of a human child or with the maturation of an individual human being.

I am not in the business of describing language origins, but I can be a curator of metaphors. In the episode from Abbasid Arabic literary history

I have described in this chapter, we can watch a language undergoing a transformation that has no plausible relation with human biology. Aristotle, describing the dramatic tradition of the Greeks, used a word that signified "tale" or "narrative" to name the narrative backbone of Greek drama: μῦθος, *mythos*. A millennium later, when Aristotle's *Poetics* entered the Arabic language by way of a lost Syriac intermediary, Abū Bishr Mattā used two words to render Aristotle's *mythos* in his translation of this statement: خرافة, *khurāfa*, which refers to a fantastic tale; and حكاية, *ḥikāya*, which connotes imitation or mimicry. The meaning of *khurāfa* today is essentially the same as it was for Mattā: today, it still means "fantastic tale." *Ḥikāya*, however, was a word in motion during the Abbasid era. It meant one thing before Abū Bishr Mattā used it as part of a portfolio of Arabic words that rendered the Aristotelian theory of mimesis in Arabic. After Mattā's translation of the *Poetics*, after al-Azdī's *Ḥikāyat Abī al-Qāsim*, after the skirmishes over language, languages, and logic that characterized the intellectual life of eleventh-century Baghdad, it came to mean something different. Many factors no doubt influenced the shift in meaning that pushed the word *ḥikāya* out of its comfort zone. I emphasize the significance of the collision of languages that occurred during the translation movement, and the communication between Aristotle's Greek and Mattā's Arabic in particular, for two reasons. In the first place, the long historical reach of the cosmopolitan language, its ability to bend and stretch under pressure yet retain communicative power through the centuries, is my topic in this section. Second, there is a delightful irony in the reading I offer here, in which the use of Arabic by a nonnative speaker may have a decisive influence in transforming the meaning of an Arabic word. The cosmopolitan language may be used to snub men with accents; but sometimes these men have the last word. Sometimes, they send that word skimming over the surface of the cosmopolitan language, like a pebble skipped over the surface of a pond; sometimes, it dances over the depths of the language for a millennium or more.

[CHAPTER 9]

"I Became a Fable"

Arabic and Latin in twelfth-century al-Andalus;
Latin and Italian in fourteenth-century Italy

"What's that supposed to mean?"

"We don't know how to read it yet. All we can do right now is pay witness."

COLSON WHITEHEAD, *Zone One*[1]

The Aristotelian corpus reached the Latin West by multiple routes. Some of Aristotle's treatises had been translated from Greek into Latin during late antiquity and had cultivated the full complement of commentary and elaboration in their Latin transmission during the course of the first Christian millennium. The philosopher Boethius (d. ca. 526 CE) translated the first six treatises of the Aristotelian Organon (the treatises on logic and debate) into Latin and wrote commentaries on them.[2] The Latin West received other philosophical works through Arabic-Islamic transmission. In some cases, the treatises translated from Arabic into Latin were already known in translation from the Greek; other treatises entered the orbit of the Latin language through translation from Arabic. The whole of the Organon—including the *Rhetoric* and *Poetics,* incorporated into the Organon during its late-antique reception history—would appear in Latin when the Averroistic commentaries on them were translated from the Arabic. This transmission history—through generations of translation, retranslation, and commentary—introduced the Latin West to Aristotle's *Poetics.* The commentaries of the Andalusian philosopher Ibn Rushd (known to the Christian West as Averroes, he was born in Cordoba in 1126 and died in Marrakesh in 1198) were not in fact *translations* of Aristotle's works. However, they were understood as such by Latin scholars who knew that Ibn Rushd embedded the text of Aristotle in the fabric of his own readings of the text alongside the filters of late-antique Greek commentary, Syriac translation and commentary, Arabic translation, and generations of Islamic commentary incorporated into the Averroistic commentaries.

Ibn Rushd, like Aristotle himself, was the hired philosophical gun of a great leader. Aristotle tutored Alexander the Great when Alexander was young and continued to mentor him by correspondence when Alexander went on to greater things. Ibn Rushd wrote his commentaries in order to explain the works of Aristotle to the Almohad caliph Abū Ya'qūb Yūsuf (r. 1163–1184), whose conquests were more modest than Alexander's—he toppled the Almoravid dynasty in Seville, Spain, in 1172—and who would die fighting the advancing Christian armies in al-Andalus. Unlike Aristotle, and unlike Abū Bishr Mattā (whose translation of and commentary on Aristotle I discussed in the previous chapter), Ibn Rushd worked in a geo-chronological hinterland. Al-Andalus was the far western marches of the Arabic-Islamic world, and during Ibn Rushd's life it was beset by conflict between the rival Almohad and Almoravid dynasties and between Christians and Muslims. Furthermore, Ibn Rushd wrote at a moment when the Arabic-Islamic philosophical tradition was entering a period of decline. It is a profound irony, and wholly unpredictable from Ibn Rushd's own perspective, that his commentaries would have their greatest impact not in the Arabic-Islamic world but in Latin translation and in the Christian West.[3]

The commentaries of Ibn Rushd would be translated into Latin en masse shortly after they were written, all within a half century of his death. These interpretations reintroduced the work of Aristotle to the Latin West, becoming the topic of intense and focused study. Scandalized bishops banned the works of Aristotle, along with the commentaries on Aristotle by Avicenna and Averroes, at the universities of Paris and Oxford multiple times during the thirteenth century.[4] But that was (as the old saw goes) like closing the barn door after the cows are gone. Thomas Aquinas (1225–1274), who lived exactly a century after Ibn Rushd, cited Averroist concepts some 503 times in his own works, by one scholar's reckoning.[5]

In this chapter, I continue to trace the path that Aristotle's *Poetics* followed, via translation and commentary, through Arabic into Latin. As in the last chapter, my intention is in part to watch while cosmopolitan languages flex their muscles: while they pass a philosophical work hand to hand, from the Islamic heartland to the back of beyond and from al-Andalus to Paris. The currency of Arabic in tenth-century Baghdad and twelfth-century al-Andalus allowed it to manage the challenge of translating this literary curiosity—a treatise on the poetic arts from another language and another age altogether—and to argue for its relevance in the present. Mutatis mutandis, the same holds for Latin. At the same time, by watching a translation tradition like this one—like the Mississippi or the Nile, it is both wide and long—the attentive observer can discern the cosmopolitan language tinkering with its own workings. In the last chapter, we watched the Arabic word *ḥikāya* grow new meanings, perhaps in part in response to the translation tradition into which it was drawn. Pressed into service to translate the Aristotelian theory of mimesis, the word learned a new behavior. In this chapter, that history continues, as both Arabic and Latin respond to ambient changes and to the challenges specific to this translation tradition. The two languages struggle to explain ancient Greek poetics to a new audience. In so doing, they push words to bear new weight, sometimes to delightful effect.

∴

Unlike other treatises in the Aristotelian corpus, Aristotle's *Poetics* had not been translated from Greek to Latin in late antiquity. It entered Latin by means of a thirteenth-century translation of Ibn Rushd's Arabic commentary on it. Ibn Rushd, of course, had no access to (and no interest in) the Greek "original" of the treatise, which was much contested even within the orbit of the Greek language.[6] He seems to have known Mattā's translation, along with the (much briefer) syntheses of Ibn Sīnā and al-Fārābī;[7] there may, of course, have been other works at his disposal that are not known to modern scholars. He chose among these options, selecting the readings that he found most provocative and useful and ignoring others.[8] In his manipulation of this received tradition, Ibn Rushd made two decisive innovations. He elaborated the text by adding a multitude of citations from the Arab poets and (much less frequently) from the Qur'an to illustrate Aristotle's points. He was, remarkably, the first of the commentators to use poetic citation to illustrate Aristotle's poetic theory. In addition, fortunately for the Western transmission history of the *Poetics*, Ibn Rushd accepted the transformation of *tragedy* and *comedy* into *poetry of praise* (or *encomium*) and *poetry of blame* (or *satire*). He rejected the technical terms transliterated from the Greek that al-Fārābī and Ibn Sīnā had used to translate *tragedy* and *comedy* in their discussions of the *Poetics*, which communicated little to an Arab audience. In his decisions regarding terminology and the use of Arabic poetry to illustrate an ancient Greek philosophy of poetry, Ibn Rushd's treatment of the *Poetics* represents a typical "domesticating" translation: he reworks a foreign and unfamiliar tradition in order to create something of use to contemporary readers in their own language and in the context of their own culture.[9]

Given the distance that separated them both geographically and historically—Mattā lived and worked two and a half centuries earlier than

Ibn Rushd in what is now Iraq—it is no surprise that Ibn Rushd's account of Aristotle's poetic theory should differ radically from Mattā's. Along with the transliterated Greek rhetorical vocabulary, the Arabic noun *ḥikāya*—one of a portfolio of words that Mattā used to translate Aristotle's theory of mimesis—has dropped out of Ibn Rushd's treatise. Ibn Rushd uses verbs derived from the same lexical root to express the concept of mimesis.[10] However, the nominal form *ḥikāya* does not appear in his commentary. Ibn Rushd responded to an Arabic literary tradition that had undergone significant development since the early tenth century, when Mattā took on Aristotle's *Poetics*. The narrative tradition that was emergent during Mattā's lifetime, the tales that both related a sequence of events and engaged in sophisticated, witty wordplay (exemplified by the *Ḥikāyat Abī al-Qāsim* and the *maqāmāt*), has proved less central to Arabic letters than has poetry. Poetry in myriad genres—there at the beginning of the Arabic language, even before the Qur'an—is now, in twelfth-century al-Andalus, what Arabs embrace as the heart and soul of their literary tradition. Arabic poetry, like Greek drama, entangles ethics (praise of the virtuous and blame of the vicious) and linguistic pyrotechnics, and the commentaries on the *Poetics* strive to explain the symbiosis between the two. For these reasons, Ibn Rushd has dismantled those reflections on the plot construction of Greek drama in Aristotle's treatise (or disregarded the fragments of this argument that reached him), replacing them with notions more appropriate to a literary theory that speaks to poetry.

But there still remained vestigial traces of the passages in Aristotle's *Poetics* that analyzed plot construction, in order to explain how narrative—a complex sequence of events not true but plausible, mimetically enacted on the stage—can teach an audience important truths. To comment on these portions of the work, Ibn Rushd must choose from the lexical options that the Arabic language makes available to him in order to respond to the provocation he finds in the Arabic-Aristotelian tradition that has reached him. "Plot (*mythos*) is the *mimesis* of action (*praxis*)": when he renders this key phrase in Arabic, Ibn Rushd rejects *ḥikāya*—the word (one of them) that Mattā used to translate the Greek *mythos* and thus to describe the narrative sequence of events that drive drama. *Ḥikāya* in Ibn Rushd's time, two and a half centuries after Mattā's translation, has presumably settled into its modern meaning: "story, tale." The word is too narrow to convey the meaning that Ibn Rushd intends. Instead, Ibn Rushd uses the other term that Mattā made available, one used by Ibn Sīnā as well: *khurāfa*, which designates a tall tale or fabulous story, particularly one deemed pretty, despite its falsehood.[11] Ibn Rushd's translation of Aristotle's programmatic statement on the construction of plot reads: "Poetic statements are fabulous tales" (*al-aqāwīl al-shuʿriyya khurāfāt*).[12] Ibn Rushd imagines the confections of the poets as aural and conceptual baubles, inventions that create meaning through imagery that strikes the ear and the mind's eye simultaneously. The sound of the poetry, the image it generates: this is the stimulus his commentary must evoke and explain. *Khurāfa* connotes tales that deliver vivid images to our imagination; this is the word that Ibn Rushd uses to convey and analyze Aristotle's meaning in this passage.

In Ibn Rushd's commentary on Aristotle's *Poetics*, the poet is a moral actor, someone whose verbal inventions convey the fundamental truths that should guide our lives as thinking beings. At the same time, the poet is an inventor: one whose words bring into being creations that need have no mimetic link to historical realia. The poet's tall tales should help us to live a better life, by showing us examples of virtue and heroism that we might emulate and by satirizing the vicious life we should avoid. Or poetry may lead us astray. In one of the aphorisms that would make its way into the Latin translation of his treatise and the Latin florilegia culled from the translation, Ibn Rushd warns that love poetry, if not conceived to elevate the reader, may incite its audience to lust.[13] The *khurāfa*—the tall tale spun by the poet, the words that float like bubbles, then burst—may infect the audience with a moral virus, goading them to actions that will bring them and those around them to grief.

Ibn Rushd's treatise on Aristotle's *Poetics* was translated into Latin in 1256, less than a century after it was written.[14] Like most of Ibn Rushd's writings, this treatise had much greater success in the Latin West than in the Arab or Byzantine world (at least for the first seven centuries of its reception history). The translator of Ibn Rushd's commentary on the *Poetics*, Hermannus Alemannus, has been—like Mattā ibn Yūnus before him—roundly mocked by modern scholars for his presumed miscomprehension of the treatise he translated. Yet Hermannus's version of Ibn Rushd's commentary enjoyed a modest success among a late medieval and early modern readership. It was copied and its content excerpted and disseminated in florilegia, and in this way it came to be much more widely known than the version of Aristotle's *Poetics* translated directly from the Greek into Latin at roughly the same time. That version of the *Poetics* (created by William of Moerbeke just a few years after Hermannus's, in 1278) survives in only two manuscript versions and was unread during the Middle Ages.[15] Even after the Greek text of the *Poetics* reached Italy (following the fall of Constantinople to the Ottomans in 1453), it would take a full century of debate for scholars to push away Hermannus's version of Ibn Rushd's commentary on Aristotle's *Poetics* (and the subsequent Latin translations of Ibn Rushd's treatise made via a Hebrew synthesis of Ibn Rushd's Arabic) and to accept the Greek version—

with all its peculiarities—as Aristotle's authoritative statement on poetic composition.[16]

Hermannus's Latin generally follows Ibn Rushd's Arabic very closely. Thus Aristotle's statement on the plot of epic comes to be translated word for word from Ibn Rushd's Arabic in Hermannus's Latin version: "sermones poetici fabule sunt."[17] Poetic statements are *fabule*—"fables" or "fantastic tales": here, Hermannus dutifully renders Ibn Rushd's perception that the poet might dissemble in order to represent a greater truth. Like Ibn Rushd's *khurāfa*, Hermannus's *fabula* proposes an image of the poet as a spinner of tall tales. In medieval Latin, *fabula* most often refers to the improbable, complex narratives of Ovid's *Metamorphoses* and to the simple teaching tales of Aesop, often used for Latin education—not fantastic like Ovid's, although they do typically feature speaking, reasoning animals.[18] But the word was not frequently used in medieval Latin manuals on poetic composition. It appears only twice in the best-known Latin treatises on poetics, the *Ars versificatoria* of Matthew of Vendôme and the *Poetria nova* of Geoffrey of Vinsauf, when Matthew uses it as pejorative to name the fantastic tales produced in school exercises.[19]

The absence of the technical term *fabula* in medieval Latin poetic treatises makes Hermannus's use of it all the more striking. When *fabula* appears for the first time in Hermannus's translation, reflecting the word *khurāfa* in the Arabic, Hermannus, like Ibn Rushd before him, is describing the portfolio of rhetorical strategies that the poet uses to buttress lyric invention: devices like metaphor, simile, metonymy, and so on. Here, Hermannus discusses the use of a representational strategy that encompasses both realistic representation and fantastic invention:

> Sunt *fabule* que referuntur per assimilationem et representationem seu imitationem; et dico "*fabulam*" compositionem rerum quarum intenditur representatio aut secundum hoc quod sunt in semetipsis, aut secundum quod assuetum est in poeticis fingere eas, quamvis sit fictio mendosa. Et propter hoc dictum est quoniam sermones poetici *fabule* sunt.[20]

> *Fables* are those things that are depicted through likeness and representation or imitation; and I call "*fable*" a composition of those things that embrace representation either according to that which they are in themselves, or according to what is customary to pretend them to be in poetic [compositions], although they are false fiction. For this reason it is said that poetic statements are *fables*.

The word *fable*, which I have italicized in both Hermannus's Latin and my translation, identifies the modus operandi of poetry. It describes poetic invention as composite: derived from both mimetic representation of reality ("according to that which [things] are in themselves") and nonmimetic strategies, poetic conventions that don't pretend to be realistic (that might even be "false fiction"). Following this passage, in which the term is defined, whenever Ibn Rushd uses the noun *khurāfa* or the adjective *khurāfī* to describe the derivation and ethical dimension of poetic invention, Hermannus follows suit with *fabula* or *fabularis*.

Thus, once again, translation has taught an old word new tricks. But here, it seems, the trail grows cold. Unlike the Arabic *ḥikāya*, which acquired a new range of meanings under the pressure of translation and changing literary fashions, *fabula* seems not to have metamorphosed after Hermannus's repurposing of it. This phrase—"sermones poetici *fabule* sunt"; "poetic statements are *fables*"—was among those collected and disseminated in the earliest known florilegium of Hermannus's translation of Ibn Rushd's commentary on Aristotle's *Poetics*.[21] Men of letters might have encountered it in florilegia like this, extracted from Hermannus's argument, a maxim to be pondered if not thoroughly plumbed. It's difficult to know what they might make of it. Poetic statements are *fantastic narratives*: tales of transformation (like Ovid's), tales in which animals speak (like Aesop's). Poetic statements are *chatter*. Poetic statements are *gossip*. All these interpretations are possible. Since antiquity, the Latin *fabula* has referred to a fantastic invented tale, but also to any kind of common talk passed between people: conversation, rumors, idle chat.[22]

Certainly that last sense is what Petrarch means when he uses the word in the opening sonnet of the *Canzoniere*. Of course, Petrarch uses the *Italian* cognate of the Latin word; but here the distinction between Italian and Latin is academic. The Latin is *fabula*; the Italian is *favola*; and Petrarch himself is the fable.

Ma ben veggio or sí come al popol tutto
favola fui gran tempo, onde sovente
di me mesdesmo meco mi vergogno. . . .[23]

But now I see well how for all the people
I became a fable for a long time, wherefore often
I am ashamed of myself within myself. . . .

Here, *favola* signifies "chatter, gossip." Commenting on this line, the editor Marco Santagata quotes a number of scriptural and classical Latin passages in which a speaker laments being made the *fabula* of the crowd.[24] In English, these lines are typically translated "Now I see how I have become *the target of gossip*." But in light of the foregoing discussion of the fates of the Latin *fabula*, it is tempting to see a plurality of meanings in Petrarch's use of its Italian cognate. It might connote "idle talk" or "gossip." It might signify "a fantastic tale, a fable": Petrarch as the fourteenth-century equivalent of a reality star of the twenty-first century. And it might mean, in addition, "a poetic invention, combined of both mimetic and nonmimetic elements spun out of the personality and ethical stance of the poet, that sustains a lyric poem or a collection of lyric poems": we might see in it some of the connotations that it acquired through engagement with the Arabic philosophical-poetic tradition. In the line that follows ("di me mesdesmo meco mi vergogno"), Petrarch circumambulates a monument of self, circling slowly like a leaf settling to the ground, like a funeral dirge in three-quarter time. "I myself, within myself, am ashamed of myself": the line foreshadows much that is to come in the *Rime sparse*, as if *me* were another way to say *you* ("*Voi* ch'ascoltate"; "*You* who listen"), as if *I* were both the point of origin and the vanishing point of the collection as a whole.

Petrarch uses the word *favola* one more time in the *Rime sparse*, in the second half of the collection:

> La mia *favola* breve è già compita,
> et fornito il mio tempo a mezzo gli anni.[25]
>
> My brief *fable* is already complete,
> and my time brought to a close midway through my years.

In his gloss on this passage, Marco Santagata sends the reader to Petrarch's letters, where Petrarch uses the Latin *fabula* to refer to the span of his years.[26] In fact, Petrarch has just written "la mia vita" ("my life"), in rhyme position, in the tercet that precedes the lines quoted above. Again, the connotations seem clear. *Favola* signifies the poet's life as compass of years and as narrative thread that links a series of brief poetic components. Petrarch's personal experience is (as always) both present and irrelevant in this sonnet, because his poetic inventions are (as always) both mimetic and antimimetic: a love poem placed squarely between two people; a meditation in which his beloved, Laura, is both omnipresent and superfluous.

Petrarch's use of the Italian *favola* here, understood as an Italian resurrection of the Latin *fabula*, embodies a combination of mimetic and nonmimetic features, an artisanal cocktail mixed by language workers (philosophers, translators, commentators, poets, copyists, and compilers of digests), distilled from multiple languages. Like the Arabic *ḥikāya* before it, the word has metamorphosed under pressure. Mattā's *ḥikāya* translated Aristotle's *mythos*; but by the time Ibn Rushd got into the commentary game, *ḥikāya* had moved on. Its meaning changed, until it could no longer respond to the *haecceity* of a passage in which Aristotle describes the plot of tragedy. For philosophers, the word *haecceity* designates the "this-ness" or "such-ness" of a thing: the unique qualities that distinguish each individual thing or being from others of its kind.[27] Literary historians don't use the word, although we could—in particular, to describe the linguistic characteristics privileged by the national language system of Europe and by modern literary and aesthetic revolutions. Modern literature in a realist or naturalist mode aims for immediacy, contemporaneity, and continuity with lived life. In the same way, modern literature written in the European national languages aspires to *linguistic* continuity with contemporary life. *Haecceity* might be used to name the "such-ness" of lived experience represented in a literary text written in the same language in which that experience was lived: the dynamic vitality of the literary text written in the mother tongue. The gut punch delivered by Dashiell Hammett's tommy-gun sentences, Raymond Chandler's exquisite, oppressively florid prose, William Faulkner's plaintive vernacular genius, F. Scott Fitzgerald's gauzy neo-Romantic phrasing: if these authors had written in a learned register, their works would lack the haecceity for which they have been treasured by generations of readers. They would not likely have been written were the vernacular not available as literary medium and would never have been read (as today they might) under the bedsheets with a flashlight or in a hammock under spreading summer leaves or by the fireside on a winter afternoon.

In the context of translation between languages, *haecceity* might signify the dynamic of linguistic contiguity and intimacy that connects the modern translation to the present. Modern publishers have little interest in retranslations of scientific works, which lose their relevance with the passage of time. The exceptions are retranslated for their cultural merits: the works of Galileo or Freud, for instance. Classic literary works, however—like the Homeric epics or Virgil's *Aeneid*—must be retranslated for every generation, and some (Dante's *Commedia* is the classic example) much more often. The modern translation pushes aside the textual network of the transmission tradition—the pedigree that links translation to translation, commentary to translation, and new philosophical treatise to commentary to translation, stretching from the moment when the original text was written to the present day. Each modern translation vaporizes this textual tissue, seeking to represent the haecceity of the original in the linguistic present: it aims to recreate the original in the contemporary idiom.

Hikaya, in contrast, proposes a different relationship both to the textual prehistory of the translation and to its representation of that past in the present. The Arabic word *ḥikāya* meant "mimicry" until, under the pressure of the Abbasid translation movement and the swift evolution of the Arabic literary tradition, it came to mean something more: a constellation of linguistic performances that conspire to produce a tale. Here, I use the (barely) anglicized word *hikaya* to designate one behavior of the premodern translation movements. The modern translation observes a mimetic convention when it aims to push aside the rubble of centuries and reproduce the premodern text in contemporary garb. But hikaya is nonmimetic or even antimimetic. It is written in continuity and in communication with a deep tradition of linguistic and literary affiliations. In the case of translations, even scientific translations, the text affirms and annexes those works—the previous translations, retranslations, and commentaries on philosophical treatises, as well as the literary works that riff on those traditions—that connect it in a complex but unbroken chain to its "original." The scare quotes caressing that word signal the complicated affiliation between the text viewed as initiator of a tradition and its distant avatar. *Hikaya* names the strategies that the translation uses to respond to a submerged textual history: when the language expresses its fidelity to its own past, to historical and extralingual influences not visible to the naked eye, rather than remaining faithful to the linguistic present.

Or, in reference to literature (rather than scientific translation), *hikaya* might signify the text's refusal to engage in linguistic actuality: its choice of the deep history of the language rather than or in addition to linguistic usage in the present. In the opening sonnet of the *Canzoniere*, *favola* means "chatter," the gossip that torments the beleaguered lover. But not to see in it other meanings, simultaneously and without detracting attention from this primary meaning, is to impoverish it. In sonnet 254, *favola* means "life": the eventful charade that will end all too soon. It also denotes the biographical fiction that sustains Petrarch's invention, at once truth and conceit. To illustrate my point, I'll turn away from premodern translations and from the world of literature to consider another representation of the complications of mimesis. In the movie *Playtime* (1967), director Jacques Tati allows his camera to linger on large pools of glass: the sheath of the classic modernist office building.[28] Sometimes the exterior glass walls of his office buildings are transparent and sometimes they turn opaque; sometimes they reflect an exterior surface and sometimes they reveal the interior life of the building. They might act as invisible barrier (to the chagrin of the businessman who collides with them). They might be illuminated pools that attract the eyes of passersby to interior tableaux or might reflect ground or sky when seen from outside. In a similar way, in my reading, Petrarch's *favola* is at once Italian and Latin; in a similar way, it allows diverse meanings, sometimes at tension with each other, to be present simultaneously. So too, like Tati's modernist office buildings, the premodern translation sometimes works diligently to reveal the workings of the original beneath the sheath of a new language. At other times, it deflects the gaze from the original, so that the reader sees other scenes reflected in its surface: the long tradition of responses to the original, or newly detected relevance to the moment in which the translation is being made. Not mimesis, then, but a more playful relationship between present and past and between "translation" and "original": hikaya.

Like the surfaces of Jacques Tati's windows—at once transparent and reflective—Petrarch's poetry keeps multiple truths in play. The personality of the poet, who speaks always in his own voice, is the thread that links the discrete compositions that make up his diwan. After all, Petrarch did write something like the Arab poet's diwan, a collection of poems in diverse styles and on diverse topics, bound together by the personality of the author himself. Petrarch's collection has a hint of a framing fiction: his love and conversion; the life and death of Laura. But this through line doesn't distract us from the main action of the *Canzoniere*. The poet's bravura performance, the divagations of genius, the *path* or *lane* or *alleyway* (as the manuscript Conventi Soppressi G.IV.936 expresses it; see the epigraph to chapter 5) of the Italian language itself; the conscience of the poet, the personality as plot: these are the story lines that pull us onward, that compel us to turn page after page and to lose ourselves in the labyrinth (in Petrarch's own metaphor). Like the diwans of the Arab poets, Petrarch's *Canzoniere* is a collection of poems in which life and language meld.

Of course, my point is (merely) comparative: one cannot responsibly argue that Petrarch was inspired by the example of the Arab poets.[29] One could, however, suggest that Petrarch intended to invest a specific word—the Italian *favola*, cognate to the Latin *fabula*—with the connotations and associations of the Latin *fabula*. Petrarch, after all, was deeply invested in Latinity (see the discussion above, chapter 3). He saw Latin as the language of past and future: Latin, not the vernacular, was the language with the ability to erase time. When he turned to Italian, which he did periodically throughout his life, he was in a sense cheating on Latin. The *Rerum vulgarium fragmenta* is an arabesque embroidered on the hem of Latinity: a work that he dallied with—intensely, to be sure, but without (as it were) hope of issue—particularly at certain periods of his life, including his final years.[30] In the case of Italian, more so than the other Romance vernaculars, the veil between Latin and the vernacular is exceptionally diaphanous. Because of their shared history, because Latin remained the language of the Roman Church, Latin and Italian had a peculiarly symbiotic relationship. Therefore Petrarch could, if he wished, give the word *favola* the connotations of the Latin *fabula*—as Marco Santagata argues, in order to make the word mean "chatter" or "gossip" (in sonnet 1), or to make it mean "life" (in sonnet 254). He might at the same time be thinking of Hermannus's definition of poetry: "sermones poetici *fabule* sunt"; "poetic statements are *fables*." As a young man, Petrarch lived in Avignon, where the florilegium of Hermannus's translation of Averroes's treatise on Aristotle's *Poetics* was known to circulate, so it's possible that he knew the text, in one form or another. Perhaps he uses the deep history of the word *favola* in sonnet 1 in order to reveal the topic of his collection: the poet himself as fantastic invention, created and sustained by chatter; the poet himself as subject of his poetry.

Do we love the *Canzoniere* for its hikaya or its haecceity? Do we love it because it is fresh, true to life, vibrant, dynamic, living, relatable, seductive in its music and the vitality of its message? Or do we cherish it because it sends us deep into a labyrinth of language, obliging us to feel the presence of a dappled plurality of meanings?[31] The word *labyrinth* was given a programmatic meaning by Petrarch, and I mean my English word to echo Petrarch's Italian:

> Mille trecento ventisette, a punto
> su l'ora prima, il dí sesto d'aprile,
> nel laberinto intrai, né veggio ond'esca.[32]
>
> Thirteen hundred twenty seven, exactly
> at the first hour, on the sixth of April,
> I entered the labyrinth, and still I see no way out.

Here, Petrarch (again) collapses the personal and the poetic: he names the precise hour when he first saw Laura, and time was elided into an infinite poetic regress. Petrarch's Italian is not mimetic in any straightforward or simplistic way. It possesses some of the timelessness of his Latin, and it requires us to work to bring ourselves to its level and to unlock its meanings, as the Alexandrian languages do. In part, this is because the categories I have identified using the literary-historical neologisms *hikaya* and *haecceity* do not name qualities that can be isolated and analyzed through experimentation, like elements in the periodic table. In part, it's because Petrarch writes on the boundary between the two systems: the cosmopolitan and the vernacular; the premodern and the modern styles of literary performance. His vernacular is simultaneously current, expressive of the haecceity of his plight, and timeless—noodling with lexical memories in part borrowed from the Latin prehistory of Italian and in part created in the play between poems within the work itself. This second quality—timelessness, lexical play, an investment in deep linguistic history; neither mimetic nor antimimetic, but consumed with the music of the medium itself—encompasses the behaviors that I have called *hikaya*. Petrarch's language is not at all fresh, dewy, or spontaneous: it is at times practiced, studious, and circular in its logics. His vernacularity draws into itself some of the ponderous depth and the Alexandrian acrobatics of the cosmopolitan language itself: the *late work* of Latin, as I argued in chapter 3.

But Petrarch lived during a watershed moment in the history of the Italian language: during an age when prominent men of letters wrote both in the vernacular and the cosmopolitan language. This period would last for several centuries in the Italian context. Most regions of Europe moved decisively toward vernacular composition during the late Middle Ages. But in Italy, because of the symbiotic relationship between Latin and Italian and also in large part in response to Petrarch's authority and Petrarch's influence, men of letters executed a volte-face. More authors in the Italian Peninsula embraced Latin as a viable and dynamic literary instrument during the fifteenth century than in most other parts of western Europe: a ratification of Petrarch's deep feeling for the language and of his sense that Latin was central to Italy's future.

I conclude this tour through the translations of Aristotle's *Poetics*—this portrait gallery of subsequent translation movements, from the Abbasid East to the Latin West—with a portrait of Petrarch hesitating:[33] Petrarch hovering between Latin and Italian; Petrarch investing in his vernacular compositions some of the qualities that he associated with and loved in his Latin. Later in this book, we will meet a man who, in a sense, *became a language*: the dragoman, whose function as negotiator between languages was usurped by the Mediterranean lingua franca (see chapter 12). Petrarch was *the man who became a fable*: he himself the premise and the organizing fiction of his collection of vernacular fragments. Petrarch invested in the vernacular poetry his hunger for a language that might convey at once the plangent music of desire and the gravitas of literary history. In his late work on the *Rerum vulgarium fragmenta*, Petrarch showed us—using the humble medium of his Italian—how he felt about his Latin: not because his Laura was a metaphor for his Latin, but because in the vernacular poetry, he performed the nomad writer's desire for the once and future language.

[CHAPTER 10]

A Spy in the House of Language

Arabic in Egypt and England, nineteenth century

> Earlier scholars only worked with the noble language, but I have loved it: my affection for it is so true that I prick up my ears to its parchments; I have lit my wicks with it, and I spend my nights in it.
>
> AḤMAD FĀRIS AL-SHIDYĀQ, *Sirr al-layāl fī al-qalb wa-al-ibdāl* (*Secrets of the Nights: On Metathesis and Substitution*)[1]

If Petrarch was the man who became a fable, the shadowy, long-dead figure Khurāfa was the man who became a tale. The Arabic word *khurāfa*—the word used by Ibn Rushd to signify poetic inventions, which would be transformed in Hermannus's Latin translation into *fabula* (see chapter 9)—has a curious lexical status. According to the Arabic lexicographic tradition, it was the proper name of the man whose experiences inspired the word. I excerpt from the definition found in Edward William Lane's great *Arabic-English Lexicon* (1863–1893):

> خُرَافَةٌ—*Stories that are deemed pretty.* . . . خُرَافَةٌ was the name of a man, of the tribe of 'Odhrah, whom the Jinn (or Genii) fascinated, as the Arabs assert, and carried off, and who related what he had seen of them when he returned, and they pronounced him a liar, and said of a thing that was impossible, خُرَافَةٌ حَدِيث [*a story of Khuráfeh*]: but it is related of the Prophet, that he said, خُرَافَةٌ حَقٌّ, meaning *What Khuráfeh relates* [as heard] from the Jinn [*is true*]. . . .[2]

In classical Arabic, *khurāfa* meant "fantastic tales," and the word retains that meaning to the present day. The basic meaning of the lexical root from which it derives, however, is "to gather or pluck," referring in the first instance to fruit. Perhaps the distance between the fundamental semantic range of the root and the meaning of this outlier noun, which designates a story that is both fantastic and beautiful, accounts for the legend of a man fed fabulous stories by the jinn, stories that scarcely seemed credible although the Prophet affirmed their truth. Lane's definition begins with an unwonted aesthetic note, not typical either of his dictionary or of modern definitions of this word: "stories that are deemed *pretty*." Twentieth-century dictionaries don't judge the aesthetic merits of the tales that Khurāfa told. They define the word as a fantastic, fabulous tale; a funny tale or joke; or even a superstition.

I reproduce Lane's definition here with nearly all the typographic tics and lexicographic arcana intact because the tissue of this dictionary is part of my topic in this chapter. Edward William Lane (1801–1876) created a tribute to the classical Arabic language (for him, this term referred to the usage of the Bedouins, who possessed "the utmost chasteness of speech," and the Qur'an[3]), a work that represents the rich Arabic lexical tradition with marvelous fidelity. At the same time, the dictionary sometimes reads like a *khurāfa* itself: a fantastic tale, one that takes unpredictable turns and is occasionally difficult to parse. In this brief excerpt, we see most of the hallmark literary characteristics of Lane's style. Lane wrote before a standard transliteration system had been established, and as a result his transliterations at times appear eccentric (using the Library of Congress system, Lane's *'Odhrah* would be transliterated *'Udhra*). His reasons for preferring transliteration rather than the Arabic alphabet sometimes are mysterious, and his use of square brackets rather than parentheses and italic type rather than roman seems at times whimsical. His learned interjections are usually illuminating and erudite; here, however, the use of the Latin *genii* to gloss the unrelated Arabic *jinn* mystifies. Lane was a fastidious scholar, and I do not mean to call into question the depth of his knowledge or the reliability of the dictionary. Rather, I point out a fact that all who have used the dictionary have, at one time or another, noticed. Lane's *Arabic-English Lexicon* is a macaronic confection in which the English language translates the great Arabic lexica with fidelity but, at the same time, mysterious transferences occur: Arabic infests English, and English itself seems to be prone to sudden flights of fancy.

In this chapter, I will set Lane's experiences and achievements alongside the life and work of a man who was his contemporary and who (like Lane) possessed a passionate enthusiasm for the Arabic lexicon. Literary author and newspaper editor Aḥmad Fāris al-Shidyāq (1804–1887) felt a deep attachment to the lexicographic tradition and the historical memory of the Arabic language. Like Lane, he recognized the need for a reformation of Arabic lexicography and, in particular, for a modern Arabic dictionary. Both men experimented with the tissue of language, though their sensibilities and strategies differed. In this chapter, I will pay tribute to their lexical shenanigans in order to reflect not upon *translation* (the focus of the previous two chapters) but rather upon *time,* the other of the twin themes of this section of the book.

In their discussion of the temporality of medieval icons, art historians Christopher Wood and Alexander Nagel explain that the icon "stitched through time, pulling two points on the chronological timeline together until they met."[4] The cosmopolitan language, like the icon, has the capacity to bundle discrete historical moments: to put contemporaneity in colloquy with the past and even with multiple moments from the past simultaneously. It does not always achieve this transhistorical range by virtue of its lucidity and transparency. It is valued for its capacity to sustain meaning through the centuries, so that the noun *khurāfa,* for instance, means fundamentally the same thing to a reader of Arabic in the twenty-first century as it did to a reader of Arabic a millennium earlier. However, at times a word's meaning may change, as did the Arabic *ḥikāya* (see chapters 8 and 9) or the Latin *gramatica* (see chapter 3). This expanded lexical range is often additive, rather than substitutive: a word (like Nagel and Wood's icons) may hesitate between multiple meanings, so that it is the lexicographer's job to describe and account for multiple meanings (and the reader's job to choose among them for the best sense).[5] All words may acquire new meanings, of course. The cosmopolitan languages challenge the language worker because they may reach so far, historically and geographically, for lexical arsenal. Tracking the journey a word has traveled through time and space—as a lexicographer (like Lane) or literary author (like al-Shidyāq)—at times requires prodigious effort. This is, to use the technical term, the work of the philologist: the *lover* of the *logos,* of the word and the logics that grant it meaning.

The intertwined lives of the language workers in this chapter depict the choreography of the cosmopolitan language by knitting together words (and indeed a whole language) with the human labors that sustain them. The material history that feeds the cosmopolitan languages—papyrus, parchment, and paper; inks; the hands of copyists, printing presses, inkjet printers, and screens; scrolls, codices, books, and digital documents—is also a part of the story, though only a sliver of that can be reflected here. My aim is to map a psychogeography of the wanderings of Khurāfa, the man who became a word, in two segments: by relating episodes from the lives of Edward William Lane, a man whose life leeched away into his dictionary, and of Aḥmad Fāris al-Shidyāq, whose lexical exercises followed a very different itinerary through the dictionary. Both of these men traveled across the Mediterranean, and their peregrinations were crucial to their intellectual formation. But both were nomads (in the sense I use that word in this book) not because of their travels but rather because they lived in and through a language that itself was not rooted either to time or to territory. The first chapter in this section on time and translation investigated the claim that the lingua sacra could allow humans to level up from time to eternity. The story told in chapter 7 was also about language politics: What language will grant access to the divine; and what mortals merit access to this precious tongue? This chapter tells a similar story in a secular register. This book is a ballad for a language that is dead, and for those philologists who pick the lock and carry its corpse back to the world of the living.

∴

Edward William Lane began his scholarly life as an Egyptologist, during an age when Egypt was every schoolboy's dream world. Napoleon's expedition to Egypt at the turn of the nineteenth century had enflamed the European imagination. The exquisite, massive *Description de l'Égypte* (1809–1829)—with its illustrations of Egyptian flora and fauna and the material culture of antiquity—brought the wonders discovered by Napoleon's teams of explorers into sitting rooms and gentlemen's clubs throughout Europe. A traveling exhibition of Egyptian artifacts came to London in 1821 (when Lane was an impressionable twenty-year-old). Captivated by new images of an ancient world, Lane—then working as an engraver in London—made plans to travel to Egypt in order to document the antiquities. He had the notion of using the camera lucida to create more accurate reproductions of the monuments. But his interest from the beginning encompassed not only long-dead pharaohs but also contemporary Egypt and contemporary Arabs and their language, culture, and society. In order to prepare for the trip, he undertook to study the language, both classical Arabic and the Egyptian colloquial.[6] After three years of study, Lane left England. He spent the years 1825–1827 in Cairo; while there, he twice made the journey to Upper Egypt to see the spectacular, still largely unstudied antiquities.

Lane left England for Egypt in a glow of youthful enthusiasm; and in 1828, a year after his return, he wrote to a friend that "probably the greater part of my life will be spent in a foreign country."[7] But over time, he was obliged to recognize harsh financial and personal realities. Despite his affection for Egypt, a combination of factors would keep him in England for most of his life: money woes, family responsibilities, his demanding work schedule, health problems, and presumably, in later years, the increasing timidity of age. He made two extended trips to Cairo following the first, spending the years 1833–1835 and 1842–1849 there. Though he was an adventurous traveler in his early years—his journeys to Upper Egypt could provide a model for Indiana Jones—in midlife he would settle into a regime of impressive discipline. In 1841, when he had already completed a number of projects that did not earn him a living wage (including a translation of the Qur'an that prominent orientalist A. J. Arberry referred to as a "pot-boiler"[8]), he first began to discuss with Algernon Percy, his patron, the possibility of creating a new, modern Arabic-English dictionary.[9] He returned to Egypt a year later with the aim of gathering the lexical resources necessary for that project. During this period, and for the rest of his life, Lane lived essentially as a shut-in.[10] Protected by the women of his house, he worked relentlessly on the dictionary. Lane's household has inevitably attracted comment: the sister, an evangelical Christian with two children who had been abandoned by her preacher husband, class-conscious and haughty toward Muslims, even when keeping house for her brother in Cairo; and the wife, Nefeeseh, an enslaved Greek woman whom Lane had bought and manumitted on his first trip to Egypt, who suffered from numerous physical ailments and who seems to have been no match for the sister. The ladies refused all visitors with the exception of one day a week (Fridays while the family was in Cairo, Sundays after their return to England).[11] Even on these days of rest, Lane did not venture far from home. He lived a retiring life, pouring his energies into the dictionary.

Here, I hesitate: how should I convey the achievements of a man of inaction? In *Orientalism*, Edward Said sketches a damning portrait of Lane's reticence and his withdrawal from public life. Said condemns Lane's "refusal to join the society he describes" while Lane was writing his first book about Egypt, *An Account of the Manners and Customs of Modern Egyptians*. Here, Said is making a point about the "European" observer of Egyptian customs (although he writes exclusively about the English and the French). Lane refused marriage, even as he observed and recorded the marriage customs of Egyptians. This, Said argues, allowed Lane to be a dispassionate and scientific observer: it made possible "his definition of the Egyptians, since had he become one of them, his perspective would no longer have been antiseptically and asexually lexicographical." In Said's reading, Lane's obsessive reclusiveness carries through to his later works (which, to be fair, do not interest Said): the translation of *The Thousand and One Nights* and the *Arabic-English Lexicon*, in which

> his individuality has disappeared entirely as a creative presence, as of course has the very idea of a narrative work. Lane the man appears only in the official persona of annotator and retranslator (the *Nights*) and im-

> personal lexicographer. From being an author contemporary with his subject matter, Lane became—as Orientalist scholar of classical Arabic and classical Islam—its survivor.[12]

Said's condemnation seems tetchy to one who knows Lane's biography. Lane's retreat from the world outside his doors began early; it defined his habits even back in England. Following his return from the first trip to Egypt, when he was still in his twenties, Lane lived in London but did not leave his house for months on end, on his doctor's advice.[13]

I quibble, too, with Said's definition of Lane as "survivor" of "classical Arabic and classical Islam." In 1842, Lane and his entourage undertook their last journey to Egypt in order to gather materials for the dictionary. There, Lane worked alongside the Azhari scholar Ibrāhīm al-Dasūqī (1811–1883)—or, in Lane's transliteration, "the sheykh Ibráheem Ed-Dasooḳee"—to transcribe the dictionaries that he would use to compile the *Lexicon*.[14] Lane returned to England in 1849, carrying with him the transcriptions completed at that point. The work of transcription in Egypt would continue in Lane's absence; Lane deplored the delays in his copyist's work, but Dasūqī pled the extenuating circumstances of political regime change, which affected his access to manuscripts, and incompetent assistant copyists.[15] Lane would continue the work on the dictionary for the rest of his life, and the preface to the *Lexicon* evidences a preoccupation with decadence and mortality: Lane is aware that his work is a race against time. On the opening page of the preface to volume 1, he laments the death of his first benefactor, French orientalist Fulgence Fresnel, who started Lane on his path as lexicographer by generously giving him precious Arabic lexical manuscripts and introducing him to Dasūqī.[16] The manuscripts themselves are mortal: the ink is corrosive and the pages rotting or crumbling, so that they will soon be illegible.[17] Lane worries about language entropy. As it ages, the language becomes unintelligible even to those who consider themselves its custodians: "many explanations perfectly intelligible when they were first given became less and less so in succeeding ages, and at length quite unintelligible to the most learned of living Arabs."[18] Most poignant of all, he expresses anxiety that he himself will not outlive the language:

> I considered also that the undertaking which I had thus long been prosecuting was one which would require many more years for its completion; and that it was incumbent on me to take into account the uncertain duration of my appointed term of life, and to occupy myself first with what was most important.[19]

Following the preface, before the opening page of the *Lexicon*, a stark notice mourns the death of the first patron of the dictionary and recognizes that the work now depends on the beneficence of his widow.[20]

Pace Said, I am sorry to report that Lane did not "survive" Arabic; he died before completing work on the *Lexicon*. The *Lexicon*, however, survives Lane: a monument to Lane's engagement with Arabic, so invested in the early Islamic lexical and intellectual tradition that those of us who use it seldom open it without a moment of hesitation. Here, for instance, is a passage from the article on the root عرف (*ʿ-r-f*), which produces one of the fundamental Arabic verbs meaning "to know":

> It is said in the Baṣáïr that المَعْرِفَةُ differs from العِلْمُ, in meaning, in several ways: the former concerns the thing itself [which is its object;] whereas the latter concerns the states, or conditions, or qualities thereof: also the former generally denotes *the perceiving* a thing *as a thing that has been absent from the mind*, thus differing from the latter . . . ; and the former is *the knowing* a thing itself as *distinguished from other things*; whereas the latter concerns a thing collectively with other things.[21]

The sample, excerpted almost at random, displays the qualities seen in the passage quoted earlier: Arabic alphabet interspersed with the Roman alphabet and with transliterations of Arabic (eccentric nineteenth-century translations, as they appear today). Typical, too, is the learned discussion of distinctions between ways of knowing that makes little intuitive sense to a mind trained by other lexical and grammatical systems. From here, we might pass equally to a mereological discussion of parts and wholes or to God's knowledge as distinguished from human knowledge. In fact, we instead learn that differently vocalized, the same root form of the verb might signify "*He requited him*"; "*He clipped the* عُرْف [i.e. *mane*] *of the horse*"; "*He was patient on the occasion of the affliction*, or *misfortune*"; "*He* (a man) *was*, or *became, pleasant*, or *sweet, in his odour*."[22] Nor does the pageantry of the word stop here—though I am certain that my readers' patience will. The book is a market in which two languages barter words, a fever dream in which two languages dance with each other—ever more louche as the definition advances.[23]

I beg my readers' patience to linger a moment longer over one of the definitions just quoted, to elucidate the final ingredient in the cocktail that is Lane's prose. "*He was patient on the occasion of the affliction*, or *misfortune*," Lane writes, translating from the *Tāj al-ʿArūs*, a standard Arabic lexical reference. Yet the prose here has an irresistible rhythm, as if in departing from the one language the sentence had been carried off by jinn and emerged chanting spells in the other. In addition to its odd macaronic quality, its habit of veering precipitately from one language to another; in addition to the extraordinary prisms of meaning gathered in each definition; in addition to the typographic eccentricities, Lane's dictionary also includes passages like this one, marked by the sudden incursion of a poetic meter. Consider a phrase from Lane's definition of one of the basic Arabic words signifying "boundary," *thaghr*: "You say, *This is a city in which are gaps*, or *breaches*."[24] The framing of the definition—"You say"—is a literary habit borrowed from the Arabic lexicographical tradition. All the great Arabic dictionaries tell us how we speak; the verb here is in the indicative rather than the imperative. The galloping rhythm of the definition, however, is all Lane's, as is the curious decision to include this phrase without further explication. *Why* do I say "This is a city in which are gaps"? Is the fabric of the city itself riven, shot through with interstices? Are these interruptions of the space-time continuum, or simple potholes, priest holes, and beggars' hidey-holes? The linguistic and literary texture of the *Lexicon* (its juxtaposition of languages and alphabets; the array of disparate meanings; the occasional lapse into the most homely English poetic rhythm) at moments invites such grasping interpretations: something like a lexical sublime, in its luminous discontinuity.

The lexicographic tradition holds special importance for the Arabic language, in part because the lexicon is so large and includes so many rare words with such precise (often peculiar) definitions. It sometimes seems that Arabic words emerge through spontaneous generation, but formulas determine much of this process. Three-consonant roots generate most Arabic words. Each of these roots is associated with a range of meanings, and some arrangements of the root consonants with vowels—of which Arabic has only three, in long and short versions—produce words that convey predictable meanings. So, for example, the word *faʿala* is a verb that means "to do, to act." *Fāʿil* is the active participle. Because Arabic active participles are frequently used as nouns, *fāʿil* means "doing; the doer, the one who acts." *Kataba* means "to write"; *kātib* means "writing," "the writer," or "the scribe." It seems a laudably logical and transparent process, but the rules that govern the production of lexical matter are legion. For instance, verbs may generate "derived forms," with doubled root consonants or different patterns of vocalization or supplementary letters inserted before or between the root consonants. Each verb, the patriarch of each family of derived forms, has its own "aspects" (the Semitic equivalent of verb tenses), passive and active voice, participles, and so on, along with an attendant family of nouns and adjectives—all formed by following established patterns. Each derived form, in turn, conveys a specific meaning—in some cases predictable, given the meaning of the root; in others, not. Ten derived forms, including the base form of the verb, occur fairly frequently, although not every verb is attested in all ten forms. An additional four derived forms exist, although they are rarely seen in the wild.

The first chapter of the first book of *Al-sāq ʿala al-sāq* (1855), or *Leg over Leg*, by Aḥmad Fāris al-Shidyāq—published while Lane was at work on the dictionary, before the first volume of the *Lexicon* was published in 1863—begins by exulting in the lexicographic treasure house of the Arabic language. Following a dedication, an "author's notice" (that pays effusive tribute to dictionaries and to the exuberance of the Arabic lexicon—a spoiler for much of what is to come), a publisher's introduction (although al-Shidyāq was publisher of the book as well as author), and a "proem" in the form of a poem, chapter 1 begins with eleven synonyms equivalent to the English "Hush!" and calls on the reader to be silent and mind the author's words. The author's self-justification and self-elucidation (some would call it hedging and stalling) continue for several pages before he turns to the real meat of the chapter: a pileup of words naming the sexual organs, male and female, and their qualities, attributes, and conditions.[25] In Humphrey Davies's sparkling translation, a glance at these pages reveals their remarkable quality. The Arabic on the left-hand page is terse—a scant eight lines of words, each preceded by the Arabic connector *wa* (which may have many lexical functions but here means simply "and"). On the right-hand page a full thirty-six lines of English text translate, gloss, explicate, atone for, and pay tribute to the Arabic. I select just three elements from the melee:

والخبوق والخقوق والغقوق[26]

> . . . the woman whose vagina makes a sound when entered, the woman broad-buttocked as a donkey whose vulva also makes a sound, the one whose vagina makes another kind of sound . . .

The delirium of the passage is generated not only by the precise and abstruse meaning of the words but also by the sound they make. These three lexical exhibits are all aurally similar to each other: each word changes just one root consonant in order to produce the next: *wa-l-khabūq wa-l-khaqūq wa-l-ghaqūq*. . . .

Because the Arabic language is a lexicon-generating engine, because of its long history, and because Islamic revelation occurred in the Arabic language, dictionaries are essential to the maintenance of the language. I discussed the life and career of the first grammarian of Arabic, Sībawayhi, in chapter 6. Sībawayhi's work had immense importance for a Muslim community held together by a book written in a language that had scant literary history predating the appearance of the book itself. Mutatis mutandis, the same can be said of the lexicographic tradition. The Qur'an includes both grammatical structures *and lexical matter* that the emergent Muslim community struggled to interpret. The poetry of the pre-Islamic Arabs, as it was collected by the early litterateurs who were Sībawayhi's contemporaries, added its own lexical curiosities to the mix. As the language grew and spread, as it was learned and used by a population speaking a wide variety of mother tongues, dictionaries remained important to its maintenance. The lexicon grew apace: in response to words absorbed from adjacent tongues (sometimes through translation; see chapters 8 and 9) and to adjust to new phenomena that demanded new words.[27]

Lane's *Lexicon* belongs in this long tradition: it stabilizes the language by looking back to the earliest sources, pinning it to the Qur'anic and classical traditions in which it first took shape. Al-Shidyāq provides a useful counterweight to Lane. His career epitomizes distinct but equally important tasks that the language worker must take on, and like Lane's, his career illuminates how the language negotiated a transition to modernity. The brief passage quoted above illustrates a salient difference between Lane's and al-Shidyāq's methods and sensibilities. Lane courted and coveted an illusive quality that he termed linguistic *chastity*. He uses the English word *chaste* no fewer than ten times in the preface to the *Lexicon*, sometimes translating from the Arabic.[28] His sources likely use the word *'afīf*, which means "chaste" or "abstaining from what is unlawful." Al-Sīrāfī uses a verb derived from the same lexical root in his linguistic takedown of Abū Bishr Mattā, discussed above.[29] Lane's sources used the concept of "chastity" to characterize authoritative or beautiful Arabic, and to refer to the language of the pre-Islamic Bedouin poets, the Qur'an, and the generation of the Prophet. In contrast, as even the very brief passage from *Leg over Leg* quoted above makes clear, al-Shidyāq is not interested in linguistic chastity. He seeks the opposite: language that plays and dallies and hooks up—and that describes sexual organs and acts in exhaustive, exacting detail.

Al-Shidyāq was Lane's contemporary. But his life was as adventurous as Lane's was constricted.[30] Al-Shidyāq moved restlessly—driven by both necessity and ambition—from Lebanon to Egypt to Malta (where he lived, improbably, for fifteen years);[31] from the eastern Mediterranean to England and Paris; from western Europe to Istanbul (in 1859), where, finally, he settled for the last twenty-eight years of his life. His spiritual life, too, was measured out in a series of conversions. Born to the Lebanese Maronite community, he converted first to Protestantism, under the influence of

American missionaries, and later to Islam. Before his death he left instructions that he should be buried in the same Maronite cemetery as his family but that a crescent, symbolic of the Islamic faith he had embraced, should mark his tombstone. Finally, al-Shidyāq worked across linguistic boundaries. He translated Christian scripture and Protestant publications as well as literary texts from English into Arabic. But he is remembered today for his contributions to the modernization of the Arabic language. He was instrumental in the early history of the Arabic printing press in both Cairo and Malta. In Istanbul, he was the founder and editor of an important Arabic-language newspaper, *Al-Jawā'ib* (or *News from Afar*), and he wrote and (using the press he founded with his son) published extended studies of Arabic lexicography. Al-Shidyāq was nomad writer and language worker par excellence.

Al-Shidyāq's life was eventful and complex—too complex to do justice to here.[32] So, too, is his masterpiece a layered and multifaceted confection. I will not attempt to describe all the features of *Leg over Leg* here—the page upon page of lexical mummery, the inspirations for the work from both the Arabic tradition (al-Jāḥiẓ, Abū Ḥayyān al-Tawḥīdī, al-Hamadhānī's *maqāmāt*, and especially the *Qāmūs* of al-Fīrūzābādī—a dictionary in which al-Shidyāq seemingly took up residence) and the European (in particular, Rabelais's *Gargantua and Pantagruel* and Sterne's *Tristram Shandy*). Rather, I will focus on the "characters" who populate the work: not the fleeting personas based on real contemporaries of al-Shidyāq, but his protagonist, the Fāriyāq, and in particular the protagonist's mysterious consort, known as the Fāriyāqiyyah. The Fāriyāq's name was born of al-Shidyāq's lexical playfulness. It is a compound of the first syllable of al-Shidyāq's given name, Fāris (he took the name Aḥmad only when he converted to Islam), and the second syllable of his family name. The novel follows the Fāriyāq as he traces the stations of al-Shidyāq's life—moving to Egypt, to Malta, to Britain, to Paris; meeting missionaries and newspaper reporters; and so on. The Fāriyāq is both true to life and, verbally at least, larger than life, a man inclined to speak his mind—especially when the conversation turns to the topics of women or the Arabic language. The Fāriyāq, in brief, is a man of robust sexual and lexical appetites.

In the Fāriyāqiyyah, al-Shidyāq creates a suitable match and helpmeet for his protagonist. The novel is not in the least realistic. It has no interest in being mimetic or true to life. Rather, like *Tristram Shandy*, the novel gives us the life "and opinions" of the protagonist (and his consort). The Fāriyāq speaks his mind; and because he is a contrarian and a libertine, his rants consume pages. The plight of women, in particular, exercises him. In the chapter that introduces the Fāriyāqiyyah (appearing in volume 3 of the four-volume novel), he laments the narrow-mindedness of women and chastises custom—the isolation of women from society in particular—for keeping them ignorant and forcing them to rely on their mothers and maids for news of the world.[33] He and the Fāriyāqiyyah have just married, and she lashes out at him. He wishes to take her from Egypt to Malta, and the thought of the journey by sea terrifies her. In a snit, she turns her back to him. The Fāriyāq responds with a long meditation on the backsides of women, which culminates in a word list (yet another word list): Arabic words that name women's rears by referring to their size and shape.[34]

The Fāriyāqiyyah is nominally present for the rest of the novel, although the Fāriyāq travels away from her a great deal. The scenes in which we see the husband and wife together play out like a lascivious, dazzlingly erudite version of a Hepburn-Tracy movie. As the Fāriyāq prepares to leave, the two discuss conjugal relations between men and women (book 4, chapter 2). When the couple is reunited on his return from London, they talk about the appearance and customs of English men and women (book 4, chapter 6). Later, they converse about the sartorial customs of various parts of the world and the shapes that local clothing gives to the male and female bodies (book 4, chapter 9). Here, as the two discuss conjugal duties and obligations, the conversation turns to the gendered teachings dished out by the dictionary (the *Qāmūs* in particular).[35] This allows the Fāriyāqiyyah to rail against men's manipulation of language

> to serve their exercise of tyrannical power over and violence against women. This is despite the fact that language is a female,[36] and had women created it (which would have been more proper, given that all generation and creation must be female in nature), they would have created words denoting men who think only of their wives, and how men should avert their glances from all but these. . . .[37]

The Fāriyāqiyyah's thoughts continue in this vein until she runs out of steam; her sexual-lexical gymnastics and banter with the Fāriyāq fill the rest of the chapter.

Who—or what—is the Fāriyāqiyyah? Clearly, al-Shidyāq did not intend to create a realistic representation of a woman. In her excellent foreword to Davies's recent translation of the novel, Rebecca Johnson speculates that the Fāriyāqiyyah should be seen as an extension of the Fāriyāq: both a dimension of the Fāriyāq's personality *and feminine* at the same time.

> She might thus be thought of not as a stand-in for a historical personage . . . but as a second apparition of the self. Writing not simply *about*

women but *as if a woman*, al-Shidyaq uses gender as another permutation of his thought-experiment in radical difference and belonging.[38]

Kamram Rastegar has pointed out that the formation of the Fāriyāqiyyah's name suggests not that she is a feminine version of the Fāriyāq but rather that she is an expression of Fāriyāq-ness.[39] Rastegar adds that, in his author's notice, al-Shidyāq promises a narrative of progression for the Fāriyāqiyyah—but not for the Fāriyāq.[40] Yet the novel follows a classic travel narrative trajectory, in which the protagonist moves through new landscapes and learns by observing and admiring or criticizing the customs of the people he meets. Both the Fāriyāq and the Fāriyāqiyyah travel; when the Fāriyāq travels on his own, he brings back stories for her; together, in their page-gobbling banter, they digest what he has seen. The Fāriyāqiyyah's farewell, when she makes the decision to travel on to Istanbul toward the end of the book, summarizes the shortcomings of the men and in particular the women of Paris:[41] a formal announcement that her travels in the land of the Franks have ended.[42] Her final words are the last spoken by a character in the novel; her farewell serves for her and the Fāriyāq both.[43] In the protagonist and his consort, then, we have a composite character who is both female and male, both self and other.

Or, quite possibly, the Fāriyāqiyyah represents woman, and an extension of the masculine protagonist, *and the language* that the Fāriyāq courts like a suitor throughout the book—which, as the Fāriyāqiyyah points out, "is a woman." She might, at times, stand in for the Arabic language—the Fāriyāq's silent consort as he travels in non-Arab lands—which, like the Fāriyāqiyyah, will grow in the course of the book, responding to the people and the scenes that the Fāriyāq encounters as he journeys. In the most poignant family scene in the novel, when the couple's young son dies in London, the Fāriyāqiyyah is all but absent.[44] The character is not a mimetic representation of a woman, nor is she a realistic projection of the protagonist's character. She is a confection that al-Shidyāq uses to explore the social place of women, to represent the internal musing of the protagonist, and to show the great language at play: challenged by the stimulus thrown at it by the Franks, stretching itself to express the thoughts and desires of the protagonist, and amusing itself in the halls of its own lexical history.

I have chosen Lane and al-Shidyāq to illustrate the strategies that the cosmopolitan language uses to adjust to modernity because both men were exemplary language workers, and because their devotion to the language took parallel but strikingly different forms. Lane and al-Shidyāq never met, to my knowledge. But their lives overlapped chronologically and, at moments, geographically. Both were in Cairo in 1833 (when Lane arrived on his second trip to the city) and 1834 (the year when al-Shidyāq relocated to Malta), and both were known to have frequented the salon of Rifāʿa Bey al-Ṭaḥṭāwī (1801–1873), author of an important book about his travels in France, published in 1834. Both were in England, at least fitfully, between 1849 and 1857. Both men had a passion for lexicography and a predilection for, as A. J. Arberry puts it, "ransacking the dictionary."[45] From this point, however, their tastes and methods diverged drastically. Lane turned to the "chaste" Arabic of the pre-Islamic poets, the Qurʾan, and the era of revelation. The title page of the great dictionary promises "all the classical words and significations commonly known to the learned among the Arabs." Lane also planned a second dictionary that would compile words "that are of rare occurrence and not commonly known": that is, precisely the words that seduced al-Shidyāq.[46] However, so Herculean a labor was the first dictionary that Lane died before completing it, and the second remained a twinkle in its would-be father's eye. But the dictionary he produced did much to modernize the lexical tradition: Lane standardized the order in which regularly generated lexica (like the present active participle, e.g., *al-fāʿil* ["the doer"] or *al-kātib* ["the scribe"]) appear within each definition.[47] This is no small feat, given the fact that each article—representing the lexical matter spun off by each three-letter root—may stretch on for pages, much like the conjugal banter of the Fāriyāq and the Fāriyāqiyyah.

Al-Shidyāq chose a different path to modernize the language. Linguistic chastity spoke to Lane; al-Shidyāq was as randy a lexicographer as ever lived. Lexical curiosities fascinated him, as they did Lane. But his aim in exhuming philological oddments was not (as was Lane's) sober and scientific. His modern translator, Humphrey Davies, calls al-Shidyāq's tone in *Leg over Leg* "ludic," which seems *le mot juste*.[48] Al-Shidyāq adored the deep lexical history of his mistress tongue—but she meant little to him if he couldn't tease and goad her into extraordinary new behaviors. His effort to modernize the language, especially later in his career, extended to the invention of new words to describe the new world emerging in both Europe and the Ottoman Empire. He coined words at a furious rate: his coinages, which number in the thousands according to one scholar's estimate, include some of the modern standard Arabic words for the technical and technological innovations of modernity, like "railway" (*sikka al-ḥadīd*) and "newspaper" (*al-jarīda*).[49] The novel expressed a different kind of interest in the lexical abundance of the Arabic language: at once deeply rooted in lexical history and ecstatically innovative. In this sense, *Leg over Leg* represents a path not taken for literary modernity in Arabic. Other writers would create Arabic literary fiction in a realist mode, taking as models from the European tradition not Rabelais and Sterne but rather Zola and the Russians. That strand of Arabic literary modernity would be anointed as uniquely Arab and uniquely modern, while al-Shidyāq's contribution—playful, melodic, besotted with the language itself—would be largely forgotten. It is only in recent years that *Leg over Leg* has begun to attract its due attention.

For those who don't read Arabic, Humphrey Davies's translation of *Leg over Leg* performs a marvelous service. Even those who know Arabic quite well but would prefer not to lose themselves in dictionaries will appreciate Davies's work. *Leg over Leg* makes al-Shidyāq's accomplishment accessible to a much wider public in an energetic translation and in a handsome edition. The press and the editors of the series in which these volumes appear, too, deserve their share of the credit for this accomplishment. The Library of Arabic Literature, an imprint of the New York University Press produced with the support of the NYU Abu Dhabi Institute, makes available works of Arabic literature that have not before been translated in English (most of them never translated into any of the national languages of western Europe). The series promises "authoritative Arabic editions and modern, lucid English translations."[50] Loosely modeled on the Loeb editions of Greek and Latin classics, the volumes give original text and translation on facing pages. It is a labor of love and dedication to the Arabic language that will help to transform nonspecialists' perceptions of the Arabic literary heritage. As al-Shidyāq's career demonstrates, all these actors—writers and translators, editors and publishers—are essential language workers, without whom the life of the great language will be at best attenuated, and at worst in danger of being extinguished.

In a review of *Leg over Leg*, Tarek el-Ariss, a scholar of modern Arabic literature, describes visiting Davies in Cairo while the latter was working on the translation. He saw Davies's desk, piled with the word lists Davies had generated as he worked his way through the text: lexical curiosities to track down and, somehow, render in English. Davies, el-Ariss wrote, "was re-creating the scene of writing *Saq*, its degree zero, restaging al-Shidyaq as a way of entering his text."[51] El-Ariss's description of Davies's desk as a replication of al-Shidyāq's desk may stand in as an image of Lane's desk, as he worked on the great dictionary; or of the desk of al-Fīrūzābādī, author of *al-Qāmūs*, a dictionary consulted by both Lane and al-Shidyāq; or of the desk of Abū Bishr Mattā or Cyril or Sībawayhi, for that matter. The image may be imprecise and anachronistic (did eighth-century scholars have desks?). But I aim for the sort of emotional verisimilitude for which Hollywood is celebrated, not the mimetic realism of the nineteenth-century novelists. Davies and Lane; Abū Bishr Mattā, al-Shidyāq, and Sībawayhi: none of these men was born into Arabic—not into the classical language, at any rate, although al-Shidyāq learned it very young—and none was born Muslim. Indeed, al-Shidyāq contributed to the effort among Lebanese Christians to take possession of a language so closely associated with the Islamic past, and to prepare it for the next chapter of its life: modernity.[52] These are language workers and this is the *cura linguae*, the human ministrations upon which the superhuman language depends.

Latin had no such friends to wait upon it at the dawn of the modern age. Latin, to quote al-Sīrāfī, "has withdrawn long ago, and its people have died, and those who were joined in conversation in the language have perished, along with those who understood each other's intentions through its grammatical distinctions."[53] To this day, the great machinery of the language still functions in pockets of its former domain. Programs in Rome (Father Reginald Foster's Aestiva Latinitas Romae, today run by the Paideia Institute as "Living Latin," or the Accademia Vivarium Novum, for instance) teach Latin as a spoken and written tongue. Some would like to see it used as the language of state at Brussels;[54] and now that the UK is no longer part of the European Union, why elevate English as common tongue? Yet that happy ending seems unlikely to materialize for Latin. It is perceived as a difficult language: it has too many declensions, too many tenses and moods. Latin has too much baggage. In part for that reason, Latin faltered while the attention of its people was pulled away by another drama, the flashy arrival of the vernaculars. Latin (like Icarus in Bruegel's famous painting) slipped quietly into the sea, while the vernaculars (like the farmers, shepherds, and sailors in Bruegel's canvas) toiled and dallied and dreamed, pulling the viewer's eye to the foreground.

[PART FOUR]

∵

Beyond the Cosmopolitan Language

[CHAPTER 11]

Silence

It was said of him that he could be silent
in more languages than any man in Europe.[1]

During the centuries known in the Christian West as the Middle Ages, between the eighth century and the fifteenth, Arabic and Latin passed through some of the same developmental stages.[2] Their profiles looked different before this period. Latin had previous experience as imperial language; Arabic was a new language of literature, science, and bureaucracy, with the energy of revelation behind it. Yet, despite their differences, during this period both languages went through phases of intellectual and creative expansion and used translation movements to pad their lexicon and their scientific and literary repertoire. By the sixteenth century, however—at the most conservative estimate—the two languages had parted ways. Between the seventeenth and twentieth centuries, in most of the regions where it was used as lingua sacra and literary language, Arabic learned to share dominion with other languages: Persian and Turkish in the Middle East, Persian and Urdu in South Asia, French and Amazigh in the Maghrib, French and English in the Levant.[3] But it maintained its status as language of literature into the modern period, as evidenced by the devotion paid to it by men like Edward William Lane and Aḥmad Fāris al-Shidyāq in the nineteenth century (see chapter 10). Medieval Latin had a much narrower regional jurisdiction than Arabic. It was used as language of letters and record only in western Europe. But even in western Europe, by the fifteenth century, its fortunes were in decline. The Persian poet Niẓāmī (1141–1209) and the French poet Chrétien de Troyes (fl. ca. 1160–1191) were contemporaries. Five centuries later, both Arabic and Persian remained important languages, in the spoken and written registers, east of the Mediterranean. Meanwhile, north of the Mediterranean, Latin had begun its long decline, and the vernacular cultures—like Chrétien's French—celebrated their Renaissance.

I cannot resist using that term, *Renaissance*, discredited though it is—long contested in the visual arts, no longer fashionable in literary studies—

because it is so ironic, in the context of the story I tell in this book. Was it a Rebirth or the wholesale invention of new linguistic and literary media and practices? Why not call it a Funeral—for Latin? Leonardo Giustinian (ca. 1388–1446), to cite just one example, was a Venetian litterateur who wrote in both Latin and Venetian Italian. During his lifetime, his peers knew him best for his funeral orations in Latin honoring the lives of the great men of his age: celebrations of the dead that provided models for the living. Today, however, scholars remember and celebrate the love lyrics in Venetian Italian, which embody the sparkling, salacious culture of fifteenth-century Venice. Only the specialists in Renaissance Latin know Giustinian's elegies.[4] In late medieval Europe, rising vernacular cultures challenged the literary hegemony of the one language of written culture. Latin didn't just go away, of course. It endured, and even thrived, in some circles. But life happened elsewhere.

This last section concerns itself with the last act in the life of the great language in western Europe. In this chapter, we watch as Latin stumbles and falls silent. The Mediterranean lingua franca, discussed in chapter 12, could not replace and never aimed to replace Latin. Yet in the spoken register, it aped some of the ambitions of Latin: it was transregional and was used as professional idiolect by nomad actors with multiple languages in their portfolio. The final chapter circles back to Arabic—still a viable language of literature and bureaucracy, although today it has currency mainly among ethnic Arabs—and reflects on the ethics of the cosmopolitan language system. This chapter, too, is concerned with language and ethics, with morality and mortality. It acknowledges the ethical shortcomings of the cosmopolitan language system: what it passes over and who it relegates to silence.

Medieval misogyny makes a dreary object of contemplation. Chauvinism and abuse, along with an unforgiving maternal mortality rate, made premodern women's lives a misery. In the face of all the existential trials they faced, the cosmopolitan language played a relatively minor role in marginalizing women and limiting their access to the world. The long training demanded by the language was not accessible to women. And so the intellectual and aesthetic sublime expressed in the language, which compensated in some measure for the difficulties of life, was also denied them. It's true that individual women (remarkable individuals) slipped through the perimeter fence and into the precincts of the one language of intellectual history. Most men, too, died illiterate and anonymous, without access to the great language. But women were, as a population, brides of silence, unless plucked out of the herd by a lucky marriage (or, in the Islamicate world, enslaved to a wealthy man). The life of the mind can grant the human being dignity, and this compensation was refused to women on the basis of gender.

In the circumstances, it seems churlish to refuse what the European vernacular revolution offered to women: access to the capacious world of literature that transcends the ghettos of the here and now. In truth, at its origins, the vernacular revolution provided little sustenance for the life of the mind. Dante formalized what many vernacular writers must have been thinking: "The first to write in the vernacular," he writes in the *Vita nova*, "did so that his words might be understood by a woman, who would have been hard-pressed to understand Latin verses."[5] Here, the writer is masculine; his target audience is feminine; and she is understood to be a reader of (or a listener to) the text in order to be seduced by the poet (or the performer). But even if the original intention was to speak to women, rather than to enable their literacy, in practice vernacular literacy had a knock-on effect: by the fourteenth century, Italian women (like the men) were keeping commonplace books and recording registers of their interior lives. *Volgarizzamenti*—vernacular translations from the Latin (and some from the French)—made important philosophical works accessible to a wider population.[6] The vernacular revolution opened the door to literacy for constituencies who had been denied access, including women; the cosmopolitan language, through sins of both omission and commission, did not.

In this chapter, I recognize the drama of vernacularization that threatened Latin hegemony in some quarters, the movement gaining force on the margins of the page, but I maintain my focus on the Alexandrian language of the life of the mind. The vernacularization movement began much earlier in northern Europe and the British Isles (places imperfectly colonized by the Roman Empire and hence by Latin). By the late Middle Ages, finally, the vernacular movement reached Mediterranean Europe. Local tongues put texts in the hands of a much larger public. Voluble rivers of vernacular literary production joined to form pools, then lakes, then an ocean, stranding promontories of Latin at the universities and churches. From the perspective of the national languages of western Europe, this is a story of liberation. Once they have systematized their grammar and vocabulary and established their literary credentials, the national languages do a victory lap. Europe emerges as a network of villages where local identity is entrenched in history, customs, and first and foremost in a distinct local language. The French are those who speak French (and eat frog legs, as the British point out); others do not.

At the same time, the nigh-immortal language of culture falls silent. Scientists continue to write in Latin—Galileo and Kepler, for instance, into the seventeenth century. The Roman Church uses Latin as lingua franca into the twenty-first century. But it is no longer a medium that the writer can trust to deliver her message to an audience far away in space or time.

Here, I aim to tell the story of European vernacularization (mainly) from the perspective of Latinity. As always, I use vignette to drive my narrative and textual analysis as methodology. I discuss a small group of scribblers: an obscure cleric, Philip of Harveng; the Abbasid Arabic prose writer al-Jāḥiẓ, as contrast and point of reference; and mainly, I focus not on a historical individual but a fictional character—a shadowy man known as Secundus the Silent Philosopher. In this chapter, I call for a moment of silence for the fallen cosmopolitan language of western Europe. But, as we will see, silence has many meanings from the perspective of the cosmopolitan language.

∴

The story of Secundus the Silent Philosopher dramatizes the gender politics behind literary representations of the motif of controlling the tongue. In this dismal tale, a boy named Secundus is sent away from home to be educated. Soon after he leaves home, his father dies; the boy remains with his tutors for some years. They teach him, along with their other lessons, that all women are dishonest and lascivious by nature. When he finally returns to his home village, he decides to prove or disprove his tutors' claim by testing the chastity of his own mother—who, at this point, has been a widow for some time. He negotiates through a maid to pay for the pleasure of spending the night with her, and she accepts the arrangement. In some versions of the tale, she is eager to say yes. In others, her maid uses lengthy arguments to convince her. Implausibly, when her son arrives, the mother does not recognize him. He has been gone a long time, his sedentary life has transformed his appearance, and "Secundus" was not imagined by a writer committed to mimetic psychological realism. She is amenable to his designs and is puzzled when—after apparently offering her a night of pleasure for profit—he withholds. When morning comes, he reveals his identity. She, horrified and shamed, responds by hanging herself.

Only after his mother's suicide does the son recognize the consequences of his actions. In recognition of his guilt, he takes a vow of silence. So committed is he to silence, and so renowned was he for his wisdom before he stopped speaking, that the Emperor Hadrian becomes interested in his case. He beseeches Secundus to speak and put his wisdom on display; Secundus refuses. In the Latin version of the tale that Vincent of Beauvais included in his *Speculum historiale*, the emperor's question to the philosopher is particularly succinct and poignant: "O Secunde, quare tacens morieris? Loquere et vives" ("O Secundus, why will you go to death silent? Speak and you will live").[7] But Secundus maintains silence, even when confronted by so imperious a presence, and even under the threat of immediate execution.

His silence has been complete up to Hadrian's confrontation of him: "In observing silence you have imposed upon yourself a kind of law," the emperor says, "and that law of yours I was unable to break down."[8] He puts a pen in Secundus's hands. Now, Secundus is able to write his apologia. With his first words, he tells the king: "You have the power to kill me, because you are the ruler of today. But you have no power over the voice that comes forth from me."[9]

This narrative core draws together elements that are both bleakly familiar and unique. The lustfulness of women, the betrayal of the husband, the protagonist whose self-control is his superpower: these elements appear in the story of Joseph from the Bible (Genesis 37:1–46:7) and the Qur'an (surah Yūsuf) and in the framed narrative known as the *Book of Sindbad* in the East and the *Seven Sages of Rome* in western Europe. However, the exchange between the emperor and the philosopher is unique. "Secundus" circulated widely and was translated into many languages, although it did not pass from Latin to the European vernaculars. It is extant in Greek, Arabic, Armenian, Ethiopic, and Latin. In the multiple languages in which the tale is extant, the emperor refers to the philosopher's self-imposed silence as a "law."[10] In each language, the emperor's accusation is the same: by obeying his own idiosyncratic law, Secundus has abrogated the laws of the state. Secundus does not fear the personification of the state, the emperor, because he does not fear the ultimate punishment that the emperor can impose: death. Only his knowledge matters to him. Wounded by the scandalous knowledge of his mother's lust, he cures himself by rehearsing the healing knowledge learned through his study of natural philosophy. His ability to write that knowledge allows him to separate himself from the indignities of life: the squalor of his mother's sexual appetite and self-murder.

When the emperor puts a pen in his hand, Secundus bursts into a voluble stream of speech, and his written communications fill the bulk of the book. The emperor asks the philosopher a series of questions, and the philosopher records his answers. In most versions of the text, Secundus's responses do not take the form of lectures or philosophical discussions. Rather, they are an exercise in definition, a series of nominal phrases in apposition with key words in philosophy and ethics.

> What is the Universe?
>
> A circumference beyond our reach, a theoretic structure, an eminence not easily perceived in its entirety, a self-generated object of contemplation, a conformation with many aspects, an eternal establishment, nourishing ether, a globe that does not wander from its place, the light of the sun, day, stars, darkness, night, earth, air, water.[11]

> What is the Ocean?
>
> An embrace of the world, the crowned frontier, the Atlantic bond, what skirts all of nature, what stays the globe, the impudence of the road, the limit of the earth, the division of realms, the home of rivers, the fountain of rains, a refuge in danger, grace in pleasures.[12]

These are the first two questions and responses in, respectively, the Greek version and the earliest known Latin translation.[13] The syntax of the book invites confusion.[14] Each definition strings together abstruse words and startling images. Because the substance of the book consists of sequences of nominal phrases and there is little context from which a translator might derive the sense of an unknown word, errors are frequent and are nearly impossible for subsequent translators, adaptors, or copyists to correct.[15] The result is a kind of jazz: abstract images pile up, or are pruned by a more economical writer. Each definition is a series of riffs, a bouquet of nouns held together by the tether of grammatical rules: genitives hugging their noun, the series of nouns bound by apposition to that first Noun which they define.[16]

In the story of Secundus, silence is a powerful narrative motif; it signifies a dignified retreat from the petty passions that create confusion and sow discomfort in the human psyche. The relatively chatty seduction scene between son and mother does not end well, after all. The philosopher's silence presents itself in the first instance as a defense mechanism. As the plot advances, silence provides the circumstances for the genesis of substantive, philosophically significant ideas. Once Secundus falls silent, he fulfills his promise as philosopher by passing on the knowledge gained from his teachers and through study and contemplation. Of course, this second shoe drops only following the shock of the primal scene, as Freud would call it: the mother's body presented as sexual offering to her son, her shame and self-destruction when she understands who he is. The mother's silence is not made legible in "Secundus." She has no hermeneutic tool to allow her to distance herself from the suffering caused by her son's actions or her own appetites. "Secundus" is not a story about the silence of women and the absence of a linguistic instrument that women might use to filter out pain and produce knowledge, although it could be.[17]

The story of Secundus combines distinct modalities of silence: the silence of exclusion (of women); the silence of remorse; silence as self-imposed law; the silence of meditation. These last two categories came together in the Christian West in clerical communities, within the cloister, where silence formed the core of spiritual practice. For men who lived in community, restraint in communication was so important that a monk and prolific writer, Philip of Harveng, wrote a treatise to instruct his fellow

Premonstratensian monks in the discipline of silence. Philip became abbot of Bonne-Espérance (in present-day Estinnes, Belgium) in about 1157 and died in 1183.[18] Before his appointment as abbot, Philip had been a member of the community of Bonne-Espérance, until an obscure scandal drove him out of the abbey. He lived for about two years in exile from the abbey, probably in another abbey in the neighborhood. In time, his name was cleared, and he was granted permission to return. He remained at Bonne-Espérance until his death. Philip's treatise, *De silentio clericorum*, reflects upon silence as prerequisite for meditation and study and as communicative strategy. In good scholastic fashion, he begins his treatise by dividing silence into species and subspecies: silence from speech and silence (or restraint) from doing good or evil deeds; silence of speech then further subdivided into silence from speaking or from communicating in signs; and so on.[19] Philip's discussion of the "signs" that communicate in place of speech extends to the written language as sign. Signs of this variety, he writes,

> juxta grammaticos littera, quasi legittera nominatur, eo quod per eam iter legentibus praebeatur, vel quia in ceratis tabulis antiqui scriptitabant, a lituris litteras nominabant.[20]

> are called by grammarians *littera*—or as it were *legittera*, either because through it the path [*iter*] is opened to readers, or because the ancients used to write on waxen tablets, so that they called it *littera* after *lituris* [i.e., the rubbing out of errors on a wax tablet].

Philip's splendid mash-up word *legittera* names the formal language as the combination of laws (*leges*) and a repertoire of physical traces that communicate not only with those present but also with people distant from the moment of communication in time and space. As an example of the *gramatica* effect—the ability of the language to fix meaning on the page for those distant from the living voice—Philip cites the tablets that God sent down the mountain with Moses.[21] For this reason, he sees the *gramatica* as a path leading to knowledge (like Remigio [see chapter 5] and Sībawayhi [chapter 6]). This path metaphorically represents the book, which by synecdoche stands for the linguistic code—"of service more to the eye than to the ear"[22]—that will open up fields of knowledge to the reader, revealing its meanings only after diligent (and, in an ideal world, silent) study.

Philip recognizes that the one, unified language of written communication, sufficient in all times and places, has enemies: the vulgar tongues. In a letter to a patron, Henry I—count of Champagne and Brie, known as Henry the Liberal (1127–1181)—Philip acknowledges the failure of Greek and Hebrew, the first languages in which God communicated with his earthly community. Now, he says, only Latin stands between humanity and the abyss. Yet Latin, too, is under threat.

> Recte ergo viro nobili litterarum placet nobilis officina, cujus exercitio cuditur salutaris morum, scientiae, fidei disciplina, ita ut si cuilibet vulgares linguae praesto sint caeterae, non Latina, ipsius pace dixerim, hebetudo eum teneat asinina.[23]

> Rightly, therefore, does the noble man take pleasure in the noble workshop of those letters in the exercise of which he forges salubrious training in customs, knowledge, faith; so that if any of the vernacular languages be present, not Latin—I should say in the silence of that language—an asinine dullness takes hold of him.

Latin binds us to God and to the history and customs of the Christian Church. The vernaculars are the sworn enemies of the unified and unifying divine message. Only diligent application (*otium* is the word Philip uses: the leisure to devote oneself zealously to this pursuit) allows us to understand the written word of God. Philip hopes that the support of the patron to whom he directs this letter will buy his community the leisure to make such study possible, in order to hold the vernaculars—sowers of confusion—at bay.

Philip's aim is to tease out what is most fruitful in the silence of the cloister and to discourage those who use silence as cover for ignorance, subterfuge, or deceit. At the same time, in both the letter to Henry and *De silentia clericorum*, he recognizes the frailty of human language. Hebrew and Greek have stumbled. They are (as Philip explains in the letter to Henry) no more than a rumor to us; only Latin remains present to the Christian West.[24] Western Christians struggle to strengthen their Latin as bulwark against entropy, but with equivocal success. Meanwhile, outside the small circle of Latinity, the vernaculars rage. Three centuries later, Thomas à Kempis (1380–1471), a German-Dutch cleric, would argue a similar point:

> Potius eligerem ab aliis dictata in silentio legere quam rusticitate mea claritatem illustrium virorum barbarizando obscurare.[25]

> I should rather choose to overhear in silence things read out by others, than in my rusticity to obscure the brilliance of illustrious men by barbarizing it.

Restraint and probity compel the man of discernment who is not eloquent in Latin to choose silence in the company of those who wield it well. In a delightful phrase, scholar Arno Borst summarizes the argument that Philip makes in *De silentio*: "The essence of the development thus resulted in *Latin silence*."[26] Men of discretion ought to hold their tongue *in Latin* rather than open their mouths and babble in the vernacular.

All the stories I am telling in this chapter share a similar backdrop: communities of men who retreat into silence, turning their backs on the vitality and dynamism (and, truth be told, the confusion) of life, unedited. This commonality demonstrates what is, to many audiences, least palatable about the cosmopolitan language in the European orbit: its association with a monastic or a scholastic milieu. Within the sphere of influence of the cosmopolitan language, a circle of pale men stooped over the leaves of their manuscripts, covered with obscure signs; without it, life, in all its abundance and variety. This is the prison house of language that the vernaculars have chipped away at, achieving finally the jailbreak of the vernacular revolution. As Latin subsides into silence, how do men of letters respond? Do they share in the embarrassment of the cosmopolitan language, hold their tongue, and mimic the silence of Latin, a language increasingly contained to the page? Is the best response a "Latin silence"? Or should the man of letters give in to the scandalous chatter of the vernaculars?

Given that a monkish scandal drove him from his abbey, it seems that Philip had ample reason to distrust the silence of his brothers. For silence, as Philip acknowledges in *De silentio clericorum*, may have many meanings. The story of Secundus, too, illustrates the duplicity of silence. It may mark the place of diligent study and meditation. But it may, equally, represent the failure or absence of meaning: confusion or ignorance. The mute face of an interlocutor sometimes signals the desire to conceal hidden intentions: this is the silence of subterfuge and scheming, or of shock and disapproval. The silence of the man who contracted a night of sex, then withheld the sex he paid for, may conceal a dark purpose. Finally, silence may indicate the will to exclude others from the circle created by the light of the language: this is the silence of knowledge withheld, the son who refused his companion the creature comforts of sex and slept silent in her arms, until the morning when he revealed the terrible truth. The mother, it seems, had no tongue in which to accuse her son or confess the motives of her actions. The narrative converts hers into the most resolute silence of all: the silence of the grave.

The Abbasid Arabic litterateur al-Jāḥiẓ wrote an essay about the meaning and consequences of silence that puts verbal performance—what we say and what we don't—in a broader perspective. We met al-Jāḥiẓ briefly above (see chapter 8) extolling the pleasures of mimicry. He was born in the new city of Basra (it had been founded a bit less than a century and a half earlier) in about 776 CE, and, like other architects of early Arabic letters I have discussed in this book, he was a non-Arab. He is thought to have been Abyssinian, though it's difficult to know anything about his biography with certainty at this distance. One of al-Jāḥiẓ's essays tackles the problem of keeping secrets: maintaining silence about matters on which you have privy information, especially when that information, if released, may harm others. Al-Jāḥiẓ approaches his topic with typical energy, restless attention, and (ironically) volubility. News reports, al-Jāḥiẓ argues, have long made the experiences and knowledge of distant people present to those who receive them. When important news was passed on, he writes, it "was accepted as though from an eyewitness even when there was no direct contact."[27] Given its immense communicative capacity, language—implicitly, the cosmopolitan language par excellence: Arabic—can be a force for good or for evil. For this reason, al-Jāḥiẓ counsels his reader on strategies for holding the tongue, when indiscreet communication will cause pain, confusion, or destruction.

Handling the cosmopolitan language, thus, places an immense burden and substantial responsibility on a man's shoulders. In one of the most memorable phrases from the essay, al-Jāḥiẓ quotes the words of "a wise man":

إنما الإنسان حديث، فإن استطعت أن تكون حديثاً حسناً فافعل.[28]

People are a narration, so if you can be a beautiful tale, do so!

Curate yourself, al-Jāḥiẓ advises his audience, so that your words and silences alike, the things you choose to say and those you chose to withhold, are *beautiful*. The word that al-Jāḥiẓ uses is *ḥasan*, "good" or "beautiful": the same word that Sībawayhi uses to describe correct grammar (see chapter 8). Be beautiful, al-Jāḥiẓ urges us; be accurate, good, and correct! Like Petrarch, the man who became a fable (see chapter 9); like Khurāfa, the man who became a tale (chapter 10), al-Jāḥiẓ imagines human character as a performance unbounded by time and space. Life is coextensive with the words we speak (and the silences we keep), which may be reported and passed on through the ages, buoyed by the tensile strength of the Arabic language.

The cosmopolitan language grants immense expressive power, but only to a privileged few. It cordons off knowledge as territory forbidden to those refused access to the training in the language that allows its practitioners to learn and communicate sophisticated concepts. Arabic tussled with its linguistic competitors early in its career as great language. Itself young, inquisitive, and acquisitive, it met and tangled with older, more established languages in its skirmishes with the *shuʿūbiyya*—the resistance to Arabic mounted by Persians and other linguistic minorities conquered in the Arab expansion (see chapter 2). Al-Jāḥiẓ's life coincided with this movement; he, evidently, made a separate peace with Arabic. The fictional philosopher, Secundus, must have learned about the malfeasance of women in his learned tongue. What language did he use to seduce his mother? To confront her? What tongue could express the scandal of the mother who offers her body to the son who knowingly entraps her? What law did she—a widow, bereft of both husband and (for, apparently, many years) son—violate when she agreed to a night of revelry with a man who presented himself as a stranger? These topics, it appears, are beyond the ken of the cosmopolitan language: they must be expressed in the mercurial vernacular, the linguistic code of seduction and hook-ups, of those carnal pleasures as ephemeral as the words used to describe them. Would you, dear reader, turn back the page on that liberation, chase the voices of the populace back into the cage, and return to the dignity and grandeur *and exclusions* of the cosmopolitan language?

But my aim in this book is to celebrate the Alexandrian code of literary history and to celebrate those practitioners who trained themselves to use it. This narrative trajectory obliges me to pass over in silence (as so many have done before me) the sufferings of Secundus's mother, as well as the countless others who did not record their lives because they lacked linguistic facility. I close this meditation by reflecting on another potential interpretation of silence: it may conceal a meaning we cannot understand *yet*. It may connote enigma, the site of potential understanding: the book that the would-be cosmopolitan wants to read badly enough to learn the language in which it is written. This is the dance of seduction performed by Arabic and Latin throughout its long history. I cannot resist quoting a *very* vernacular text to illuminate this face of the cosmopolitan language. In the song "I Will Possess Your Heart" by Death Cab for Cutie, the singer describes his love for an elusive beloved. She, it seems, cannot see the potential for deathless love between them. He uses a simile to describe his attraction to her: "It's like a book elegantly bound," Ben Gibbard sings, "in a language that you can't read . . . *just yet*."[29] The lyric structure of the song emphasizes the surprise of those last two words. Both rhythm and rhyme lead us to expect the verse to end with "you can't read": his love is like a book in an incomprehensible language. The singer drops the last two words of the verse—*just yet*—as an afterthought. They hold out the promise that she *will* be able to read the book of his love for her, if only she dedicates to his language the time it merits.[30] Unlike Dante and the vernacular poets of the Middle Ages, the lyric persona of the song wants to pull the beloved away from her mother tongue: he beckons her to follow him into the terra incognita of his language. The cosmopolitan languages used this siren song to seduce their acolytes, until the vernaculars offered a much headier and much more alluring promise.

[CHAPTER 12]

The Shadow of Latinity

Lingua franca in the Mediterranean, seventeenth century

Tiel Ni sendis ĝin kiel klaran araban instruon.
Thus We have sent it as a clear Arabic instruction.
QUR'AN 13:37[1]

How do new languages come into being? Glossogenetic language change—the changes introduced from one generation to the next—may transform a language so thoroughly that study is required to understand the form of the language spoken two hundred years ago. The identity of the language, however, remains the same. The versions of English written by Hillary Mantel, Jane Austen, and Margery Kempe are discernibly different, but nomenclature poses no difficulty: we call all these historical registers "English." The origination of planned languages can be documented, of course. But few linguistic experiments find success outside the laboratory. Test-tube languages like Esperanto, to date, have not provided a solution for the Babelian confusion of tongues.[2] Pidgins and creoles are the exception. We know where pidgins come from, and in some cases we can document their progress toward creolization. One party (generally, native speakers of a language) speaks a simplified form of the language to another (people who do not speak the language). Over time this linguistic exchange occurs repeatedly, in a narrow range of situations. Trade languages are spoken around the bargaining table. Languages of the enslaved are spoken in the household or the field. A limited vocabulary and bare-bones grammar allow essential communication to happen, and a pidgin is born.

Pidgins are spoken only by people who have other languages that they use in more linguistically demanding circumstances. They do not function as a mother tongue or first language. If a pidgin becomes a language of place and develops the full complement of grammar and vocabulary necessary to operate outside the environments that necessitated its invention, linguists say that it has creolized. French, Portuguese, Spanish, and English colonialism created creoles in the Americas, in the South Pacific, and in sub-Saharan Africa. Many of these are still spoken today, although few have become so well established or so widely used as to generate literary traditions. Exceptions include the French of nineteenth-century Louisiana Creole literature and Haitian Creole literature, still written today.

The Mediterranean lingua franca is in one sense the ur-pidgin: not because it was the first pidgin but because it gifted its name as a generic term for languages of convenience, used to traverse linguistic divides. The language has no documented origin, although we can reconstruct some details of its origin. It had a Romance structure, and its vocabulary in the earliest texts that attest its existence was largely Italian. But it was a movable feast; the Italianate words used in the eastern Mediterranean might be swapped out for Spanish vocabulary in the western Mediterranean. Later, after the rise of French colonialism, the number of French words found in the language increased. It seems that the language emerged in exchanges between traveling sailors and merchants, who spoke simplified forms of their own languages to those they bargained with and negotiated with in the Mediterranean port cities. The lingua franca used pidginization strategies typical of the Romance languages. The infinitive replaced finite verbs, for instance, and all nouns and adjectives appeared in the masculine singular form. It flourished, after a fashion, in the early modern Mediterranean. But it never creolized and never generated a written version of itself. It never became a language of record; it never came to be used as bureaucratic medium. As far as I am aware, nobody ever wrote a lingua franca text in the first person. It is recorded only in the form of snatches of overheard language, when a traveler describes how he heard people speak on distant shores. Its simplified grammatical and lexical structure, the narrow range of life experiences in which it was used, and its ephemerality all are representative of its status as pidgin: a linguistic make-do, a rough-and-ready form of communicating necessary information across linguistic boundaries.

In this chapter, I am interested in the lingua franca as a shadow of the cosmopolitan language. In order to understand both what we know and what we can't know about it, I will briefly discuss the language itself: its name, its structure, and the historical record that attests its existence. More interesting, for our purposes, is the provocation the language poses for anyone interested in the problems posed by linguistic complexity across the Mediterranean. Mediterranean connectivity—the word becomes a term of art in Mediterranean history, describing human mobility and trade[3]—presupposes the existence of a relatively sophisticated linguistic instrument to support the circulation of people and goods from port to port around the sea. Those who created and used the lingua franca were (like the agents of the cosmopolitan language) linguistic nomads. It emerged from a dynamic of circulation and sporadic, repeated communication, akin to circulation of both merchants and cosmopolitan elites that generated the cosmopolitan languages. Actors whose mother tongues were mutually incomprehensible used the lingua franca as a communicative vehicle. Like the cosmopolitan language, it furnished a strategy that language used to bridge the gap that language created. The historian can read the record that the language left of itself as both a success story (demonstrating how transits were successfully negotiated) and an aporia; for the moments when the language failed to speak are, on balance, more evocative than the traces of the language that remain.[4]

∴

The name by which the language was known in the early records indicates the historical, ethnic, and linguistic complexity of the choreography of the language. *Lingua franca* may be understood as Italian (producing an Italian plural: *lingue franche*) or as a Latin phrase naturalized in English- or French-language scholarship (producing the plural *lingua francas*). The noun *lingua* is unproblematic. In both Italian and Latin it means "tongue," in either the anatomical or the abstract sense, and here signifies "language." The formation of the adjective *franca*, however, is more complex: it is a Romance borrowing of an Arabic borrowing of a Greek borrowing of a Latin word. The word emerged from the murky depths onto the stage of history as the ethnonym that the Romans used for the Germanic tribes beyond the Alps, presumably derived from the Franks' own name for themselves. After the coronation of Charlemagne, King of the Franks, as emperor of western Christendom, Byzantines used the term *phrangoi*—a Greek appropriation of the Latin *franci*—to refer to western Christians in general. The borrowing was necessary for a simple reason. Both eastern Christians and western Christians referred to themselves as Romans. The term "Franks" disambiguated competing imperial claims made on two shores of the Mediterranean. Subsequently, the Arabs acquired the term from the Byzantines and used an Arabized form (*ifranjī*) to refer to western Christians. Western Christians themselves learned the word when they started to travel in the Levant in large numbers, during the era of the Crusades.[5] *Frank* (in whatever linguistic coloration it occurred) meant western Christians, sometimes Romance-speaking western Christians in particular, as viewed by eastern Christians or Arabs. Finally, during the sixteenth century, the adjective was attached to the noun *lingua*. The term *lingua franca*—the language of the Franks, the western Christians—referred to a language of convenience used throughout the Mediterranean, essentially a simplified form of Italian with an infusion of vocabulary from other languages, especially Arabic and Spanish.

However, other names for the language appear in various sources, an early indication of the vaguely defined nature of the language itself: "small Frankish" (*piccolo franco*), "bad Italian" (*italien corroumpu* or *italien baragouïné* in the French sources, *italiano corrotto* in Italian).[6] Antoine Galland (1646–1715), best known as French translator of the *Thousand and One Nights*, would refer to it as "un certain langage par mi et ti" ("a certain language using *mi* and *ti*").[7] Later, French-language sources from colonial Algeria would call it *sabir*, taking the name from the lingua franca verb meaning "to know." These monikers capture the amorphous, changeable nature of the tongue. The lingua franca was a vehicular language used as a means of communication by people who did not share a common language. It used a simplified Romance grammar and largely Italian lexicon, but it cherry-picked lexica from other languages of the Mediterranean as well. It seems likely that the lingua franca was long used by traders and travelers on the Mediterranean circuit: merchants, pilgrims, sailors, corsairs, and captives. Yet the first detailed documentation we possess dates to the opening decades of the seventeenth century, when three European travelers describing three different parts of the Arabic-speaking world each undertook to describe the language. François Savary de Brèves was the French consul to Constantinople, and his aide Jacques du Castel wrote an account of his journey to Tunis in 1604 to sort out some difficulties that had arisen with the corsairs there. In describing Tripoli (in present-day Lebanon) he includes an account of the lingua franca, which he calls "Italian, but a corrupt speech, or more precisely a jargon."[8] Antonio de Sosa—a Portuguese traveler taken captive and held in the bagnio in Algiers from 1577 until 1581—mentioned the language among those used in Algiers and recorded a number of comments in the lingua franca in a Spanish-language memoir published posthumously in 1612. He refers to it as "what the Moors and Turks call *franca*, or *hablar franco*."[9] Pietro della Valle described the lingua franca—*franco piccolo*, or "little franco"—in a letter that he wrote about his visit to Damascus in 1616.[10] These early witnesses to the language disagree about what to call it. But the language they describe in each case is the same: a simplified form of Romance used to communicate between speakers of diverse languages in the bagnios of the Barbary republics and the markets of the Levant.

None of these early descriptions supply enough detail to allow us to reconstruct the language. Of the early sources, I cite Savary's, because it is the most succinct and detailed of the three, and because it is less often cited than Sosa's:

> Il est bien composé de termes Italiens, mais sans liaison, sans ordre, ny syntaxe, ne gardant és noms la concordance des genres, meslans les masculins avec les feminins, & ne prenant des verbes, que les infinitifs, pour tous temps & personnes, avec les pronoms, mi, & ti : neantmoins on les entend aussi bien que s'ils y observoient toutes les reigles de grammaire, & faut que ceux qui ont affaire avec eux, en usent de mesme, s'ils veulent estre entendus.[11]

> It is composed of Italian words, but without connection, order, or syntax; not respecting, in the case of nouns, the agreement of gender, but mixing masculine with feminine; and using only the infinitive of the verb for all tenses and persons, with the pronouns *mi* and *ti*; nevertheless they are understood just as well as if they observed all the rules of grammar, and it is necessary that those who do business with them use the same [language], if they wish to be understood.

Early descriptions largely concur with Savary's—the lingua franca consisted of nouns without markers of gender or number and infinitives without the terminations that designate tense, mood, voice, and person—although they are not always so frank in describing it as simplified Italian. As we have seen, Pietro della Valle also calls it Italian. But Sosa refers to it as "a mixture of various Christian languages, largely Italian and Spanish words with some recently added Portuguese terms, since a great number of Portuguese captives were brought to Algiers from Tétouan and Fès after the king of Portugal, Don Sebastian, lost the battle in Morocco."[12] Sosa was, naturally, more sensitive to the Portuguese words which have entered the language recently, because he himself came from Portugal and was (presumably) a native speaker of Portuguese. Here, he describes the effect that linguists call *relexification*. The language could shed vocabulary and repopulate its lexicon with words better suited to the demographics of a specific time and place. More Spanish was heard in the western Mediterranean and more Italian in the eastern Mediterranean. More Greek appeared in the Adriatic. Over time, as France became the great colonial power in the western Mediterranean, more French vocabulary was introduced. The lingua franca was less a clearly defined language than a template that could be pressed into service as needed, using current, local linguistic raw materials.

The origin of the language is impossible to determine. After the year 1000, Italian ships traveled between the Italian ports and the eastern and southern Mediterranean with increasing frequency. The nature of the lingua franca, in the few early written texts that survive, suggests that it must have been generated by Romance-speaking sailors traveling that Mediterranean circuit. It seems evident, given the typical formation of pidgins, that sailors and merchants spoke simplified forms of their own languages to the locals in the port cities of the eastern and southern Mediterranean where the language would later be attested. It became a distinct language when the locals learned it and spoke it back to the "Franks."[13] The lingua franca was, as its name attests, always a foreign language ("frankish"), always someone else's tongue. From the perspective of local populations, it was the language of western European travelers. From the perspective of the western European sailors and merchants, it was *our* language, as spoken by *them*.

The historical record preserves very little trace of the language, especially in the early centuries of its use. Indeed, the category of what we do not know and cannot know about the lingua franca is in some ways more compelling and provocative than the evidence we possess. An extensive body of negative evidence suggests its absence or failure: travelers in territory where the lingua franca is attested by others who say nothing about the language themselves. An anonymous English-language guide for pilgrims published in 1500 includes glossaries of useful words in Greek and Arabic but makes no mention of the lingua franca.[14] During the 1580s, Giovanni Francesco Alcarotti traveled overland from Constantinople to the Holy Land. He compiled a detailed, bracingly pragmatic guide for the pilgrim, including a list of words that one would need on the road (most of them Turkish); in it, he advises the traveler going by land from Tripoli to Jerusalem to learn a bit of Greek.[15] He says nothing about the lingua franca. A 1583 report written for the Venetian Republic laments the loss of souls on ships at sea: extracommunitarians who do not know the lingua franca must die without confession or absolution.[16] Lanfreducci and Bosio, Knights of Malta, wrote a detailed work of reconnaissance about the coast of the Maghreb in 1587. They tell us that Christian sailors off the Tunisian coast use what Turkish they know to communicate with the local population.[17] In 1612, Giovanni Paolo Pesenti passed through nearby Aleppo with a company of Italian merchants on his way to the Holy Land and left a lively description of Ramadan nights spent drinking coffee and smoking tobacco in the cafes of Aleppo (before either coffee or tobacco were familiar to western Europeans). He says nothing about the lingua franca; he tells us that the traveler must rely upon dragomans in order to communicate with the locals. Santo Brasca in the Holy Land in 1481, Henry de Beauvau in the Holy Land in 1619, Domenico Magri in Mount Lebanon in 1664: this is but a partial list of the mountain of negative evidence, travelers who wrote books about their journeys through the Mediterranean that tell us nothing about the lingua franca.

The language, that is, seems to have had a wide *but discontinuous* valence among transient populations in the Mediterranean. It would have a robust conceptual afterlife as a symbol of the triumph of language over cultural differences: viewed, in a sense, as a ghost of Latinity, emerging as Latin itself retracted to become the idiolect of scientists and the Roman Catholic Church. One late eighteenth-century writer represents it as a transregional megalanguage: "a kind of dialect, which, without being the proper language of any country on the coast of the Mediterranean Sea, has a kind of universal currency over all that quarter of the world."[18] An early American novel views it as transhistorical: it "appeared to be the shreds and clippings of all the tongues, dead and living, ever spoken since the creation."[19] A third author sees it as "that barbarous jargon which serves to render Italian so useful in every part of the Mediterranean."[20] The lingua franca was both language and a parody of language; both culturally or ethnically specific—identified most often as Italian—and transnational. Like Latin, the lingua franca emerged from these descriptions as a transregional superlanguage, a professional jargon not learned as a mother tongue but, rather, absorbed by a certain segment of the population as trade language. It did not saturate a given territory (as a national language or, in the premodern context, a vernacular is understood to do) but, rather, was acquired by those needed it: merchants, corsairs, enslaved people and their enslavers, dragomans, and so on. The choreography of the language drew together such actors and witnesses: the marginal characters—both honest laborers and scam artists—of the late medieval and early modern Mediterranean, and the contingent textual witnesses that recall these men and women's fleeting presence on the historical stage.

But most eloquent of all are the lacunae that mark moments where the lingua franca failed or operated beneath the notice of the historical record. The scarcity of the early record and the contradictory record left by the early witnesses invite readings of the lingua franca as metaphor. During the centuries of early modernity—when the lingua franca left the first traces of itself, like words traced in the sand while the tide is out—the cosmopolitan language regime in Europe faced a series of challenges that would prove fatal. Western Europeans wrote love poetry, chivalric romance, epic, prose narrative, and finally even works of philosophy in the vernacular—and in vernacular after vernacular, until Europe itself was balkanized, its knowledge parceled out into linguistic packets that had currency only in the immediate linguistic environs. It's tempting to read the lingua franca as a shadow of Latinity, like the skeleton of the firework traced in smoke after the lights have fallen to earth.

Or we could see the lingua franca as a parody of the cosmopolitan language.[21] To those living east of the Mediterranean, all western Christians were "Franks"—a risible reduction of local identities, to European eyes.[22]

Yet Europe's cosmopolitan language had unified the continent in a similar way. It created an umbrella identity for western Christendom: a language that disregarded microidentities and arced above the local in order to promote transregional communication. True, the lingua franca was a sideshow language, clownish in its reduction of the linguistic palette: a pastiche of epithets, slurs, and commands, at its most elegant nothing more than a trade language. A mockery of a cosmopolitan language, then, that put the cosmopolitan register in the mouths of criminals and scam artists, the demimonde of Mediterranean trade.

A third metaphorical reading of the lingua franca might see it not as shadow or parody but, rather, as a nostalgic vision of a Mediterranean unified by language, as it had been under Roman rule—a sad, poor language, perhaps, but a shared linguistic medium nonetheless. The lingua franca made its last stand in the "empire cinema" of Italy, the movies made during Italy's brief, ignominious colonial adventure (brought to an end by the unrelieved catastrophe of World War II). In these movies, set generally in Libya or the Horn of Africa, a pidginized Italian that bears a strong resemblance to the lingua franca is used by natives and imperial subjects.[23] The caricature is loathsome, analogous to the crude English spoken by Native Americans in cowboy movies. But the use of pidgin Italian as the linguistic currency of empire—and thus as a nod to both the lingua franca and Latinity, as pan-Mediterranean languages of convenience and imperial aspiration—could not be clearer.

However we read the significance of the language, the timing of its emergence makes it tempting to hear the lingua franca as the death knell of the cosmopolitan language. There can be no argument that the Alexandrian language is a bad fit for European modernity. It is rococo and recherché. Its grammar is unnecessarily complicated and requires too much time to learn, with its proliferation of moods, tenses, and voices, its nouns that decline and oblique adjectives, and its thickets of paradigms to memorize. Its lexicon is an attic bursting with the disused effects of hundreds of generations. It gives no quarter to those who like to tailor language to their purpose. It demands that we learn its ways and, haughty and supercilious, will override any attempt to engineer or modify it.

What would Occam's razor do with this language? The answer is there, in the literary record of the centuries of early modernity. The vernacular revolution cut Latin away like old growth to reveal the shoots and sprigs of a new grove of languages hiding in its shadows. Using these languages, the literatures of modernity emerged—at first halting and stammering, then with increasingly fluency as the years passed. Since September 2013, the European Union has recognized twenty-four official languages: Bulgarian,

Croatian, Czech, Danish, Dutch, English, Estonian, Finnish, French, German, Greek, Hungarian, Irish, Italian, Latvian, Lithuanian, Maltese, Polish, Portuguese, Romanian, Slovak, Slovenian, Spanish, and Swedish. Other languages, like Basque, Welsh, and Catalan, may be used officially on an ad hoc basis, on request.[24] Some of the official languages of Europe are robust international languages with their own extensive literary history. Others are spoken by tribal elders, propped up and kept alive through mandatory language classes in the primary-school system, linguistic media relegated to the demographic extremes: the classroom and old age. This linguistic dispensation is poised for change. As I write, the United Kingdom has recently exited the European Union. The British take with them a small handful of minority languages (Scottish Gaelic, Welsh). They also remove from the EU the largest European nation that uses English as a national language. It remains to be seen whether the European Union will continue to rely upon English as lingua franca, in recognition of its global status, once the native speakers of English in Europe no longer send representatives to the European parliament.

For Westerners, and for Europeans in particular, language constitutes a major component of the speaker's identity: speakers of German are Germans, speakers of Italian are Italians, and so on. In this book, I have tried to complicate this understanding of language. The cosmopolitan language contributes to the speaker's identity. But it is an attribute that the speaker takes on consciously, that one acquires, most often, as an adult. It is—to use the formal philosophical term—a *habitus*: an acquired habit; a discipline; linguistic, aesthetic, and ethical training for both mind and mouth. It conditions the user's interactions with the world. But its practitioners do not receive it as birthright. On the contrary, one must study it, learn it, and earn it before using it. The lingua franca displayed some similarities to the cosmopolitan language. Like an Alexandrian language, it was no one's mother tongue and had to be learned. Like a cosmopolitan language of culture and bureaucracy, it was associated with specific trades and specific functions. But unlike Arabic and Latin, the lingua franca had to be learned as professional jargon—generally (in the vernacular phrase) in the school of hard knocks. Its public used it only in order to fulfill a narrow range of duties and obligations. The colorful, sometimes unsavory cast of characters who spoke it, who were identified with the language in early modern travel narratives—merchants, enslaved people and their enslavers, pirates of the Mediterranean—personified its purpose and lexical range. The cheerful English pirate whom Jacques du Castel and François Savary de Brèves met in Tunisia, who told them that he would sell his own father if he captured him at sea, did so in "Italien baragouïné" ("garbled Italian")—a French term for the lingua franca.[25] The language allowed characters like this to speak in travel narratives. But it did not claim to represent the entirety of a speaker's character. Lingua franca gave voice to illiterate characters in recorded narratives about the premodern Mediterranean, though it gave them precious little to say.

In a sense, rather than functioning as a vehicle for self-expression, the lingua franca provided an instrument of character assassination. The language was a work-around, compensating for the absence of more formal tools of translinguistic communication. In that sense, it allowed its users to forego the dragoman, the professional agent whose primary business was linguistic negotiation. Indeed, the presence of the dragoman (in some cases, at least) explains the absence of the lingua franca from the accounts written by those who traveled beyond the reach of their linguistic competence. Santo Brasca, in the Holy Land, recalled "el nostro trucimano ditto abelquadro" ("our *trucimano* [dragoman], called abelquadro [presumably, Abd al-Qadr]").[26] Giovanni Paolo Pesenti traveled through the eastern Mediterranean with "a Christian of the country, who served as servant and as translator." He continues, "Indeed, there are many who have the languages necessary for the country, and wait upon this matter."[27] Lingua franca outsourced the skills of these language professionals, allowing premodern agents to negotiate their own destiny at sea and in the marketplaces and streets of the southern and eastern Mediterranean.

If the Arabic Khurāfa was a man who became a tale (see chapter 8), the lingua franca gives us another kind of merging of linguistic and psychological identities. It was a debased and debasing language, perhaps. Yet it emancipated those who used it, granting them mobility. It could not be used for artistic expression. Nobody ever wrote a text in the lingua franca. A language without fine-tuning, with little range of expression, geared to express commands and epithets, it could not capture the nuance or aspiration of the individual personality. Without historical memory, it could not record and play back the thoughts and emotions of those who spoke it in centuries past. Geographical continuity was its strong suit: it granted ease of movement across the sea. But it lacked both the expressive range and the textual memory for aesthetic expression or cultural memory. What it achieved was more visceral and more ephemeral. It was roguishly populist. It delivered a gut punch to Latin, a Bronx cheer aimed at Arabic, by taking the capacity for transregional communication out of the hands of the textual languages of the elite. It displaced the industry professional, the dragoman—whom (according to the clichés of premodern Mediterranean travel narratives) no one trusted, anyway.[28]

The lingua franca can be read as a pale imitation or a mockery of the cosmopolitan language, or as nostalgic look back at the cosmopolitan language regime. Another metaphorical representation of the language sees it as a megalanguage that has shed the baggage associated with Alexandrian languages. The lingua franca was an inclusive linguistic dispensation. It created a space where Venetians could communicate with Turks, where Algerians and Portuguese spoke the same language. It pushed aside the dragoman and inhabited the identity of the man who performed in linguistic drag. It certainly was not a habitus; one could not *live in* the lingua franca, so meager a dwelling did it furnish. It provided a rough-and-ready linguistic tool, contingent but functional. It could not express the soul of the man. Yet, like the cosmopolitan language, it provided a linguistic bump-up.

At the risk of buckling this groaning board of metaphorical readings of the lingua franca, I offer one last image of the language. The lingua franca may be understood as the refusal to offer the cosmopolitan language to extracommunitarians. Scholars have long asked why Arabs would deign to learn the language of a subject people. Why, in the markets of the eastern and southern Mediterranean—that is, in a predominantly Arabic-speaking environment—would local merchants condescend to learn a pidgin Romance to communicate? Why, in the Algerian or Egyptian household where people were enslaved as housekeepers and field hands, would the enslaver and the ladies of the house learn lingua franca? Why would jailers learn the language of their prisoners? Some have speculated that the Arabs learned lingua franca not out of deference to the linguistic sensibilities of the people they enslaved but in order to withhold their own language from the subject population, in the belief that the cosmopolitan language was not a mere convenience but a privilege granted to the worthy.[29] Such a sentimental reading of the genesis of the lingua franca is, of course, difficult to sustain in a scholarly argument. Yet the notion that the elevated language of culture must be withheld from extracommunitarians who have not studied it and suffused their soul with its history seems consistent with the jealous attention with which the Arabic language has at times been safeguarded.

When the scholar reads the history of the lingua franca from the perspective of the meager historical record—written, of necessity, in one or another more successful linguistic register—he might view it as shadow, parody, or yearning memory, or as reappropriation of or exclusion from the cosmopolitan regime. Viewed from the perspective of its inventors and practitioners (if such an approach were possible), it would be seen differently: as a tribute to the linguistic ingenuity of the transients of the Mediterranean. As the cackling class unleashed the voices of vernacularity in Europe, the casual travelers and professionals of the port cities of the Mediterranean generated the bottom-feeder language that they would use to negotiate, harangue, and cajole. With time, the Mediterranean lingua franca might have become a linguistic contender itself. The inversion of the dream of the lossless language (which the vernacular promises to deliver), it would be the language of loss joyously embraced. It would emancipate those who used it from their landlocked identities, the linguistic regime of the territorial state. It would float free of paradigms and declensions and sequence of tenses; the language of incarceration and slavery and hard-nosed barter would become the register of the absolutely, abjectly free, those who owed allegiance to no state. Every day would be Talk like a Pirate Day! To spin out the counterfactual yarn to its illogical conclusion, if some utopian pan-Mediterranean state had emerged from the crucible of Mediterranean trade, it might have recognized the lingua franca as imperial language, the tongue of a new tribe: the register of the nomads of the Mediterranean ports and currents and breezes; to paraphrase a memorable expression from a British modernist manifesto, the new *Arabs of the Mediterranean*, plying the surging waves as they sail away from the continents of the old cosmopolitan tongues.

BLESS ALL SEAFARERS. THEY exchange not one LAND for another, but one ELEMENT for ANOTHER. The MORE against the LESS ABSTRACT.

BLESS the vast planetary abstraction of the OCEAN.

BLESS THE ARABS OF THE ATLANTIC. THIS ISLAND MUST BE CONTRASTED WITH THE BLEAK WAVES.[30]

[CHAPTER 13]

Life Writing

Arabic, Latin, and Italian in sixteenth-century Italy;
Arabic and English in twenty-first-century California

[L'éthique] est langage, c'est-à-dire responsabilité.

[Ethics] is language: that is to say, responsibility.
EMMANUEL LEVINAS[1]

Was bleibt? Er bleibt die Muttersprache.

What remains? The mother tongue remains.
HANNAH ARENDT[2]

Literary historians often represent the vernacular revolution in western Europe as a liberation. During the late Middle Ages, the voices of the people vanquish Latin—the dark lord of medieval letters—and the modern vernaculars and their literary traditions emerge to express the *genius loci.* At the same time, there is a tendency in studies of the Islamicate languages to duplicate this narrative arc and to represent Arabic as a language that suppresses popular literary expression and that should be pushed aside to make room for literatures in the colloquials or in other local languages.[3] My aim in this book has been to construct a contrarian version of this history: to celebrate the ability of the cosmopolitan language to transcend regional and historical difference and bring its community together, across the continents and the centuries. I do not wish to demonize the boutique languages of Europe. High-school French first introduced me to the allure of foreign languages, and Italian was the first foreign language I truly loved. And yet, I know the urgent pleasure of languages that demand exertion from the language worker: I relish the sense of order that comes from construing a medieval Latin sentence or supplying vowels to an unvocalized Arabic text. Most important, I have spent enough time in the languages of others to respect those who—by choice or by compulsion—have made a new life for themselves beyond their mother tongue. For these reasons, I celebrate the nomads who live in their cosmopolitan language as a refuge from linguistic confusion on the ground.

But the Alexandrian language is a harsh taskmistress. She demands exacting attention from her acolytes, and she dismisses those unable or unwilling to meet her requirements. In chapter 11, I discussed the exclusions of Latin: those to whom it refuses access, who are struck dumb as a result. In chapter 12, I constructed a counterfactual narrative in which an uneducated public creates an open-access antilanguage, understood from shore to shore of the Mediterranean. In this last chapter, the cosmopolitan language strikes back. I return to early modern Italy to discuss the strange and little-known history of the first printed Qur'an—and how the cosmopolitan language exacts a punishment for crimes against it. I tell the story of a powerful metaphor still used today to describe the relationship between Latin and the vernaculars, which was born in sixteenth-century Italy. Finally, I discuss the ethics of the cosmopolitan language: the language that the nomad chooses—or that he takes on *as if it were a choice*, as if one could choose one's linguistic fate. Finally, I pay one last tribute to a language worker whose devotion to his mistress tongue allowed him to give new life to a literary classic written in a deathless language.

∴

The story begins in Venice in 1537—a scant century after the first use of movable type in western Europe—when an Italian printer undertook to print the Qur'an in Arabic. Before this, European printers had experimented with printing non-Roman alphabets. During the early years of the printing press, Venetian printers in particular published books in the Greek, Cyrillic, and Armenian alphabets, some intended for scholarly audiences in western Europe and some for export to a larger overseas public. But Arabic posed particular technical challenges. The printer must create three forms for most letters depending on where the letter occurs within a word: initial, medial, and final forms. In order to print the Qur'an, the printer must also add vocalization to indicate short vowels. Most printed texts don't require full vocalization. But because ambiguity must be avoided at all costs in the sacred text, it is regularly copied or printed with all short vowels indicated. Doubled consonants, too, must be indicated by an added diacritical sign. Other letterforms—the *lām-alif* ligature; the multiple ways of writing the *hamza*; the final *alif maksūra* and *tā' marbūṭa*—must be created. Taken together—three forms of most letters, with all possible vocalizations, notation of doubled consonants, and compulsory ligatures—the printer must create roughly seven hundred possible letterforms in order to print Arabic using movable type. Most technically difficult of all for the printer, the letters must connect.

Who would undertake such an ambitious enterprise? Obviously, the task required someone with exhaustive knowledge of and deep passion for the language and the text. Instead, the man who aspired to print the Qur'an was Alessandro Paganini: an inventive printer, a man with a genius for innovation—but, I am sorry to say, a language worker manqué. Alessandro was the natural son of Paganino Paganini, a printer who had made a name for the Paganini press by publishing large-format, fine editions of the Bible and an important mathematical treatise.[4] Alessandro, to judge the man solely by the books he printed, was both more experimental and more impetuous. Starting in 1515, Alessandro printed a series dedicated to vernacular poetry in a new format: the *ventiquattresimo*, tiny books (84 × 39 mm) intended to put the vernacular poetry of Petrarch, Bembo, and Sannazaro into the hands of a new reading public. He designed a new typeface, between italic and roman, to make these tiny books more elegant and more readable. In 1517, Alessandro rushed to print a remarkable book—the *Opus macaronicarum*—without permission of its author, Teofilo Folengo. This rambunctious work, written in a macaronic mash-up of Italian and Latin and full of vernacular regionalisms, became an unlikely best seller for the press. It appeared in three subsequent editions, including the deluxe 1521 Paganini press edition with fifty-four woodcut illustrations and extensive corrections and emendations introduced by the author. It would enrapture audiences, and its hero—crude, larger than life, and all too human—would inspire Rabelais. In a catalogue dedicated to the work of Alessandro Paganini, Edoardo Barbieri refers to Alessandro as an "open-minded, at times bizarre typographer."[5]

Printing the Qur'an, however, requires more than impetuous daring. The book demands the care of a courtier, devoted to the language and attentive to every detail of the exceptional text. Alessandro did not know Arabic. The press didn't leave records, and it has proved difficult to reconstruct both his motives for attempting the experiment and the methods he used to achieve it. Scholars have concluded that he must have had an adviser, someone who did understand the language, as well as a copy of the text. It seems unlikely that the press worked with a Muslim, who would have understood why the project was doomed to fail. In fact, it's hard to believe that their informant knew Arabic well, given the nature and number of errors in the Qur'an that the press produced.

For the Paganini Qur'an is full of errors. Because the diacritical dots which distinguish the consonants are misused, for instance, there are systematic errors in the printing of consonants: there is no *dāl* in the whole of the text, only *dhāl*; and there is no *thā'*, only *tā'*. The *shadda* (which indicates doubled consonants) is used only in the name *Allah*. Perhaps the most shocking error—because it is attested in nearly every word of the volume—is the *ḥarakāt*, or vocalizations. The only short vowel indicated in the Paganini Qur'an is the *fatḥa*, or the /a/ sound; it is used everywhere, even where a *kasra* /i/ or *ḍamma* /u/ or *sukūn* (no vowel following the consonant) is required. In addition to these systematic errors, the Qur'an attests numerous errors of substance: words misspelled and words or phrases omitted or repeated.[6]

From the perspective of an observant Muslim, the Paganini Qur'an is a monstrosity. It mutilates the text that is, in Islamic teaching, the earthly expression of the Divine Word. Yet it seems that Alessandro intended to market the sacred book precisely to a Muslim audience. The Paganini Qur'an has none of the Latin apparatus that would have made it accessible to European readers. It is printed entirely in Arabic and contains only the substance of the Qur'an. Furthermore, the sole extant copy of the book is printed on fine paper—finer than the paper used for the press's other books. It has taken historians years to reconstruct what happened. It appears that the Paganini press intended to sell the printed Qur'an on the Ottoman market. When a representative of the press arrived in Constantinople with his wares, he was arrested and brought before the authorities. He was at first sentenced to death; when a Venetian ambassador interceded for him, the sentence was commuted to amputation of his right hand.[7]

Today, a single copy of the Paganini Qur'an survives in a monastery in Venice.[8] Teseo Ambrogio degli Albonesi, a student of Oriental languages, owned the book. He made notations only on a handful of pages, and we don't know whether he knew enough Arabic to be able to discern the systematic printing errors that turned the text into an incomprehensible alphabet soup.[9] The Paganini press was apparently ruined by the investment they made in the Qur'an, money they failed to recoup. The elder Paganino Paganini died, at the age of eighty-eight, in the year the book reached Constantinople, but he had largely left the press in the hands of his son in his late years and so likely was not involved in the printing of the Qur'an. Alessandro published two more books in 1538—the last books the Paganini press ever printed.[10] He lived another two decades but published nothing more after 1538.

It's hard to know what lesson to take away from this sad story. The Paganini Qur'an surely could be turned into a cautionary tale for those who approach the cosmopolitan language without adequate preparation: if not used with due reverence, it may have its revenge. Certainly, Alessandro's cultural insensitivity is reprehensible by twenty-first-century standards. Yet, at the same time, one must admire his technical daring. The Paganini Qur'an was not the first book printed in Arabic using movable type. An Italian printer, Gregorio de' Gregorii, had printed a Roman rite book of hours for export to the Arab Christian market twenty years earlier.[11] The typeface of Paganini's Qur'an, however, is a considerable improvement on that book. The letters are more elegantly formed (the Gregorii Book of Hours gives many of the letters childish, oversized loops). There is a flow similar to handwriting in the typesetting of some words in Paganini's Qur'an, a slight northeast-to-southwest alignment that mimics the look of a text written by hand.

Most tantalizing of all is the thought of what might have happened had Paganini's experiment succeeded. In a counterfactual version of this story, the Ottomans would look at Paganini's mangled text and see it not as monstrosity but as intriguing possibility. They would send a representative to Italy to correct Paganini's printing plates. Together, Ottoman experts and Italian printers would produce a Qur'an accessible to a vast market. In the Ottoman Empire during the sixteenth century, many families had to content themselves with sharing communal mosque Qur'ans. Before Paganini's experiment, the Qur'an was known only in manuscript versions; copying the Qur'an was viewed as an act of devotion, typically undertaken by calligraphers who specialized in creating copies of the sacred scripture.[12] But the Paganini Qur'an could be reproduced for a fraction of the cost of the lavish handwritten copies of the Qur'an available at the time. Every household could have its own copy. In this alternate universe, like Alessandro's tiny *ventiquattresimo* editions of the Italian poets, the printed Qur'an would make the sacred text available to a vast new audience. It would make Alessandro Paganini a very rich man. It would also give the Ottoman Empire access to print media, just twenty years after Suleiman the Magnificent acceded to the throne and at a moment of booming growth for the Ottomans and their culture.

In chapter 10 above, I introduced Aḥmad Fāris al-Shidyāq and Edward William Lane: nineteenth-century men of letters who wrote works knowing that they would be typeset and printed in Arabic, using movable type and modern printing methods. That chapter was a smash cut into the distant future from the premodern Mediterranean where most of this book is set. Modernization brought a number of changes to the languages of literature used around the Mediterranean, none more important than the printing press. In sixteenth-century Venice (and in Lyon and Paris, the other centers of publishing during the sixteenth century), entrepreneurs printed books in Latin and, increasingly, the vernaculars. It would take longer for a printing press to be established in the Arabophone world, partly because of the technical difficulties of printing in the Arabic alphabet. The first printing press that printed in Ottoman Turkish—that is, using the Arabic alphabet—opened in Istanbul in 1727, but it printed relatively little.[13] The first printing press in Egypt published its first book—an Italian-Arabic dictionary—in 1822.[14] The Qur'an would be printed in Iran in the 1810s, in India in 1850, and in Istanbul in 1872; the first Qur'an printed in the Arab world was published in Bulaq, Egypt, in 1864.[15]

Yet mechanical reproduction of the printed word did not bring a vernacular revolution to the Arabophone world. Al-Shidyāq (discussed in chapter 10) supervised the printing of his own novel in Arabic in Paris, and the last act of his long career was entangled with the early history of the Arabic-language printing press in Istanbul. But his approach to modernizing his mistress tongue represents, among the linguistic vignettes I have presented in this book, something of an anomaly, a counterfactual history although it is true. For al-Shidyāq, literary modernity is print-adjacent, but not linked to modern spoken usage. The beloved tongue must modernize by diving deep into its historical reserves. Rather than mimicking the way that people speak on the street today—the European vernacularization model—the cosmopolitan language must be reminded of words and behaviors it has forgotten. In the alternate version of modernization that al-Shidyāq showed us, the language worker who has dedicated himself to the study of the mistress tongue awakens her by reminding her of her deep history and restoring the tether lines that connect her to her past. Rather than modernizing the language by streamlining and simplifying it, he resuscitates it, quickening dead words and using them to name the artifacts and phenomena of modernity. Mechanical reproduction simply provides a means of bringing the fruits of this linguistic labor to a wider public.

Literary moderns write in the language in which they live—generally, the language in which they have lived since infancy: the mother tongue—because, tautologically, it is a *living language*. The writer can't invest the cosmopolitan language with the same vigor and dynamism because it is a *dead language*. Throughout this book, although I have played with the metaphor of the language that lives, I have avoided using those two loaded terms. But for the general population, they are familiar designations, used as taxonomic labels to categorize language. A living language is spoken by a population; somewhere on the planet, it remains the language of daily life. A dead language is a textual language. It survives only in books. The living must learn it not by following the sweet music of the mother's voice but by memorizing verb paradigms and vocabulary lists, chanting the rhythmic conjugations and declensions of the dead. The distinction between living language and dead feeds into the definition of the cosmopolitan language, which (in the premodern past) was not a language of daily life but rather a language of the page.

The distinction between living and dead languages has the appearance of an objective system of classification. Like the family trees that scholars use to represent relations between languages and language change over time, *living language* and *dead language* seem like inert labels that describe categories that exist in nature. But languages do not breed; they are not born and they do not die. Furthermore, the metaphor of the "living language" was invented at a specific point in history: it first appeared (as far as I am aware) just three years after the publication of the Paganini Qur'an, in 1540. It was coined in the context of the language wars that consumed Italian intellectuals during the fifteenth and sixteenth centuries. During the first half of the fifteenth century, Italians tried to reset the clock. Unlike writers in any other part of Europe, they turned away from the emergent vernacular and resurrected their dear cosmopolitan language, Latin. The experiment could not last, of course. Humanist Latin would give way by the close of the fifteenth century to a vernacular resurgence. Then, Italians had a second language war to fight: choosing the best vernacular in which to write. The Italian language was divided into dialects, most of them considered foreign languages beyond their native city. If the author was to write in the language of daily life, which of these myriad vernacular varietals should he or she choose? This battle would continue throughout the sixteenth century, becoming a war of attrition. In the end, Italians chose to write in an updated version of the vernacular code devised by the *Tre corone* (Three Crowns) of the fourteenth century: the elevated Tuscan in which Dante wrote the epic, Boccaccio wrote narrative fiction, and Petrarch wrote his lyric poetry.

In the course of the debates over language that consumed Italian men of letters during the late fifteenth and early sixteenth century, a relatively obscure figure, Alessandro Citolini, devised a new metaphor to describe the opposition between Italian and Latin. He seems to have been the first to use the locutions *living language* and *dead language* in print.[16] His aim was to discuss the vernacular, but first he had to dispense with Latin. After examining the arguments made by those who would still elevate Latin at the expense of the vernacular, Citolini notes that the defenders of Latin "do not notice that Latin is dead and buried in books; and that the vernacular is alive; and it holds in Italy today that same place that Latin held while it lived." He clearly enjoys the power of his image, and elaborates it at some length, dwelling on the cold comfort of dead languages, like Latin and ancient Greek: "If one wishes to make use of them, he must seek them in books; and he must be content with that alone which he receives from books."[17]

Without detracting from the credit due the man for his invention, the metaphor has an air of inevitability. The one language summons images of dusty library shelves and fusty old men. The other has the bloom of youth and urgency; it is the language used to pursue and court. With this epitaph, the Italian vernacular dances on Latin's grave. The "living language" metaphor, of course, would have a long and fruitful life following Citolini's coinage. It is still standard practice to represent language history as if it followed the arc of a human life: languages have a youth, must learn and grow to become mature, and finally become senescent and die. Reading out from this metaphor, both scholars and nonspecialists represent language change using the metaphor of genetics, with predictable confusion. In a recent, lamentable use of the metaphor, a report written by an Oakland, California, school board in 1996 represented Ebonics (an older term for African American English) as "genetically based." The report meant to say that linguists had traced certain grammatical features of Ebonics to languages spoken in sub-Saharan Africa, but politicians and the public understood the phrase to mean that African Americans were genetically incapable of speaking "correct" English. At the end of a brief, inflammatory debate, stoked by this and other rhetorical infelicities, the Oakland schools were obliged to abandon their effort to bring the complexity of spoken American English into the classroom.[18]

At roughly the same time that Latin was pronounced dead, it lost one of the pillars that supported it: its close relationship to religious practice in western Europe. It maintained its status as lingua sacra for the Roman Church. But that church itself lost market share as the Protestant Reformation gathered steam. The vignette that I used to illustrate the category "lingua sacra" in this book—the adventures of Cyril and Methodius, apostles to the Slavs (chapter 7)—was, by design, eccentric. Cyril invented a new alphabet, not a new tongue. He used it to write not a cosmopolitan language but a local vernacular. The drama of that episode derives from the contest between Cyril and the Latins, the cawing birds on the Venetian dock who accuse the upstart missionaries as language traitors. Cyril and Methodius arrived in Moravia (in the middle of the ninth century) some 650 years before Luther nailed his Ninety-Five Theses to the door of the Wittenberg Castle church (in 1517); it is with some satisfaction that I note that Luther wrote his Theses in Latin. The widespread translation of the Bible into the vernaculars and the celebration of church services in the vernaculars became a pillar of Protestant practice, as Latinity (and all its hocus-pocus) came to symbolize Roman Catholicism.[19]

Arabic, on the other side of the Mediterranean, lost none of its dazzle as lingua sacra during the late medieval and early modern period. Arabic has a much more intimate relationship with revelation in the Islamic context than any Christian language can claim. The substance of revelation in Islam is embedded in language, in a unique register of one tongue: Qurʾanic Arabic. The doctrine of the inimitability of the Qur'an, articulated in response to Qurʾanic assertions of the unique status of the Qurʾanic text on the one hand and poets' attempts to duplicate Qurʾanic diction on the other, is just one recognition of the unique status of the language in Islamic belief.[20] For Muslims, God and Qur'an form a kind of Moebius strip, quite impossible to disentangle. The debates over the ontology of the Qur'an and the relationship between the text and divinity furnished matter for the first doctrinal battles of the nascent Muslim community: the Miḥna (833–ca. 848 CE), which centered on the question of the createdness of the Qurʾan. Was the Holy Book created in a specific historical moment or coeternal with God? The Miḥna—or, as it is sometimes termed in naturalizing translations of Islamic history, the "Islamic inquisition"—was an exercise in articulating Islamic conceptions of rule and the role played by the caliph as leader of the faithful as well as a doctrinal investigation. But it pointed to questions still important for Muslims: is it possible to distinguish between God and his Qur'an, or are they two expressions of the same eternal and continuous creation-event?

Clearly, a text believed to be so sublime that humans cannot imitate it, a text believed to exist in an eternal and unchanging state and to shadow the ontology of God, must also be fashioned of a language that cannot die. In fact, the Qur'an seems at moments to enshrine a linguistic ideal that is not held to the dispensation of life and death: a linguistic state that might be described using the twenty-first-century English term of art *posthuman*. The Qur'an does not attribute life and consciousness only to humans; therefore, it does not speak only to humans. It tells us that animals, like humans, have an *umma* (Q 6:38): the word refers to the community of believers and implies that animals, like humans, possess a consciousness and a moral faculty, enabling them to live in communities that honor God, as humans do. It tells us that all creatures that move bow down to God (Q 16:48–50) and that bees create honey in response to their own understanding of God's command (Q 16:68). The birds have their own inquisition, when Solomon interrogates them to find the hoopoe (Q 27:20), who when he returns will bring news of the Queen of Sheba. When rocks fall down in fear of God (Q 2:74), what special status does "life" or "consciousness" have? A rigorous and committed posthuman reading of the Qur'an must recognize that the text represents itself as speaking to forms of consciousness that have not been the subject of scientific study before the twenty-first century: intelligence that does not need the human brain or human body as support.

But the posthuman ontology of Qur'anic Arabic does the flesh-and-blood writers of the contemporary Arabophone world no good as linguistic model. Qur'anic Arabic takes the notion of the "aspiration language" to a new level. Arab writers of the twenty-first century may take sustenance from the Qur'an on many levels, including the linguistic. But as writers—writers of poetry, novels, comics and graphic novels, journalistic prose, histories, and so on—they need other models: they need another Arabic. Like other writers, they want a language that is responsive in the moment, one that can speak to the urgencies and quotidian minutiae of life in the twenty-first century. Arabs negotiated a new linguistic standard during the nineteenth and twentieth century: Modern Standard Arabic, or MSA, a formal Arabic less exacting than the ill-defined classical Arabic of the premodern past, with new vocabulary to describe the phenomena of modern life. But that, still, is a learned language for Arabs, not the language of the street or the kitchen or the bedroom. The movements to create a colloquial literature—literature written in the register of everyday life—have challenged the MSA of the politicians and television anchormen and the classical Arabic of the scholars and the Qur'anic Arabic of the exegetes.[21] But writers need readers, and even a language with the global muscle that Arabic still must scramble to find its reading public in the marketplace of the twenty-first century. When content can be delivered in so many ways—movies and TV shows, comics and graphic novels, songs, born-digital media like blogs and vlogs, games, texts and DMs and subreddits—how can the print media compete? When the written language must streamline itself to communicate in ephemeral digital formats, what happens to the transhistorical heft of the textual language, which I have (mostly) celebrated in this book?

This book is a ballad for a language that is dead. Yet, at the same time, I have argued that the cosmopolitan language transcends petty divisions between life and death. It is nonhuman or posthuman. Yet, at the same time, I have argued that the nomad writer, the one who writes in the cosmopolitan language, is drawn to that language by affection. One can love the mother tongue, and many people do. Whether it's a national language or a particular local dialect or accent, the mother tongue was the first we used as instrument of communication. It is bathed in the roseate glow of nostalgia. But one can also love the cosmopolitan languages: global languages, those that connect the speaker to the world; aspiration languages. The mother tongue reminds us of origins, but the cosmopolitan language reminds us of the future. A cosmopolitan language is a language that one covets and seeks to win, knowing all along that one woos in vain, because the language is bigger than the world, bigger even than the urgency with which one pursues it. It is a language that one lives in, like the nomad's tent. But like a haughty mistress, it slaps the courtier's hand when he gets too frisky: when he attempts to print the Qur'an using movable type, for instance; or when, like Sībawayhi (chapter 6), he misconstrues a verb, forgets a declension, or misplaces an essential element of vocabulary at a crucial moment and is reminded of his own limitations.

If the language worker can adore the language, he can also be a jealous lover. Trolls guarding the precincts of the beloved language have made appearances throughout this book. The Ottoman officials who amputated the hand of Paganini's representative in Constantinople; Sībawayhi's opponents in grammar; the men who questioned Bashshār ibn Burd on his non-Arab origins; the Arabs who challenged Abū Bishr Mattā; the custodians of Latin who confronted Cyril in Venice; Petrarch, sneering at King John's lack of Latin: every good story needs conflict, and this one has its fair share. Indeed, Petrarch illustrates the complexity of the affects that the language inspires. We remember him today for his sublime inventions in Italian. But Latin—the language in which he wrote the lion's share of his works, and a language he wrote with fluid beauty and grace—was his mistress for most of his life. His contemporaries, and men of letters who read his works during the century following his death, knew his Latin works best. Latin, it seems, brought out the best *and* the worst in him.

The *gramatica*, as Dante pointed out in the *De vulgari eloquentia*, is not a language that one absorbs like the waters of the Arno.[22] It is a habitus: a behavior learned through repetition, until it becomes second nature, as if one were born with it. Its acolytes earn it through hard labor. For most, it is an object of desire: those who learn it well and wield it well desired it ardently before they mastered it. Today, Arabic survives as both lingua sacra and literary language, but those who use it as literary medium are almost exclusively ethnic Arabs. Global English might be a better stand-in as the twenty-first-century equivalent to the cosmopolitan language as object of desire. Perhaps few of those who learn English as business language love it. But the global teenagers who sing along with the sounds of English or American pop songs, and only later may learn to understand those words, are motivated by desire for the mobility and connectivity that only a cosmopolitan language can grant. Glamour, sophistication, the dazzle and bustle of a big city, entrée to the most important conversations happening at the moment: the cosmopolitan language has always promised its acolytes access. It is the backstage pass of languages.[23]

The example, however, illustrates one of the difficulties posed by the cosmopolitan language—this one a difficulty related not to the elaborate structure or long history of the language, or the access to it that might be granted or denied on a whim. Those who use it don't always have the luxury of choice. Bashshār ibn Burd might have chosen not to write in Arabic; if he had, we would not know his poetry today. Bashshār had a choice between Arabic and silence. In historical circumstances in which the language of culture is imposed, not chosen, the language worker might invest the cosmopolitan language with respect, but in such cases, can we really think of the relationship between language and language worker as a bond of affection? Alessandro Paganini did not love the Arabic language. As far as we can tell, he did not know the Arabic language. The generous historian might imagine him admiring the aesthetic beauty of the alphabet; this might help to account for the relative elegance of the letterforms designed by his press. But he approached the language as an economic mercenary. He instrumentalized Arabic in the hopes of seeing an immense return on his investment. The language exacted its revenge, in the punishment inflicted on the press's representative in Constantinople and the bankruptcy of the Paganini press.

To the extent that the language worker chooses the language that she uses—despite the poverty of choice which circumstances might offer her—that choice marks the place of an ethical engagement. Alessandro Paganini approached Arabic without the proper training and formation in its grammar and history: his use of the language was heedless, presumptuous, and mercenary. I have attempted to produce a sympathetic portrait of Paganini here; in so doing, I read against the grain. While his industry and vision are laudable, his financial motivation and his complete absence of foresight make him a deeply problematic figure. Anyone reading the historical record to study the ethics of language choice would condemn Paganini on the grounds of disrespect of the Arabic language and of the sacred text in which (for believers) the Divine Word is made worldly language.

Of course, philosophers typically do not talk about the ethics of *language choice* in the way that I have in this book. Deleuze and Guattari, for instance, discuss Kafka's choice to write in German; but they do not approach the question as literary historians, and they do not see that, for Kafka, German functioned not as language of place but as cosmopolitan language.[24] In the quote used as epigraph to this chapter, Emmanuel Levinas writes, "[Ethics] is language: that is to say, responsibility." Here, he calls for mindful use of language as an instrument that can produce a relationship of justice between the self and the other. He uses "language" as synecdoche for "communication." He does not attach an adjective to the noun, to designate one language or another: he is not interested in the ethics of language choice. Rather, he refers to a portfolio of communicative strategies that rely upon language and that human beings use as citizens, to engage with either a local or a global community. In this sense, his reflections on language intersect with my discussion of a mindful commitment to the cosmopolitan language: the language worker must respect his instrument, when he engages the great machinery of the language.

Hannah Arendt, in contrast to Levinas, does talk specifically about her choice of language, and she distinguishes between the different linguistic instruments she uses both to communicate with her public and in the privacy of her own mind. In a 1965 television interview, Arendt is asked, "What remains" of prewar Germany? She replies, "What remains? The mother tongue remains."[25] Giorgio Agamben analyzes Arendt's statement as stark testimonial to the impossibility of testimony. The mother tongue—borne into exile after the rupture of those cultural and ontological ties to the defunct community that used it as cultural adhesive or as the medium of daily life—became for Agamben a "dead language" in recognition of the impossibility of bearing witness to loss on the magnitude of the Shoah. Like Levinas, Agamben uses language as a way to represent the human effort to make sense of the world and, in a narrower sense, to create justice. Arendt, however, makes a different calculus. She weighs one language against another; she talks precisely about language choice. Her "mother tongue" was German—the language she took away from her homeland with her, despite its implication in the horror she fled ("It wasn't the German language that went crazy," she explains). She chose to write in English only after a period of linguistic experimentalism. She wrote at first in French, "which I then spoke very well," because she lived in France. In the years after her arrival in the US in 1941, she wrote articles in German for expatriate newspapers. In 1942, she published an op-ed in Yiddish in a New York newspaper, in which she reflects on the complexities of language choice for cosmopolitan Jews of the war era. Finally, she settled into English as communicative medium. At the time when she filmed the interview quoted above, she lived in the United States, and she wrote in English, "but," she says of English, "I have never lost a feeling of distance from it."[26]

I am arguing that Arendt's "feeling of distance" from English describes a state familiar to all who write in a cosmopolitan language. For some, that distance is a source of comfort: they need a buffer between themselves and the work. Taking on the language might be the equivalent of putting on work clothes and going to the office, the lab, or the shop for these language workers. For others, the distance between the self and the language quickens desire, as al-Shidyāq and Petrarch, for instance, longed for their cosmopolitan mistresses (and as Dante yearned for Tuscan Italian, once he no longer spoke it in the street and the market). Arendt's "feeling of distance," in short, describes the emotional affect that attends the cultivation of the learned language as discipline. The cosmopolitan language is not "hardwired" into the mind, as the mother tongue is, to use the common metaphor for brain physiology in the twenty-first century. It is a habitus: an acquired habit. For that reason, it holds us (and we hold it) at arm's length. It is "what remains," to return to Agamben's phrase, because it speaks to the dead as well as the living, and to the future as well as the past. For the literary writer, it looks beyond haecceity, the linguistic actuality of the here and now. Because of its historical and geographical range, it allows the writer to indulge in what I have called *hikaya* (see chapter 9): a portfolio of self-reflective maneuvers, games played to amuse and instruct other lovers of the tongue.

From Paganini, language mercenary, to Citolini, who buried Latin, to Arendt, who was hounded through languages by the Nazis, the language workers who have appeared in this last chapter provide fraught examples of engagement with their Alexandrian languages. In closing, I turn the page on these brief profiles to celebrate a scholar whose manipulation of languages reflects the joy of performance in a linguistic instrument that one takes on in order to amuse and flirt with a public. In chapter 10, I discussed the Library of Arabic Literature, a new imprint that publishes Arabic works in English translation.[27] In 2020, the press published *Impostures*, Michael Cooperson's translation of the *Maqāmāt* of al-Ḥarīrī (1054–1122). The Arabic title of the book comes from a lexical root with a wide range of meanings: "to stand up," "to set out" or "depart," "to be" or "to be located." The noun *maqāma* (plural *maqāmāt*) refers to a session at which men of letters stood to recite literary compositions. Al-Ḥarīrī's *Maqāmāt* are the outstanding example of the genre most closely associated with these gatherings: dense compositions in rhymed prose that play with and in the Arabic language. Two characters appear in each of the fifty short *maqāmāt*: the narrator and the protagonist, whose dazzling verbal performances, executed to beg money from an unwitting public, are the showpieces of the book, and who appears in disguise in each sketch, only to be unmasked by the narrator at tale's end. *Impostures*, then: an English word from a Latin root (*pono*) meaning "to put down" or "set down," which in turn generates an English noun describing how things stand (*posture*, from the past participle of the Latin verb), and this counternoun designating things that stand for other things, a person who puts on a mask, a person (or a word) in drag.[28]

Cooperson chose to translate al-Ḥarīrī's *Maqāmāt* not into English, precisely, but into Englishes. Al-Ḥarīrī's Arabic is almost absurdly athletic. Some examples: his protagonist gives a formal speech that consists entirely of undotted letters—denuded prose, it appears to the eye, or archaic Arabic, written before the Arabs began to use dots to distinguish one consonant from another. In another *maqāma,* words in which every letter is dotted alternate with words in which no letter is dotted. One *maqāma* contains a number of palindromes. Another includes a sermon that could be read, word by word, front to back or back to front, and delivers a different message in the two versions.[29] Rather than try to reproduce these calisthenics in English, Cooperson chooses to write in a range of English styles: English impostures that in some manner reflect the mood or theme of the *maqāma* he is translating. He writes in accented English: Scots English in *maqāma* 14, Indian English in 15, Spanglish in 16, English using the slang of UCLA students in 37, and so on. He imitates the style of great authors of the English literary tradition. *Maqāma* 10 is written in Chaucerian English, 13 imitates Shakespearean English, 17 sounds like Jerome K. Jerome (appropriate, for this *maqāma* features palindromes), and 43 imitates the style of Henry Fielding. Cooperson channels the voice of James Boswell, and the jovial and chatty friendship between Boswell and Samuel Johnson, to translate *maqāma* 2 and *maqāma* 48 and to mirror the friendship between protagonist and narrator in the original. Al-Ḥarīrī conceived the *Maqāmāt* in a homosocial environment. Here, too, Cooperson expands al-Ḥarīrī's horizons. *Maqāma* 5 imitates the style of Virginia Woolf, 30 mimics Jane Austen, and 35 channels Gertrude Stein. The last *maqāma*—the *maqāma* of repentance, in which the protagonist returns to Sarūj (the home he fled when the Crusaders invaded) and leaves behind the flimflammery of his past—imitates the style of Margery Kempe. Cooperson supplies his own English gloss of his Middle English text, because Kempe's English is a stretch for a twenty-first century public.

Cooperson's translation is both a delight and a challenge. Here, for instance, is the narrator's account of the reformed protagonist in the final *maqāma*, when the narrator encounters him in Sarūj, in the style of Margery Kempe:

> And I fond him and hys felawshyp asunder, and hym standyng in his hirne. He was clad in a cloke ful of clowtys and a cloth of canvas as it were a sakkyn gelle. Whan I saw hym I hadde gret drede, as he were a lyon, for hys face bar the token of mech prostracyon. Whan hys paire of bedys was endyd, he reysed hys fore fynger to greten me, but never askyd for tydyns anydeel, ne spak a word of the olde tyme.[30]

Cooperson translates al-Ḥarīrī's Arabic and, at the same time, reminds us how much English has changed since the fifteenth century, when Margery Kempe wrote her account of her own (ambiguous) conversion. What a relief and what a pleasure it is to turn back to Cooperson's imitation of

P. G. Wodehouse, whose prose style (under a century old) still rings familiar to twenty-first-century ears. Here is Cooperson's translation of the parallel anagnorisis—the moment of recognition—when the narrator recognizes the protagonist in that earlier episode:

> I stuck to the Sarooji like a brother and hung like a limpet on his every word until he fell ill, poor chap, with something chronic and wasting. Rumour had it that he looked so bad that many an experienced corpse-washer would have started washing him on sight. I was in something of a reduced state myself: with his absence everything had gone to sixes and sevens, and dash it all, I did miss the poor blighter![31]

Cooperson's translation of the *Maqāmāt* is a love letter addressed at once to al-Ḥarīrī's Arabic and to the English language. In his introduction to the translation, Cooperson reflects on the ambiguity of the protagonist, Abū Zayd, the shape-shifting beggar. Abū Zayd puts Arabic through its paces in his performances, showing his audience a new face of the language in each sketch. At the same time, he himself changes so much from one *maqāma* to the next that he seems to have no stable identity, no character or qualities to call his own. "The most economical explanation for his vaporous indeterminacy," Cooperson concludes, "is that he is Arabic itself."[32] As in my reading of the Fāriyāqiyyah (chapter 10), Cooperson reads Abū Zayd as a representation of the cosmopolitan language that al-Ḥarīrī manipulates so skillfully, invested by the language worker with ties of fealty and love. At the same time, Cooperson's own performance in English inspires affection. His care for the history and varieties of English is as diligent as his research on al-Ḥarīrī's life and times and Arabic. The chapter-by-chapter bibliography includes scholarly works on the *Maqāmāt*, but also on the accents and authors whom Cooperson imitates and specialized vocabulary that comes into play in each translation. The chapter written in the style of P. G. Wodehouse, for instance, also adopts the lingo used in mid-twentieth-century American diners to convey orders to the chef (in imitation of al-Ḥarīrī's original, which uses culinary terminology). The bibliography includes a reference work called *Hash House Lingo* and a website that culls diner cant.[33] When Cooperson translates a sermon using English words of Germanic and Romance origin in alternation, and translates the surrounding *maqāma* using only English words of Germanic origin, this reader doffs her cap: this is hikaya of a high order.[34] Imitating al-Ḥarīrī's Arabic, the great language learns new melodies.

Impostures gives the reader of English access to al-Ḥarīrī's *Maqāmāt*, in its own idiom, while at the same time raising questions about English. Does the reader feel inspired, in her devotion to English, to pursue it into the thickets of Margery Kempe's prose? How far is she willing to travel to bring back the Eurydice of meaning from the underworld, and what happens to those readers content to remain in the shallows: are they left behind? Or will they lead the way forward into a streamlined linguistic dispensation, which sheds the deep historical resources of the language and the regional markers that differentiate global varieties of the language? Is this an either/or proposition, or can English be both/and: can it make itself available to some as cosmopolitan register and to others as a low-resistance vehicular language? At the same time, the book piques the reader's curiosity about the Arabic that Cooperson translates. How many readers, tantalized by Cooperson's *Impostures,* will pursue the *Maqāmāt* to the other side: to early twelfth-century Basra, and deep into Arabic?[35]

I close with Cooperson's English hikaya as a final tribute to the range of the great language. Cooperson is a polymath. He has worked to make himself worthy not only of Arabic but also of English. In the bibliography that traces his research into the world of al-Ḥarīrī and the Englishes he imitates, he shows his work: like Dante, he tracks his language into the dens and lairs where she is at home.[36] He and the press that published his translation have taken a risk with this book, and I wish them both Godspeed. Language is a public good, an instrument that each individual uses only by the grace and with the consent of a larger community, which counts among its citizens the dead along with the living. Courtesy and daring, appropriately balanced, please the mistress tongue. May she shower on Cooperson her rewards, and may this courtier's impostures bring solace and cheer to the quick and the dead!

Acknowledgments

I have been writing this book for a very long time, and acknowledging those who helped to shape it seems a Herculean task. Of the many personal encounters that left a mark on this book, I must recognize a seminar on lingua francas and cosmopolitan languages that I taught at the University of Michigan in 2011 with my colleague Michael Bonner, who—despite his astonishing erudition—never knew enough to sate his curiosity. I read Sheldon Pollock's *Language of the Gods in the World of Men* with a group of colleagues at Michigan, and I am grateful especially to Lee Schlesinger for organizing that reading group in collaboration with South Asianists at the University of Toronto and to Alison Cornish and Sara Ahbel-Rappe for their incisive contributions to our discussions. A residential fellowship at the University of Michigan's Institute for the Humanities gave me precious time to work on this book, in very good company. My students at the American University of Beirut first taught me what it means to live in a mindful way among languages, and they have been in my thoughts from beginning to end of this book. At the University of Toronto, where I taught medieval Latin as a graduate student, George Rigg was chair of the Committee for Medieval Latin Studies and my landlord, and I remember vividly his affection for both the Latin language and his garden. For intellectual camaraderie, I must single out Peggy McCracken, who does so much for medieval studies at Michigan; Kathryn Babayan, who listened to my enthusiasm and exasperation with these ideas more than once; and Suzanne Akbari, who has been part of my intellectual life since I was a graduate student.

Earlier versions of some of the arguments in this book appeared in *Middle Eastern Literatures*, *Interfaces*, *Postmedieval*, *Companion to Mediterranean History*, and *Cosmopolitanism and the Middle Ages*. I am grateful to anonymous reviewers for the University of Chicago Press, whose advice improved the manuscript substantially. I have given talks presenting material that appears here at the NEH seminar Thresholds of Change: Modernity and Transformation in the Mediterranean; the King Fahd Center for Middle East Studies at the University of Arkansas; the Department of Italian at the

University of California, Los Angeles; the Marco Institute for Medieval and Renaissance Studies at the University of Tennessee, Knoxville; the Global Georgia initiative at the University of Georgia at Athens; Medieval Studies at the University of Connecticut, Storrs; the Centre for Medieval Studies at the University of Toronto; the School of Literatures, Cultures, and Linguistics at the University of Illinois at Urbana-Champaign; the Mediterranean Seminar's University of California Multi-Campus Research Program Workshop and Conference; the Department of Literature at the University of California, Santa Cruz; the Italian Research Seminars at the University of Notre Dame; Crossing the Languages of Medieval Europe: Historical, Linguistic and Literary Approaches (organized by the Centre for Medieval Literature, Odense, Denmark) in Rome; the Medieval and Early Modern Studies workshop at Stanford University; the Medieval Studies Program at Princeton University; the Mediterranean Studies Initiative at Cornell University; the Department of Romance Languages and Department of Near Eastern Studies at the University of Michigan; the Center for Medieval and Renaissance Studies at the University of California, Los Angeles; the Department of French and Italian at the University of Minnesota, Twin Cities; the Center for Medieval and Renaissance Studies at Binghamton University, New York; the Department of French, Classics, and Italian at Michigan State University; the Western Mediterranean Workshop at the University of Chicago; and the Glasscock Center at Texas A&M University. The intellectual generosity and hospitality of many individuals made those visits memorable and enriched this book. The strengths of this book draw on what I have gained from them and from those named above; its faults are mine alone.

Notes

CHAPTER ONE

1. For an overview of diglossia as a linguistic phenomenon, see Mejdell, "Diglossia." Suleiman, "Arabic Folk Linguistics," surveys major conceptual and ideological discussions that have emerged around the subject, including what seems a basic question but proves fiendishly difficult to answer: Are colloquial Arabic (the *ʿāmmiyya*) and written Arabic (*fuṣḥā* Arabic, in his discussion) two distinct languages or two faces of the same language? Louis-Jean Calvet refers to conditions prevailing in the Arabophone world as "schizoglossia": Arabs have one name for many languages (*Towards an Ecology of World Languages*, 194–205). Niloofar Haeri studies Modern Standard Arabic (MSA) in modern Egypt from an anthropological perspective and tries to disentangle the relationship between MSA and "classical Arabic" (another ambiguous term) and to discuss how Egyptian citizens, Muslim and Christian, negotiate that complex terrain; see *Sacred Language, Ordinary People*, esp. chapter 2, 25–51.

2. See Ethnologue, https://www.ethnologue.com/language/lat (accessed June 24, 2019).

3. In recent years, a number of monographs have appeared that aim to represent the "biography" of a language—most notably, Latin—or to represent the ethnic, cultural, and linguistic complexity of a specific location (especially in the Muslim Mediterranean and central Asia). Although this book does not aim for a similar representation of a single language or place, it seems useful to point out that bibliography for my readers. I will cite those works in this chapter as general histories and background for my own project. I will also cite book-length works on Latin or Arabic written for a scholarly public. More focused bibliography can be found elsewhere in this book.

On the early history of Latin, see Penney, "Archaic and Old Latin"; for the Greek-to-Latin translation movement that birthed Roman literature, see Feeney, *Beyond Greek*. On Roman language policy in general, and the symbiotic relationship between Latin and Greek in particular, see Rochette, "Language Policies."

4. For monographs on late Latin and the emergence of the European vernaculars, see Banniard, *Viva Voce*; and Wright, *A Sociophilological Study of Late Latin*.

5. On the Latin culture of the Middle Ages, see Hexter and Townsend, eds., *The Oxford Handbook of Medieval Latin Literature*.

6. On humanism, see Ostler, *Ad Infinitum*, 233–49. For a fascinating, detailed study of the methods used to teach Latin in Italy between the twelfth and fifteenth centuries, which reveals much about attitudes toward the language, see Black, *Humanism and Education in Medieval and Renaissance History*.

7. Latin also thrived in German schools and universities into the nineteenth century,

in part because of the linguistic complexity of the German Confederation. See Bertiau, "Neo-Latin Literature in Nineteenth-Century Europe," 419 and 421–25.

8. For recent scholarship in Neo-Latin literature, in addition to Bertiau, see Helander, "Neo-Latin Studies" and Moul, ed., *A Guide to Neo-Latin Literature.*

9. For an overview of the history of Arabic and its place in Islamic culture and history, see Chejne, *The Arabic Language.*

10. New scholarship explores the extensive history predating the Qur'an and the widespread use of Arabic as textual language. The earliest inscriptions in Arabic date to the ninth century BCE (al-Jallad, "The Earliest Stages of Arabic," 315), and a corpus of epigraphy and Graeco-Arabic (Arabic written in the Greek alphabet) in documentary sources gives evidence of its early history (al-Jallad, "The Earliest Stages of Arabic," 320–24). For monographs on the early history of the Arabic language, see al-Sharkawi, *The Ecology of Arabic*; Versteegh, *The Arabic Language*; and Garbini, *Le lingue semitiche.*

11. Recent works on non-Arabophone Islamic culture include Shahab Ahmed's fascinating if problematic *What Is Islam?*—which refocuses scholarly attention on the post-Arabic, Persophone world and on the centuries which, in the European context, span the late Middle Ages and early modernity—and Green, ed., *The Persianate World*, which in important ways advances the project that Ahmed began. Both works push Islamic and Islamicate studies beyond Arabic into the Persophone world; *The Persianate World* also addresses Persian's entanglement with other languages, both local and imperial. Both works shift focus east, from the Arab heartland of the Middle East to a more capacious Eurasian canvas. Finally, both look beyond the Abbasid crucible of Arabic-Islamic culture toward the centuries of early modernity and modernity, when Persianate culture flourished.

12. I use the term *mother tongue* to describe the language of childhood and of daily life, although I recognize that it is a metaphor, not a technical term, and although the concept of the "mother tongue" is imprecise and remains unexamined in this book. Linguists—who speak without embarrassment of "language death," another metaphor borrowed from human biology to refer to language history, which I discuss below (chapter 13)—refer unsentimentally to "first language" and "second language" (L1 and L2) rather than to "mother tongue." For discussion of the history of the term *mother tongue* in the languages of western Europe, see Grondeux, "La notion de langue maternelle."

13. Gal, "Migration, minorities and multilingualism," 14–15. On language ideology in general and national language ideology in particular, see also Gal, "Multiplicity and Contention"; Irvine and Gal, "Language Ideology"; and Woolard and Schieffelin, "Language Ideology." On language ideology in early modern Spain, see Woolard, "Bernardo de Aldrete." Caviedes ("The Role of Language") discusses language ideology with specific reference to the language policies of the EU.

14. Although these books do not necessarily use the word "cosmopolitan" in this contested sense, I am thinking of works like Philip Mansel's *Levant*, Michael Haag's *Alexandria Illustrated*, Samir Kassir's *Beirut*, Tom Reiss's *The Orientalist*, and Orhan Pamuk's *Istanbul.* Though incommensurate in many particulars, these books all celebrate the complex past of cities now viewed as sadly reduced in stature—both economically and, more relevant to the current discussion, ethnically and linguistically.

15. For overviews of critiques of cosmopolitan ideology, see Pollock et al., "Cosmopolitanisms" and Werbner, "Vernacular Cosmopolitanism." For a linguistic discussion of cosmopolitanism particularly relevant to my discussions in this book, see Pollock,

"Cosmopolitan and Vernacular." Geographers have pointed out the economic inequities of cosmopolitan mobility in particular. The cosmopolitan elite is a person who travels in a certain way, consuming the cultures of the "other" as gourmand. But the poor also travel—out of economic compulsion rather than choice, and with less ability to curate and relish their experiences as travelers. See Cresswell, *Place*, 81–84; and Massey, "A Global Sense of Place," in *Space, Place, and Gender*, 146–56; and see discussion in chapter 4, below.

16. For discussion, see chapter 11 and n. 20 on p. 209.

17. For discussion of language as emergent, see Beckner et al., "Language Is a Complex Adaptive System," 14–15 and 18. The article is written by linguists and therefore asks different questions and speaks to a different audience than I do in this book. Yet some of the authors' conclusions intersect with mine. The authors point out the deficiencies associated with L2 speakers of a language (those who have learned a language not as a mother tongue but rather as a second language), because they don't have the effortless command of the spoken language associated with mother-tongue speakers. But the authors insist on nuance: "Rather than entertaining a deficit view of L2 learning, think instead of adult learners as being multicompetent, with different levels of mastery to satisfice in accomplishing what they intend for a variety of languages" (11). The sentence is delightful because it performs the quality I describe: it uses a word that few native speakers know (*satisfice*), a word which this native speaker had to look up in order to understand the sentence.

18. Literary historians often present the story of the failure of Latin and the emergence of the vernaculars as a shorthand way of describing the emergence of "Europe" and of "European literature." Although it is a complex work—not to be reduced by such thumbnail characterizations—see Auerbach, *Literary Language and Its Public*, which is deeply invested in telling the story of the emergence of the European literary traditions from the ruins of Latinity—and contributing to its preservation, at a moment when it seemed intent on self-destruction. For more recent efforts to represent the range and complexity of the literatures of "Europe," see Mortensen, "European Literature and Book History" and Wallace, ed., *Europe: A Literary History*.

19. Kristen Brustad describes the transition from descriptive to prescriptive grammars in the early Arabic grammatical tradition ("The Iconic Sībawayh," 15); in the Arabic tradition, the transition is still (just) traceable.

20. For a discussion of Mediterranean history and bibliography, see chapter 4.

21. James Strachey, first English translator of Freud's complete works, imported the word *cathexis* from the Greek to translate the German term *Besetzung*. Freud used *Besetzung* to describe "multiple concepts" including "mental energy . . . emotional investment, and the focusing of interest" (Ornston, "Cathexis," 69). Strachey's use of a neologism—a Greek word transliterated and set loose in English to express a constellation of distinct but related concepts—attracted criticism because it rendered a common German word with an initially opaque technical term. The example serves well in the present context to suggest the intralingual static generated by translation.

CHAPTER TWO

1. For discussion, see al-Jallad, "The Earliest Stages of Arabic."

2. See, for example, the opening verses of surahs 10, 12, 13, 15, 26, 27, 28, and 31, which draw attention to the book itself as substance of revelation: "*tilka āyāt al-kitāb*" ("these are the verses [*or* the signs] of the Book"). Many of these verses add the

adjective "clear" (*mubīn*) to describe the book. Some add the word *Qur'an* to describe the book: see, e.g., 15:1, "These are the verses of the Book and a clear Qur'an." Surah 2—which opens the book, following a brief prayer (al-Fātiḥa, surah 1)—uses a more succinct statement of self-presentation: "*hadhā al-kitāb lā raiba fīhi*" ("This is the Book in which there is no doubt [*or* disquiet *or* uncertainty])." These gestures of self-identification and self-presentation indicate the emergent self-awareness of the Qur'an first as (oral) "revelation" or "recitation," then as "book," and they set the Qur'an apart from the Torah and the Gospels.

3. *Lusun*, the more common modern Arabic plural for for *lisān*, is not Qur'anic.

4. *Al-lugha*, the word most commonly used in Modern Standard Arabic to mean "language," is not Qur'anic.

5. The exception to this rule is the beautiful verse 30:22: "And among His signs is the creation of the heavens and the earth, and the variations in your *languages* and your colors: truly, in that are signs for those who know."

Unless otherwise noted, all translations in this book, from Arabic and Latin as well as the modern European languages, are my own. Where a published translation exists, I cite it along with my own translation. To save space, I cite the original only where I feel it is necessary to make a philological point, or where it's too beautiful to pass up.

6. In part because of the broad comparative nature of this book and in part because of my focus on the consolidation of Arabic during the early Abbasid centuries, I will not discuss the Middle Arabic literary tradition. Middle Arabic—which blends formal Arabic and colloquial Arabic—appeared in written texts as early as the ninth century CE and was used consciously as a literary register (rather than unconsciously as grammatical lapse) especially following the collapse of the Abbasid caliphate in 1258. See Versteegh, *The Arabic Language*, 114–29; Larkin, "Popular Poetry in the Post-Classical Period"; and Hanna, *Ottoman Egypt and the Emergence of the Modern World*, 31–66.

7. This is not the standard view of the relation between formal Arabic and the colloquial forms of the language. To some extent, the comparatist framework of this study imposes such a perception: as Latin is to the Romance vernaculars, so formal Arabic is to the colloquials. Yet the parallel is not as inaccurate as linguists and litterateurs represent it. With basic training, a speaker of colloquial Arabic can follow a literary text written in formal Arabic (as a speaker of Italian might understand the gist of a Latin text). But in order to acquire proficiency in literary Arabic, the man or woman of letters must make a rigorous study of both the language and the literary sources that provide linguistic and literary standards. This regimen—and the moral, ethical, and aesthetic fallout from this education, as well as its linguistic and literary effects—is, in large part, the subject of this book.

8. My discussion focuses on the Abbasid East, where *shu'ūbiyya* was primarily driven by Persians and Nabataeans (or Aramaeans); in Egypt, during the same period, the movement gave voice to the cultural aspirations of the Copts. On the *shu'ūbiyya* movement, in addition to sources cited herein, see Bosworth, "The Persian Impact on Arabic Literature," 484–85; El-Cheikh, *Byzantium Viewed by the Arabs*, 111–12; Gibb, "The Social Significance of the Shuubiyya"; and Hanna and Gardner, "'Al-Shu'ūbiyyah' Up-Dated." Although Gutas does not discuss *shu'ūbiyya*, he does mention the changing position of non-Arabs in the Abbasid state (*Greek Thought, Arabic Culture*; see especially 63) and discusses at length the privileged position occupied by the task of translation in the Sasanian Empire. On *shu'ūbiyya* as a shift from "Arab" to "Arabic," see Brustad, "The Iconic Sībawayh," 21; and Gutas, *Greek Thought, Arabic Culture*, 191.

9. Bashshār ibn Burd, *Dīwān*, 1:379. Is it significant that Bashshār resists the tribal vocabulary that informs *shuʿūbī* ideology? The "family" (*ahl*) is the smallest social unit, encompassing only a man and his immediate dependents.

For another, particularly striking example of Bashshār's boastful account of his Persian ancestors, see Schoeler, "Bashshār b. Burd," 279–80.

10. Bashshār ibn Burd, *Dīwān*, 1:377–80; Larsson, *Ibn García's Shuʿūbiyya Letter*, 40–41.

11. Norris, "Shuʿūbiyyah in Arabic Literature," 47.

12. Abū al-Faraj al-Iṣfahānī, *Kitāb al-Aghānī*, 3:138.

13. Abū al-Faraj al-Iṣfahānī, *Kitāb al-Aghānī*, 3:135.

14. Abū al-Faraj al-Iṣfahānī, *Kitāb al-Aghānī*, 3:138.

15. Given the history of Arab and Islamic expansion outlined so briefly in this book, it was inevitable that the Arabic language would come into contact with a large number of local languages, as well as parallel systems of cosmpolitan language. On the linguistic knock-on effects of its history in multilingual environments, from the era of revelation through the twentieth century, see Versteegh, "Linguistic Contacts between Arabic and Other Languages." For a more focused discussion of the impact of the translation movement on the (relatively young) Arabic language, see below, chapters 8 and 9.

16. Al-Mahdī accused Bashshār of *zandaqa* (Zoroastrian or Manichean) leanings. On Bashshār's caliph troubles, see Gabrieli, "Appunti su Baśśār b. Burd."

17. On the life and works of Abū al-Faraj al-Iṣfahānī, see Kilpatrick, *Making the Great Book of Songs*, 14–33. Abū al-Faraj was a systematic compiler of information, but he was mainly interested in poets and songs, rather than historical accuracy.

18. Pahlavi (or Middle Persian) would be suppressed during the Arab expansion. Yet Pahlavi remained a useful language during the Greek-to-Arabic translation movement. See Gutas, *Greek Thought, Arabic Culture*, 25–27; Cereti, "Middle Persian Literature."

19. See chapter 7 for further discussion of alphabet innovation. Alphabet experimentation is a constant, and it is evident (for instance) in Karamanlı Turkish (the Turkish language written in the Greek alphabet by Anatolian Christians), in Armeno-Turkish letters, and in the Arabizi (Arabic in the Latin alphabet) used to send text messages today. Most of this experimentalism, however, occurs far beneath the notice of literary historians—and certainly beneath the notice of a poet of Bashshār's ambition. Bactria—despite preserving this alphabetic link with a Western culture—looked to the East for much of its history. Its inhabitants were Buddhists and connected by networks of trade to Buddhist centers to the east. Although linked by trade networks also to cities to the west and south, Tokharistan lay outside the control of the Sasanians for three centuries before the Arab invasions (see Van Bladel, "The Bactrian Background of the Barmakids," 46–50).

20. On the transition from Sasanian to Arab coinage, see Sims-Williams, *New Light on Ancient Afghanistan*, 21. On the dates of the recently discovered Bactrian letters, see Sims-Williams, "The Sasanians in the East," 89. In "Bactrian Letters from the Sasanian and Hephthalite Periods," Sims-Williams discusses a letter that begins with the Islamic formula "in the name of God," translated into Bactrian and written in the cursive Greek script used for Bactrian, dating to 781 CE.

CHAPTER THREE

1. On Petrarch's embassy to King John, see Barbeu de Rocher, "Ambassade de Pétrarque"; and Wilkins, *Life of Petrarch*, 173–76.

2. Petrarch, "Collatio coram Domino Johanne," 1286–89.

3. On vernacular translation in fourteenth-century France, see Monfrin, "Humanisme et traductions au Moyen Âge."

4. On Pierre Bersuire, see Pannier, "Notice biographique sur le bénédictin Pierre Bersuire"; and Barbeu du Rocher, "Ambassade de Pétrarque," 197–200.

5. On Petrarch's youthful editorial work on Livy's *Ab urbe condita* (he completed it in his midtwenties), see Wilkins, *Life of Petrarch*, 16–17; and Billanovich, *Tradizione e fortuna di Livio*. On Petrarch's role in French translation activities, see Monfrin, "Humanisme et traductions au Moyen Âge," 171–72.

6. Petrarch, Familiares XXII, 13; *Le familiari*, 4:136–38; and *Rerum familiarum libri*, 3:240–41.

7. Petrarch, *Collatio coram Domino Johanne*, 1290–91.

8. The comment can be seen in the modern facsimile reproduction of the "manoscritto degli abbozzi," the autograph manuscript of working drafts of a small number of poems from the *Canzoniere*; see Petrarch, *Il codice Vaticano Lat. 3196*, 11v.

9. *Rerum memorandum libri*, I, 37, 9, p. 40.

10. There is some speculation about Jean's motives for returning to England. A waggish chronicler, the Continuator of Guillaume de Nangis, accused him of going back to England "causa jocis" ("for the sake of sport"; Géraud, ed., *Chronique latine de Guillaume de Nangis*, 2:333)—there being apparently a lady involved. But there is undoubtedly more to the story. John arrived to festivities and a warm welcome in London in January 1364; sadly, he soon fell sick and would be dead by the end of April.

11. For a full discussion of the terminology used in this book to refer to the learned language of culture and science, see above, chapter 1.

12. Al-Fārābī, *Catálogo de las ciencias*, Ar. 20.

13. Al-Fārābī, *Catálogo de las ciencias*, 134.

14. See Dante, *De vulgari eloquentia* passim. Dante defines his understanding of the *gramatica* at the outset of his treatise: "Est et inde alia locutio secondaria nobis, quam Romani gramaticam vocaverunt. Hanc quidem secundariam Greci habent et alii, sed non omnes: ad habitum vero huius pauci perveniunt, quia non nisi per spatium temporis et studii assiduitatem regulamur et doctrinamur in illa" ("Then there is another language, secondary to us, which the Romans called *gramatica*. This secondary language the Greeks have, and others, but not all. Very few come to practiced used of it, because it is only over time and with assiduous study that we are trained and taught in the use of it"; *De vulgari eloquentia* I, i, 3). In the *Compendium studii philosophiae*, Roger Bacon balances Greek, Hebrew, Arabic, and "Chaldean" (an ethnonym used with little precision in medieval Latin), alongside Latin, as "linguae sapientiales," "languages of knowledge" or "wisdom" (cap. 6, p. 433).

15. Benedict Anderson writes: "Writing of mediaeval Western Europe, Bloch noted that 'Latin was not only the language in which teaching was done, it was the only language taught.' (This second 'only' shows quite clearly the sacredness of Latin—no other language was thought worth the teaching.)" (*Imagined Communities*, 18). In fact, the special status of Latin in medieval European schools demonstrates not the sacredness of Latin but rather the fact that Latin had rules, while other languages didn't.

16. Adorno, "Late Style," 564.

17. Adorno, "Late Style," 566.

18. Adorno, "Late Style," 567.

19. Caveat lector: these figures are based on back-of-the-envelope calculations and

are meant to give only a very rough sense of the proportion of Petrarch's Latin and vernacular work.

20. Renan wrote, "Une nation est avant tout une dynastie, représentant une ancienne conquête, conquête acceptée d'abord, puis oubliée par la masse du peuple" ("A nation is above all a dynasty, representing an ancient conquest, a conquest at first accepted and then forgotten by the mass of the people"). *Qu'est-ce qu'une nation?*, 11.

CHAPTER FOUR

1. Mayhew, *London Labour and the London Poor,* 1:1–2.

2. Deleuze and Guattari, *A Thousand Plateaus,* 370.

3. The more obvious place to look for discussions of the territorialization of language in the work of Deleuze and Guattari would seem to be their discussion of Kafka, where they address precisely the "deterritorialized" language of Kafka, the Czech Jew who writes in German (*Kafka: Toward a Minor Literature,* 16–27). Yet because they rely upon the national language model, for my purposes, that discussion is less useful. For Deleuze and Guattari, Kafka's use of German is the scar of his status as Czech and as Jew. They argue that a minor language—a language out of place; the national language of another nation—is "a deterritorialized language, appropriate for strange and minor uses"; that "its cramped space forces each individual intrigue to connect immediately to politics"; and that "everything takes on a collective value . . . because talent isn't abundant in a minor literature" (*Kafka: Toward a Minor Literature,* 17). Using the critical apparatus I construct in this chapter, Kafka is writing precisely in German as a cosmopolitan language: one which liberates the writer from territorial location, and connects his work to a public far from his own place and time.

4. Geographers also study the place of animals, things, natural and manufactured phenomena, microorganisms, etc.; place is produced by these entities and their histories as well as by human actors. See, e.g., Massey, "Landscape as a Provocation" and Pred, "Place as Historically Contingent Process." This broader understanding of space and place is relevant to the choreography of the cosmopolitan language, which draws together human actors, the material history of writing and the book, and languages themselves as actors.

5. See Twitter Tongues, http://twitter.mappinglondon.co.uk/ (accessed June 29, 2019).

6. Bull, *The Anarchical Society,* 254–55. *The Anarchical Society* was first published in 1977.

7. Strange, "The Defective State," 56.

8. Albert, "On Boundaries, Territory and Postmodernity," 56.

9. Elden, "Missing the Point," 9.

10. There is a vast and growing body of scholarship in the field known as "frontier studies." In addition to works cited elsewhere in this chapter, my discussion of frontiers depends upon the following: Turner wrote "The Significance of the Frontier in American History," published in 1893, just three years after the United States government officially declared the American frontier closed and the continent settled. He shared the intellectual errors and moral failings of his era; nevertheless, his essay is a fascinating effort to document near-contemporary social history. He seems to read the frontier as a Faustian contract between human communities and the natural environment, rather than a political convention. On this aspect of the American frontier in particular, see Power and Standen's introduction to *Frontiers in Question,* 2–3: the American frontier

designates an environmental quality, characterized by contact between people and nature; "not a barrier but a zone of passage and a land of opportunity." Berend, "Medievalists and the Notion of the Frontier," gives a thorough and thoughtful review of the scholarship, with an emphasis on premodern history. Finally, Miéville's *The City & the City* is not scholarly but rather a hybrid of speculative fiction and noir, inspired by the hyperterritoriality of divided or otherwise contested urban spaces of the late twentieth and early twenty-first centuries. It is a dazzling meditation on the way that multiple levels of sovereignty are experienced within cities.

11. Manzano Moreno, "The Creation of a Medieval Frontier," 36 and 45.

12. For a detailed overview of the merchant colonies of Venice in the sixteenth and seventeenth centuries, see Rothman, *Brokering Empire*, 29–60.

13. On medieval ships' crews, see Salvatori, "Corsairs' Crews." On petitions filed by victims of piracy and legal actions against pirates in the Ottoman Mediterranean, see White, *Piracy and Law in the Ottoman Mediterranean*.

14. For an overview of legal pluralism in medieval Cairo, see Lev, *The Administration of Justice in Medieval Egypt*, 231–58.

15. Dante intended to address the idiolects used "by a single family" in his treatise on the vernaculars of Italy (*De vulgari eloquentia* I, xix, 3, pp. 140–41), but the treatise remained unfinished and unpublished. In "Linguistic Cartography" and *Imaginary Cartographies*, Smail looks at language boundaries from a different perspective, studying the use of languages (Latin, Provençal, and, later, French) to create boundaries in late medieval Marseilles: how people from different communities and paths of life described and negotiated territorial boundaries within the city.

16. For a fascinating example of a cosmopolitan language mapping vernaculars, see al-Kāshgharī's treatise in Arabic on the Turkic languages, *Compendium of the Turkic Dialects*; and, for discussion, see Mallette, "Translation in the Pre-modern World."

17. Scholars agree that smaller-scale frontiers (e.g., property lines or boundaries between intraurban districts) were drawn with greater precision—more likely to be marked as boundaries—than larger-scale frontiers (like the boundaries of empire), which were typically zonal (Berend, "Medievalists and the Notion of the Frontier," 68; Ellenblum, "Were There Borders and Borderlines in the Middle Ages?," 110–11).

18. Lewis and Short, *A Latin Dictionary*, s.v. *limes*; Sophocles et al., *Greek Lexicon*, 667; Lane, *Arabic-English Lexicon*, s.v. *th-gh-r* (I:338–39); see also Bonner, "The Naming of the Frontier." In a discussion of the Codex Vindobonensis—a treatise written by an anonymous Muslim living in Christian Spain in 1404, after the expulsion of the Muslim population—Walid Saleh points out that the author uses the word *thaghr* as a generalized term to refer to his homeland: he and his community dwell in the interstices of sovereignty (Saleh, "Reflections on Muslim Hebraism"). For a discussion of the use of the term *thaghr* in the Andalusian context, see Brauer, *Boundaries and Frontiers*, 21–26.

19. See Barfield, *The Perilous Frontier*.

20. William Stukeley makes this claim in a collected volume of letters first published in 1754 (*The Family Memoires*, 3:142).

21. Braudel, *The Mediterranean*, 1:276. See also Braudel's poetic description of the interdependence of roads and towns in the Mediterranean: "Whatever its shape, its architecture, or the civilization that illuminates it, the Mediterranean town creates roads and is created by them. Vidal de la Blanche has said the same of the American town; the

Mediterranean region in the sixteenth century (and it must be extended to its maximum when we are talking of towns) was unique in its immensity" (*The Mediterranean*, 1:277).

22. See Wansbrough, *Lingua Franca*, chapter 1 ("Orbits," 1–75) and Horden and Purcell, *The Corrupting Sea*, chapter 5 ("Connectivity," 123–72), for detailed and systematic discussions of these concepts.

23. Wansbrough, *Lingua Franca*, vii.

24. Wansbrough, *Lingua Franca*, 169.

25. Wansbrough, *Lingua Franca*, 3–4.

26. For particularly evocative discussions of objects that cross the Mediterranean, see Sharon Kinoshita, "Almería Silk," and Kinoshita's discussion of the rock crystal vase once in the possession of Eleanor of Aquitaine in *Medieval Boundaries*, 6–7.

27. Wansbrough, *Lingua Franca*, 6.

28. Braudel, *The Mediterranean*, 1:23.

29. Bertalanffy, "Outline of General System Theory," 134; cf. Bertalanffy, "Problems of General System Theory," 302.

30. It is tempting to conclude that the cosmopolitan languages were considered coextensive not only with empire but indeed with the scope of the known—or even the knowable. Paul Claval's oft-cited statement about empire could be revised and repurposed to describe the lingua francas of premodern literature: "The *cosmopolitan language* does not have a boundary in the sense that we use the term nowadays: that is, an enclosure separating it from a different *language*. . . . It is surrounded by barbarians; where it finds peoples advanced enough to be subjugated to its *grammatical rules* and its *literary traditions*, it extends to embrace them; its expansion stops at the boundaries of the cultivated universe" ("*L'Empire* n'a pas de frontière au sens où nous entendons aujourd'hui le terme, c'est-à-dire de cloison le séparant d'un *Etat* différent. . . . Il est entouré de barbares: tant qu'il trouve des peuples assez avancés pour les soumettre *aux règles de l'administration et de la paix communes*, il s'étend; son expansion s'arrête aux bornes de l'univers cultivé"; Claval, *Espace et pouvoir*, 109–10).

31. See Garbini, *Le lingue semitiche*; and, for an application of the same ideas to the later development of colloquial Arabic, al-Sharkawi, *The Ecology of Arabic*.

32. Deleuze and Guattari, *A Thousand Plateaus*, 380.

33. For a discussion of the distinction between routes and roots and further bibliography, see Cresswell, *Place*, chapter 4.

34. Massey, *For Space*, 125.

35. Massey, *For Space*, 154–55.

36. Massey, *Space, Place, and Gender*, 148–50. See also Harvey, *Justice, Nature and the Geography of Difference*, especially chapter 11.

37. Tuan, *Space and Place*, 6.

CHAPTER FIVE

1. This phrase appears in a manuscript that records the sermons of Remigio dei Girolami, discussed later in this chapter (Florence, Biblioteca Nazionale, fondo Conventi Soppressi, G.IV.936, 289r). On Remigio, see Panella, *Dal bene comune al bene del comune*, and see Panella's website for editions of Latin texts, Italian translations, and discussion (http://www.e-theca.net/emiliopanella/remigio/index.htm). For the publication of selections from this manuscript (including this phrase) and discussion, see http://www.e-theca.net/emiliopanella/remigio2/8536.htm (accessed July 3, 2020).

2. Toscani, "Analfabetismo," Tav. 1a.

3. Dante, *Vita nova*, 31, 1, p. 231.

4. Santagata, *Dante*, 90–91.

5. Dante, *De vulgari eloquentia* I, ix, 2, p. 70

6. Dante, *De vulgari eloquentia* I, i, 2, p. 30.

7. Dante, *De vulgari eloquentia* I, xix, 1–2, pp. 139–40.

8. Dante, *De vulgari eloquentia* I, xix, 3, p. 140.

9. Mengaldo, *Enciclopedia Dantesca*, s.v. *De vulgari eloquentia*, 2:399.

10. See Machiavelli, *Discorso o dialogo intorno alla nostra lingua*.

11. Dante, *Convivio* I, iii, 5, p. 2:14.

12. I follow Santagata's dating; *Dante: The Story of His Life*, 176–84.

13. Dante, *Convivio* I, v, 7, p. 2:21. The *Convivio*, like the *Vita nova*, consists of poetry accompanied by prose explication. This definition of Latin as "noble, strong [or virtuous] and beautiful" forms part of an extended discussion of Dante's decision to write the commentary on the poetry in the vernacular, rather than Latin (I, v–I, x), and is followed by a chapter in which Dante castigates the Italians for choosing to write in vernaculars other than their own (I, xi). Taken together, the *Convivio* and *De vulgari eloquentia* demonstrate how much work it took to defend the vernacular—and make one all the more grateful that Dante abandoned the task of writing prose self-justifications and turned his attention to the vernacular poetry.

14. Indeed, in the *Convivio* Dante devotes a chapter to the discussion of his love for his vernacular; see I, x.

15. Dante, *De vulgari eloquentia*, I, i, 4, p. 32.

16. Dante, *De vulgari eloquentia*, I, i, 3, pp. 30–32.

17. Dante, *De vulgari eloquentia*, I, ix, 10, p. 78.

18. Dante, *De vulgari eloquentia*, I, ix, 11, p. 78–80.

19. Steinberg, *Accounting for Dante*, chapter 3 ("A terrigenis mediocris," 95–123).

20. Dante, *De vulgari eloquentia*, I, xi-I, xv; pp. 70–124.

21. Dante, *De vulgari eloquentia*, I, xi, 2, p. 92.

22. Dante, *De vulgari eloquentia*, I, xi, 6, p. 96; I, xii, 7, p. 104; and I, xiii, 2, pp. 108–10.

23. Steinberg, *Accounting for Dante*, 110.

24. Dante, *De vulgari eloquentia*, I, xvi, 6, p. 130.

25. Dante, *De vulgari eloquentia*, I, xvi, 1, p. 126; cp. I, xvi, 4, p. 128.

26. Dante, *De vulgari eloquentia*, I, xvi, 2, p. 128.

27. Dante, *De vulgari eloquentia*, I, xvi, 3–4, p. 128; emphasis added.

28. Shapiro, "Dante and the Grammarians," 516.

29. Dante, *De vulgari eloquentia*, I, xvii, 3, p. 132; I, xix, 1, pp. 138–40.

30. On the creation of a pan-German vernacular, mediating between regional forms of the language—precisely on the model of Dante's eloquent vernacular—see Sanders, *German: Biography of a Language*, 137–42.

31. Dante, *De vulgari eloquentia*, I, vi, 3, p. 52.

32. Dante, *Dante, De vulgari eloquentia*, trans. Steven Botterill, 13.

33. Steinberg, *Accounting for Dante*, 102.

34. Shapiro called *De vulgari eloquentia* Dante's "book of exile" not only because it was, along with the *Convivio*, the work of his first years of exile but also because of its topic: the rules of grammar, she writes, "recall man to his true linguistic heritage, restoring him from exile and confusion. This image appeared commonly in the encomia of grammar [*grammatica*: the learned language and its rational explication], viewed

as the passport to other sciences and the way of return from exile into the precincts of knowledge" (Shapiro, *De vulgari eloquentia*, 29). Shapiro's discussion of the significance of *gramatica* has obvious application to the epigraph to this chapter, discussed later in the chapter.

35. On Remigio and Dante, see Davis, "Education in Dante's Florence," 429–35.

36. The *trivium* was the name given to the three first building blocks of intellectual life: the *gramatica*, logic, and rhetoric. The trivium prepared the student for the next branches of study, the *quadrivium* (arithmetic, geometry, astronomy, and music), which in turn led to the study of philosophy and theology.

37. Dante, *Vita nova*, 16, 6, p. 150.

38. For a fascinating account of the rapid growth and increasing sophistication of the concept of "literacy" in the vernacular (not only in Latin) in fourteenth-century Italy, see Alison Cornish, *Vernacular Translation in Dante's Italy*. Cornish explores the profusion of *volgarizzamenti*, or vernacular translations, and the changing fates of vernacular and learned language before, during, and after humanism boosted Latinity. On monolingualism and national language ideology, see above, chapter 1.

39. Dante, *De vulgari eloquentia*, I, ix, 11, p. 78.

CHAPTER SIX

1. For the phrase "burning down the house" and the example from *Star Wars*, I rely on screenwriters John August and Craig Mazin's podcast *Scriptnotes*, episode 333. For a transcript of the episode, see https://johnaugust.com/2018/scriptnotes-ep-333-the-end-of-the-beginning-transcript (accessed July 3, 2019).

2. See Santagata, *Dante*, 190–94 and 210–12.

3. See Santagata, *Dante*, 254–57.

4. See Santagata, *Dante*, 298–301.

5. In Western scholarship on Islamic history, "AH" stands for "anno hegirae" (in the year of the *hijra*). The Islamic lunar calendar starts in 622 CE, the year of the first Muslim community's hegira from Mecca to Medina. I use *hijrī* dating here to underscore how close to the era of the Prophet these events unfolded: a mere century and a half after the *hijra*.

6. See Carter, *Sībawayhi*, 10.

7. Carter, *Sībawayhi*, 10–11.

8. For an overview of *iʿjāz* (the inimitability of the Qur'an), Qur'anic *āyāt al-taḥaddī* (or challenge verses, which challenge the audience to create a work as beautiful as the Qur'an), and early poetic *muʿāraḍa* (poetry challenging or honoring the Qur'an through imitation of Qur'anic diction), see Martin, "Inimitability."

9. For Sībawayhi's reliance on oral sources, see Levin, "Sībawayhi's Attitude to the Spoken Language"; and Baalbaki, *The Legacy of the Kitāb*, 35–47.

10. See Brustad, "The Iconic Sībawayh."

11. On the sources of Sībawayhi's grammatical terminology, see Carter, "Sībawayhi," *Encyclopaedia of Islam*, para. 3, and Carter, "Sībawayhi," *Dictionary of Literary Biography*, 326–27.

12. Lane, *An Arabic-English Lexicon*, s.v. *s-m-w*, 1435.

13. Lane, *An Arabic-English Lexicon*, s.v. *f-ʿ-l*, 2420.

14. Lane, *An Arabic-English Lexicon*, s.v. *ḥ-r-f*, 550.

15. Although Carter doesn't use the term "recursive," he does talk about the scalar complexity of Sībawayhi's terminology: *Sībawayhi*, 53–55.

16. For a summary of Sībawayhi's words for vocalization, see Troupeau, *Lexique-index*, 14.

17. Troupeau, *Lexique-index*, 14; Fleisch, "Esquisse," 15.

18. Carter, *Sībawayhi*, 52. Carter's article on Sībawayhi for the *Encyclopaedia of Islam*, a useful overview of Sībawayhi's thought, is even more laudatory.

19. Carter, *Sībawayhi*, 50–53.

20. Another scholar of the early Arabic language, Kees Versteegh, writes only in passing of Sībawayhi. Versteegh is not interested in Sībawayhi's curation of metaphors. But he notes that Sībawayhi's work on Arabic grammar follows a practice typical not only of Islamic legal reasoning but of the Islamic sciences in general, distinguishing between the truths derived from rational analysis (*'aql*) and those accepted as transmitted knowledge (*naql*). Sībawayhi, Versteegh suggests, is careful to distinguish between the linguistic behaviors that make logical sense and those that became habit because one generation or one region learned them from another (Versteegh, *The Arabic Language*, 59).

21. Sībawayhi, *Kitāb Sībawayh*, 1:1–6.

22. Sībawayhi, *Kitāb Sībawayh*, 1:6.

23. On the details of Sībawayhi's biography, see Carter, *Sībawayhi*, 7–17; Carter, "Sībawayhi" (both the *Encyclopaedia of Islam* and *Dictionary of Literary Biography* articles).

24. Sībawayhi, *Kitāb Sībawayh*, 1:1.

25. Romanov, "Islamic Urban Centers."

26. See Garbini, *Le lingue semitiche*. For an application of the same ideas to the later development of colloquial Arabic, see al-Sharkawi, *The Ecology of Arabic*.

27. Garbini, *Le lingue semitiche*, 18. See also Rabin, "The Origin of the Subdivisions of Semitic." My thinking about nongenealogical understandings of language change in history is strongly indebted to my late University of Michigan colleague Michael Bonner, with whom I taught a class on cosmopolitan languages called Lingua Franca in 2011.

28. For the history of tribal carpets, see Denny and Jourdenais, *Sotheby's Guide to Oriental Carpets*; and Sakhai, *Oriental Carpets*.

29. On Oriental carpets in Renaissance paintings, see Verde, "Threads on Canvas." On the presence of carpets from the East in Renaissance Italy, see Curatola, "Four Carpets in Venice" and "A Sixteenth-Century Quarrel about Carpets"; Kim, "Lotto's Carpets"; and Spallanzani, *Oriental Rugs in Renaissance Florence*.

30. Pavić, *Dictionary of the Khazars*, 61.

31. Tuan, *Space and Place*, 6 and 198.

32. Tuan, *Space and Place*, 73.

33. For the notion of psychogeography and reflections on the materiality of the landscape, see, e.g., Debord, "Theory of the Dérive"; Macfarlane, *The Wild Places*; Cornish, *Waves of the Sea*; and Hollevoet, "Wandering in the City."

34. Sībawayhi—the non-Arab father of Arabic grammar—also, inevitably, inspires resentment: see Suleiman, "Arabic Language Reforms."

35. Dante, *De vulgari eloquentia* I, i, 2, p. 30.

36. For discussion, see Carter, "The Ethical Basis of Arabic Grammar," 13–17.

CHAPTER SEVEN

1. This is the entirety of the story called "Transition"; Williams, *Ninety-Nine Stories of God*, 75.

2. Wheelock notes that "many religions have developed the idea that an entire language, usually other than the vernacular, is sacred. Such languages are then often reserved for liturgical or for other functions conveying sacred power, such as healing or magic. A sacred language usually begins as a vernacular through which a revelation is believed to have been received. This can lead to the belief that that language is particularly suited for revelation—that it is superior to other languages and thus inherently sacred" (Wheelock, "Language: Sacred Language"). Anthropologists see the lingua sacra as a function of ritual, therefore performative; as a specific genre of performative speech; as an indexical way of indicating the presence or influence of the divine; and as a means to participate in religious community, in varying degrees (for discussion, see Keane, "Language and Religion").

3. For discussion, see Rocco, "Le tre lingue usate dagli ebrei"; Giuffrida and Rocco, "Una bilingue arabo sicula"; and Bresc, *Arabes de langue*, 46–59.

4. I emphasize that the historical events described in this chapter—the mission to Moravia, the invention of the Glagolitic alphabet, and the Venetian disputation—are disputed by historians, and historical reconstructions may be complicated by national, linguistic, or religious chauvinisms. The version of the story told here relies mainly on the *Vita*s, which were devotional works rather than historical documents. For historical background and biographical background on Cyril/Constantine in particular, in addition to the works cited below, see Jakobson, "The Byzantine Mission to the Slavs"; Tachios, *Cyril and Methodius of Thessalonica*; and Dvornik, *Byzantine Missions among the Slavs*. For an overview of various theories surrounding Glagolitic in particular, see Verkholantsev, *The Slavic Letters of St. Jerome*, 34–36.

5. Even the precise region intended by the name "Moravia" is in dispute; see Lunt, "Thoughts, Suggestions and Questions," 272–73.

6. St. Cyril was known as Constantine for much of his life. Cyril was a monastic name assumed toward the end of his life.

7. *The Vita of Constantine and the Vita of Methodius*, 7. The Latin *Vita*s generally celebrate Cyril's virtue but don't make the direct association between Cyril and languages as the Slavonic lives do.

8. *The Vita of Constantine and the Vita of Methodius*, 21; *De sanctis episcopis Slavorum apostolis Cyrillo et Methodio*, col. 0020A; *Vita eorundem Sanctorum Cyrilli et Methodii*, col. 0022B.

9. *The Vita of Constantine and the Vita of Methodius*, 21.

10. *The Vita of Constantine and the Vita of Methodius*, 21–23.

11. The origin of the name "Cyrillic" for the alphabet used to write Russian is unclear. For discussion, see below, n. 33.

12. See *The Vita of Constantine and the Vita of Methodius*, 59–60.

13. For a technical discussion of the significance of the sobriquet "the Philosopher," see Ševčenko, "The Definition of Philosophy in the Life of Saint Constantine" (in *Byzantium and the Slavs in Letters and Culture*, 93–106). The *Vita*s would not call him "polyglossos," presumably, because in the Byzantine world that term had negative connotations; see Dagron, "Formes et fonctions," 222–23.

14. On plurilingualism in the Byzantine world, see Dagron, "Formes et fonctions." For an intriguing snapshot of linguistic pluralism in a bureaucratic Christian context in medieval Nubia, see Frend, "Coptic, Greek and Nubian at Q'asr Ibrim." Frankfurter, "The Magic of Writing," discusses lingua sacra and confessional and linguistic complexity from a different perspective: Egyptian and Greek views on the valence of written signs, and the influence of those distinct sign systems on each other, between antiquity and late antiquity.

15. See Griffith, "From Aramaic to Arabic." Dagron identifies a linguistic shift that has occurred in the Byzantine East by this moment. From the fourth through the sixth centuries, Greek served as a centralized language of bureaucracy, literature, and liturgy. But by the ninth century a dethroned Hellenism was replaced by a multilingual Christianity that left the task of Christianizing the countryside to individuals with targeted linguistic skills or to peripheral churches (Dagron, "Formes et fonctions," 227).

16. *The Vita of Constantine and the Vita of Methodius*, 43–45.

17. See *Vita eorundem Sanctorum Cyrilli et Methodii*, col. 0022E; *De sanctis episcopis Slavorum*, col. 0020F. One Latin source does mention the alphabet. In the opening passage, the *Lectiones ecclesiasticae* introduces Cyril as a man who "translated the Old and New Testament, along with many other works, from the Greek or Latin language into the Slavonic, using newly invented letters" (*Lectiones ecclesiasticae*, col. 0024B).

18. *The Vita of Constantine and the Vita of Methodius*, 49.

19. *The Vita of Constantine and the Vita of Methodius*, 49.

20. See, e.g., Dekker, "Pentecost and Linguistic Self-Consciousness in Anglo-Saxon England."

21. Cyril quotes Philippians 2:11: "Every tongue should confess that Jesus Christ is Lord." *The Vita of Constantine and the Vita of Methodius*, 53.

22. *The Vita of Constantine and the Vita of Methodius*, 53.

23. Andrea Dandolo praises Constantine-Cyril for being "in variis ydiomatibus peritus" ("learned in various tongues"), for converting the Bulgarians as well as the king of Dalmatia, and for translating scripture into the Slavonic tongue. However, he does not mention the Venetian disputation, either because he doesn't know about it or because he is skeptical of its historical veracity (Dandolo, *Chronica*, 156).

24. See Giovanni Diacono, "La cronaca veneziana," 1:122–23; Dandolo, *Chronica*, 157–59.

25. *The Vita of Constantine and the Vita of Methodius*, 49; italics added.

26. *The Vita of Constantine and the Vita of Methodius*, 7.

27. See Ševčenko, "Three Paradoxes of the Cyrillo-Methodian Mission," 222.

28. The reference is to John 19:19–20; see *The Vita of Constantine and the Vita of Methodius*, 47n98.

29. Darrouzès, "Le mémoire de Constantin Stilbès," 63.

30. A twelfth-century canon lawyer, Theodore Balsamon, approved the use of liturgical books translated from the Greek for Syrian and Armenian parishioners in the Patriarchate of Alexandria, provided that the books were translated directly from the Greek and that the parishioners in question could not speak Greek; see Ševčenko, "Three Paradoxes," 228n30; and Dagron, "*Formes et fonctions*," 229–30.

31. On the ongoing linguistic competition in this region, see Verkholantsev, *The Slavic Letters of St. Jerome*, chapter 2 (34–62). For centuries after Cyril and Methodius's mission, the "Glagolites" (as they became known in subsequent historical writings) used numerous languages; inscriptions dating to the eleventh century, for instance,

reveal that they were "bilingual and triscriptural" (42). See also Lunt, "Thoughts, Suggestions and Questions" for reflections on the linguistic impact of competitions between the Latin and Orthodox churches in Moravia.

32. For a perspective on the trilingual sacred language from the other edge of Latinate Christendom, see McNally, "The 'Tres Linguae Sacrae' in Early Irish Bible Exegesis."

33. In fact, the Glagolitic created by Cyril does not survive; the oldest extant texts in Glagolitic date to four centuries after Cyril's mission to Moravia (for discussion, see Verkholantsev, *The Slavic Letters*, 42; and Marti, "Philologia in the *Slavia Cyrillo-Methodiana*," 16–19). The Cyrillic alphabet was associated with Cyril, as its name makes clear, although that association dates to several centuries after the life of Cyril (Verkholantsev, *The Slavic Letters*, 17). Horace Lunt has speculated that Cyril proposed an alphabet based on Greek letters, which the Frankish clergy in Moravia rejected because they associated the Greek alphabet with the Greek language. In Bulgaria, there were no Frankish clergy to object, and the adapted Greek alphabet was used to write the local Slavic language. That alphabet was Cyrillic. See Lunt, "Thoughts, Suggestions, and Questions," 284.

34. The same was true of Bactrian—a language of central Asia, not the eastern Mediterranean, and not associated with Christianity; see chapter 2.

35. For discussion of alphabet revolutions, including those of Maltese and Turkish, see Aytürk, "Script Charisma." On Maltese, see also Mallette, "Ramparts of Europe" (*European Modernity and the Arab Mediterranean*, 100–131).

36. Pavić, *Dictionary of the Khazars*, 64. On Pavić's account of Cyril's act of linguistic invention, and the contention between Latin and Cyrillic alphabets in the publication history of the novel, see Damrosch, "Scriptworlds," 207–8.

37. Pavić, *Dictionary of the Khazars*, 66.

38. Pavić, *Dictionary of the Khazars*, 64.

39. Pavić, *Dictionary of the Khazars*, 61.

CHAPTER EIGHT

1. Deleuze and Guattari, *A Thousand Plateaus*, 11.

2. For an overview of the Abbasid translation movement, in addition to other works cited below, see Gutas, *Greek Thought, Arabic Culture*.

3. Tarán and Gutas, *Aristotle Poetics*, 85–88.

4. Tarán and Gutas, *Aristotle Poetics*, 92–93.

5. Quite possibly by Yaḥyā ibn ʿAdī; see Peters, *Aristoteles Arabus*, 28–29; and Tarán and Gutas, *Aristotle Poetics*, 96.

6. Indeed, other, more practical Aristotelian treatises were the object of even more abundant study, translation and commentary. For details, see Gutas, *Greek Thought, Arabic Culture*; and Peters, *Aristoteles Arabus*.

7. See Mallette, "Beyond Mimesis."

8. See Tarán and Gutas's description of the sole extant manuscript of Mattā's translation: it includes glosses, interlinear comments, and marginalia incorporated into the text, which make the text substantially more difficult to understand (*Aristotle Poetics*, 101–3).

9. *Kitāb Aristūtālīs fī al-shiʿr*, 29.

10. See Tarán and Gutas, *Aristotle Poetics*, 94–96.

11. Ibn Sīnā (980–1037) does not reproduce the taxonomy that transforms Greek

tragedy into praise and comedy into satire. Rather, his discussion of these categories appears to be much closer to Aristotle's text, which suggests that he worked from some translation of the text other than Mattā's.

12. For discussion of the Arabic reception of the Aristotelian theory of mimesis, see Gould, "The *Poetics* from Athens to al-Andalus."

13. Abū Bishr Mattā was by no means a marginal or insignificant figure. Scholars identify him as the "founder" or "head" of the Aristotelian school in Baghdad (see, e.g., Gutas, *Greek Thought, Arabic Culture*, 14, 101, 132), and he was said to have translated or written commentaries on almost all of Aristotle's treatises, although not all of these survive. Nor were all his contemporaries as spiteful as those present in Abū Ḥayyān al-Tawḥīdī's vignette. Al-Bīrūnī repeated an anecdote in praise of Mattā in which Mattā's knowledge of Aristotle allows him to put another, less educated scholar in his place (al-Bīrūnī, *The Determination*, 152).

14. See Endress, "Mattā ibn Yūnus."

15. For a vivid and lively portrait of al-Tawḥīdī, see Bergé, "Abū Ḥayyān al-Tawḥīdī."

16. The debate described by al-Tawḥīdī was supposed to take place in 937; see Tarán and Gutas, *Aristotle Poetics*, 92–93. Historians interpret this "debate" in the context of the contest between the logicians or philosophers and the grammarians. In brief, the logicians (inspired by Greek thought) believed that reason governs speech; the Arab grammarians saw speech as ethical, and hence inseparable from Islamic teachings. The debate lasted for centuries. For summaries, see Carter, "The Ethical Basis," 18–19; and Margoliouth, "The Discussion between Abū Bishr Mattā and Abū Saʿīd al-Sīrāfī."

17. Al-Tawḥīdī, *Kitāb al-imtāʿ wa-al-muʾānasah*, 1:111.

18. My reading of al-Tawḥīdī's account of this encounter, admittedly, tokenizes the participants in the debate, making al-Sīrāfī into a personification of the Arab claiming ownership of Arabic and depicting Mattā as an underdog whose ethnic pedigree al-Sīrāfī challenges. In a brilliant counterreading of the episode, Wen-chin Ouyang focuses our attention on the other actor in this small drama, al-Tawḥīdī. She proposes that by balancing logic against grammar in his narrative, al-Tawḥīdī plays a more sophisticated game: "It does not really matter whether we think of thought as Logic or Grammar, as long as we understand that meaning is produced in dialogism, in the ways in which language and thought define each other and give each other shape" ("Rereading al-Tawḥīdī's Transcription," 456). Ouyang argues that in al-Tawḥīdī's account of this debate, *falsafa* (the philosophical tradition) and *adab* (the etiquette of debate and literary eloquence, as represented in al-Tawḥīdī's record of the debate) prove to be symbiotic.

19. Aristotle, *Poetics*, 48–49. Only a very brief fragment of the Syriac translation of the *Poetics* survives; it does include this phrase. See Tkatsch, *Die arabische Übersetzung der "Poetik" des Aristoteles*, 1:155, for a Latin translation of the Syriac. This phrase is rendered: "Est autem fabula imitationis expositio" ("The tale [*fabula*; cf. chapter 9 below] is an exposition [or a setting forth] of imitation)."

20. Aristotle, *Kitāb Aristūtālīs fī al-shiʿr*, 51.

21. Aristotle's Greek continues to explain the terms that he has used in his terse definition of tragedy: "I use 'plot' to denote the construction of events . . ." (Aristotle, *Poetics*, 48–49). Mattā's translation incorporates a sense of action and event that is missing from the definition of "tragedy" in the preceding phrase, quoted above: "وأعنى بالخرافة وحكاية الحديث تركيب الأمور . . ." ("and by 'tale' and

'mimicry of events,' I mean the combination of the matters"; Aristotle, *Kitāb Aristūtālīs fī al-shi'r*, 51).

22. On *ḥikāya*, oral performance and pantomime, and Abbasid letters, see Moreh, *Live Theatre and Dramatic Literature in the Medieval Arab World*, 87–103; Antrim, *Routes and Realms*, 12–13; Kilito, *Les Séances*, 56–59; al-Jāḥiẓ, *The Life and Works*, 101–2; and al-Jāḥiẓ, *Al-Bayān wa-al-tabyīn*, 1:69–74.

23. Very little is known about the author to whom the *Ḥikāyat Abī al-Qāsim* is attributed in the single manuscript copy of the work, Abū al-Muṭahhar al-Azdī. Indeed, some have proposed that the book was authored by Abū Ḥayyān al-Tawḥīdī; see Selove, *Ḥikāyat Abī al-Qāsim*, 4–5.

24. See Selove, *Ḥikāyat Abī al-Qāsim*, 31–34.

25. See Moreh, *Live Theatre*, 94–100.

26. See Reynolds, "Popular Prose in the Post-Classical Period," 264–65; Pellat, "Ḥikāya." During the lifetime of al-Azdī, the *maqāma* were an emergent genre. Judging from the references made in the text, al-Azdī seems to have lived during the eleventh century (see Selove, *Ḥikāyat Abī al-Qāsim*, 4–5); al-Hamadhānī (968–1008), inventor of the *maqāma*, died at the beginning of that century.

27. In a brilliant jeu d'esprit, Emily Selove uses *Moby-Dick* as extended intertext, comparing the *Ḥikāya* to Melville's novel as a point of reference more familiar to contemporary readers (see her discussion, *Ḥikāyat Abī al-Qāsim*, 23). Indeed, al-Azdī's work seems to have a sensibility in common with Melville's—and with other works that also live in language, rather than aiming for mimetic representation of reality: Rabelais's *Gargantua and Pantagruel*, Sterne's *Tristram Shandy*, and al-Shidyāq's *Al-sāq 'alā al-sāq*, for instance. On *Al-sāq 'alā al-sāq*, see chapter 9.

28. In fact, they puzzled over the relation between (ancient) Greeks and (contemporary) Byzantines; see Cheikh, *Byzantium Viewed by the Arabs*, 103–11.

29. For discussion of the metaphor of the "living language," see chapter 13.

30. Al-Tawḥīdī, *Kitāb al-imtā' wa-al-mu'ānasah*, 1:111.

31. For discussion, see chapter 11 and n. 20 on p. 209.

CHAPTER NINE

1. Whitehead, *Zone One*, 289–90.

2. These were the *Categories*, *On Interpretation*, *Prior Analytics*, *Posterior Analytics*, *Topics*, and *Sophistical Refutations*. Boethius did not include either the *Rhetoric* or the *Poetics* in his Organon, as the Syriac, Arabic, and Alexandrian Neoplatonist commentators did. See Solmsen, "Boethius and the History of the Organon."

3. For overviews of the Arabic-to-Latin translation movement, in addition to works cited below, see Burnett, "Arabic into Latin"; for the Renaissance reception of Arabic philosophy, see Hasse, *Success and Suppression*. For a lively (if somewhat melodramatic) reimagining of the life of Ibn Rushd, see Youssef Chahine's 1997 movie *Al-Maṣīr* (*Destiny*).

4. On philosophical debates between scholars and ecclesiastical authorities and the Christian bans on philosophy, see Principe, "Bishops, Theologians and Philosophers in Conflict."

5. Urvoy, *Ibn Rushd*, 127.

6. For the vicissitudes of Greek transmission of the *Poetics* from antiquity to the twentieth century, see Tarán and Gutas, *Aristotle Poetics*, 3–76.

7. See Gutas, in Tarán and Gutas, *Aristotle Poetics*, 105.

8. On Ibn Rushd's commenting strategies, see Butterworth's introduction to Ibn Rushd, *Averroes' Middle Commentary*, xi–xii; Gould, "The *Poetics* from Athens to al-Andalus."

9. For a thoughtful discussion of this dimension of the text, see Gould, "The *Poetics* from Athens to al-Andalus," 4–6.

10. *Muḥāka* (which means *imitation*; see, e.g., Ibn Rushd, *Talkhīṣ kitāb al-shiʿr*, 57), *muḥākiyya* (which means "imitation" or "imitated"; see, e.g., ibid., p. 54; both from the lexical root *ḥ-k-y*) and *tashbīh* (which means "comparison" or "simile"; see, e.g., ibid., p. 54) appear frequently in Ibn Rushd's commentary.

11. Aristotle, *Kitāb Aristūtālīs fī al-shiʿr*, 51; Ibn Sīnā, *Al-mantiq al-shiʿr*, 47. For definitions of *khurāfa*, see Lane, *An Arabic-English Lexicon*, s.v. خرف, 726, and Ibn Manzūr, *Lisān al-ʿarab*, s.v. خرف, 1140.

12. Ibn Rushd, *Talkhīṣ kitāb al-shiʿr*, 69; cp. Ibn Rushd, *Averroes' Middle Commentary on Aristotle's "Poetics,"* 75.

13. See Ibn Rushd, *Talkhīṣ kitāb al-shiʿr*, 61, and *Averroes' Middle Commentary on Aristotle's "Poetics,"* 67–68; Hermannus Alemannus, *De arte poetica*, 44; Boggess, "Aristotle's *Poetics* in the Fourteenth Century," appendix D, no. 9, p. 287.

14. On Hermannus's translation of the *Poetics*, see Luquet, "Hermann l'Allemand," 412–13.

15. It was discovered in 1931 and published in 1953; see Tarán and Gutas, *Aristotle Poetics*, 36.

16. For discussion of the Italian humanist reception of the Greek *Poetics*, see Tarán and Gutas, *Aristotle Poetics*, 38–60. For a modern edition of Jacob Mantino's Latin translation of Todros Todrosi's Hebrew periphrasis of Ibn Rushd's commentary on the *Poetics*, see Mantino, *Averrois Paraphrasis in Librum Poeticae Aristotelis*. This periphrasis was popular during the Renaissance, it seems, because it trimmed those Latin translations of Arabic poetry that beguiled the medieval Latin readers of the treatise. For examples of Latin translations of Arabic poetry included in the florilegia, see, e.g., Boggess, "Aristotle's *Poetics* in the Fourteenth Century," appendix B, no. 9 p. 285; appendix B, no. 16–20, p. 285; appendix B, no. 23, p. 285.

17. Hermannus Alemannus, *De arte poetica*, 48.

18. In his Latin dictionary, completed in 1440, Firmin le Ver defined *fabula* as "a fictitious matter, idle speech; it comes from 'to speak' [*for, faris*] because it consists of mere words. *Fabula* also means *story* [*historia*]" (*Database of Latin Dictionaries*, s.v. *fabula*).

19. Matthew of Vendôme, *Ars versificatoria*, 4.1 and 4.16; *Opera*, 3:193 and 3:202; *The Art of Versification*, 100 and 104. For Geoffrey of Vinsauf's *Poetria Nova*, see Faral, *Les arts poétiques*, 263–320. For the use of *fabula* in the exegesis of fantastic tales, see Rita Copeland, *Rhetoric, Hermeneutics and Translation in the Middle Ages*, especially chapter 4, pp. 112–14 and 125–26.

20. Hermannus Alemannus, *De arte poetica*, 48.

21. Boggess, "Aristotle's *Poetics* in the Fourteenth Century," appendix B, no. 4, p. 284; for discussion of the manuscript in which the statement is found, see Boggess, "Aristotle's *Poetics* in the Fourteenth Century," 280.

22. In a graceful reading of medieval philosophers on the role of fiction in the spinning of philosophical and theological argument, Peter Dronke explores the meaning of the Latin *fabula*. For his twelfth-century thinkers, it has many of the same connotations

that I attribute to it here: it denotes fiction, but in particular (for the more visionary authors he discusses) those fictions that open up to deeper meanings; see Dronke's long essay *Fabula*. My reading locates in Petrarch's use of the word this significance—a confusion of fiction and truth-telling—and, at the same time, a *mise-en-abyme* that plunges poet and reader into the bottomless waters of the self, identified as the point where truth and fiction converge and where Latin and Italian meet.

23. Petrarch, *Canzoniere*, 1, vv. 9–11, p. 5.

24. Petrarch, *Canzoniere*, 10–11.

25. Petrarch, *Canzoniere*, 254, vv. 13–14, p. 1027.

26. Petrarch, *Canzoniere*, 1028.

27. Needless to say, the philosophers use the word to make other, much finer distinctions about the qualities that distinguish each individual phenomenon, or instantiation of phenomena, from others; for discussion, see Cross, "Medieval Theories of Haecceity." My discussion of the word uses it in a narrowly defined literary and linguistic sphere.

28. I'm grateful to Jason Young—now professor of architecture at the University of Tennessee, Knoxville—for suggesting the simile between mimesis and the visual games Tati plays in *Playtime*, when we were both fellows at the Institute for the Humanities at the University of Michigan.

29. For a counterexample—an attempt to link Petrarch's poetics to the work of an Arab poet—see my discussion of Pietro Valerga's translation of the poetry of Ibn al-Fāriḍ in *European Modernity and the Arab Mediterranean*, 34–64.

30. For discussion of Petrarch's late turn to Italian, see above, chapter 3; and Mallette, "Vernacular and Cosmopolitan Language in Late Medieval Europe: Petrarch at Sea."

31. I borrow the word "dappled" from Gerard Manley Hopkins's magnificent poetic description of complexity, "Pied Beauty"; Hopkins, *The Major Works*, 132–33.

32. Petrarch, *Canzoniere*, 211, vv. 12–14, p. 906. See also 224, v. 4, p. 945, for the phrase "un lungo error in cieco laberinto" ("a long wandering in a blind labyrinth") to describe his passion for Laura.

33. I borrow the term "hesitation" from Nagel and Wood; they use it to describe the work of art that *hesitates* between identifying itself as modern (reflecting and representing the moment of its creation) or historical (representing the realities of a distant past). For their definition of the term, see *Anachronic Renaissance*, 17–18.

CHAPTER TEN

1. Aḥmad Fāris al-Shidyāq, *Sirr al-layāl fī al-qalb wa-al-ibdāl fī ʿilm maʿānī al-alfāẓ al-ʿArabīyah*, 111.

2. Lane, *An Arabic-English Lexicon*, s.v. خرف, 726. I have quoted Lane's definition with fidelity, leaving out only the abbreviations he uses to indicate which lexicon each piece of information comes from. These add a further source of fascination and a further disruption to the scholar consulting the dictionary.

3. Lane, *An Arabic-English Lexicon*, vii. The term "classical Arabic" is imprecise, and it may be understood to include the writers of the Abbasid period who advanced Arabic literary practice considerably, in addition to the very early period of interest to Lane.

4. Nagel and Wood, *Anachronic Renaissance*, 32.

5. On Nagel and Wood's use of the word *hesitation* as a term of art, see chapter 9, n. 33, above.

6. For this period of Lane's life, see Thompson, *Edward William Lane*, 16–23.

7. Thompson, *Edward William Lane*, 247.

8. Thompson, *Edward William Lane*, 472.

9. Thompson, *Edward William Lane*, 473.

10. "More than once," he wrote, in the preface to the *Lexicon* (xxii), "I passed a quarter of a year without going out of my house."

11. Thompson, *Edward William Lane*, 526–28.

12. Said, *Orientalism*, 163 and 164.

13. Thompson, *Edward William Lane*, 278. Today, of course, we would see Lane's life as a shut-in as a further threat to his health.

For a pointed critique of Said's discussion of Lane, see Rodenbeck, "Edward Said and Edward William Lane." For a thoughtful account of Lane's time in Cairo and his work as lexicographer, see Roper, "Texts from Nineteenth-Century Egypt."

14. For Lane's discussion of al-Dasūqī in the preface to the *Lexicon*, see 1:v, 1:xxi, 1:xxii, and 1:xxiii. On al-Dasūqī, see Goldziher, "Al-Dasūḳī, al-Sayyid Ibrāhīm b. Ibrāhīm."

15. For the correspondence between Lane and Dasūqī, see Richards, "Edward Lane's Surviving Arabic Correspondence." Whether or not Lane's treatment of Dasūqī was shabby is a topic of dispute among historians. Dasūqī's letters sound damning; see especially Richards, 9 and 21–22. But Dasūqī himself praised Lane's erudition; see Mubārak, *Al-Khiṭaṭ al-tawfīqīyah al-jadīdah li-Miṣr al-Qāhirah*, 11:9–13. And see Roper, "Texts from Nineteenth-Century Egypt," for tributes to Lane's erudition from learned Arabs of the nineteenth century—including al-Shidyāq (249).

16. Lane, *An Arabic-English Lexicon*, 1:v. Lane also discusses the preposterous longevity attributed to early Arab poets, some of them reputed to have lived as long as 450 years. Early lexicographers artificially extended the lifespans of these poets in order to connect them to the Jahiliyya, the period before the revelation of Islam, and an era of linguistic "chastity"; 1:x.

17. Lane, *An Arabic-English Lexicon*, 1:xxi.

18. Lane, *An Arabic-English Lexicon*, 1:xxii.

19. Lane, *An Arabic-English Lexicon*, 1:xxi–xxii.

20. Lane, *An Arabic-English Lexicon*, 1:xxxiii.

21. Lane, *An Arabic-English Lexicon*, s.v. عرف, 2013.

22. Lane, *An Arabic-English Lexicon*, s.v. عرف, 2013.

23. In its fulsome style, Lane's *Lexicon* is the opposite of J. G. Hava's *Arabic-English Dictionary for the Use of Students* (first published in Beirut in 1899). The terseness of Hava's *Dictionary* struck John Julius Norwich—who also, apparently, reads dictionaries for fun. Of Hava's *Dictionary* Norwich wrote: "Almost every entry gives additional proof—if such were needed—of the impossibility of the Arabic language." He cited definitions of a single word, *khāl*, to drive his point home: "Shroud. Fancy. Black stallion. Owner of a th. Self-magnified. Caliphate. Lonely place . . ." (Norwich, *The Illustrated Christmas Cracker*, 46).

24. Lane, *An Arabic-English Lexicon*, s.v. ثغر, 338.

25. See al-Shidyāq, *Leg over Leg*, 1:42–45.

26. Al-Shidyāq, *Leg over Leg*, 1:42–43.

27. For an overview of the Arabic lexicographic tradition, see Haywood, *Arabic Lexicography*.

28. Lane uses the words "chaste" or "chasteness" in the preface to *An Arabic-English Lexicon* on page 1:vii (three times), 1:viii, 1:ix, 1:xi (twice), 1:xv, and 1:xvii (twice).

29. See above, chapter 8, n. 30, on p. 203.

30. On al-Shidyāq's life, see Alwan, *Aḥmad Fāris ash-Shidyāq and the West*, 1–73; Johnson, "Foreword," xi–xviii; and Rastegar, *Literary Modernity*, 109–15. On Fāris and his brother, As'ad, who was tortured and killed by Maronite officials under the influence of American missionaries in Lebanon, see Makdisi, *Artillery of Heaven*, 103–37. For a literary interpretation of the relationship between Fāris and As'ad, see Sacks, "Falling into Pieces."

31. On al-Shidyāq's time in Malta, see Agius, "Arabic under Shidyāq in Malta."

32. For a fascinating discussion of topics adjacent to my interests here, but beyond the reach of this study—the material history of nineteenth-century Arabic literature (in particular, al-Shidyāq's self-printing of *Al-sāq 'alā al-sāq*) and the history of the book, as they intersect with the Nahda, or the Arabic cultural renaissance of the nineteenth century—see al-Bagdadi, "Print, Script and Free-thinking in Arabic Letters of the Nineteenth Century."

33. Al-Shidyāq, *Leg over Leg*, ¶ 3.5.2, pp. 3:134–37.

34. Al-Shidyāq, *Leg over Leg*, ¶ 3.5.17–21, pp. 3:150–55.

35. Al-Shidyāq, *Leg over Leg*, ¶ 4.9.9. pp. 4:132–35.

36. Here, the witty Fāriyāqiyyah uses the Arabic word for "woman" to refer to the feminine noun for "language" in Arabic.

37. Al-Shidyāq, *Leg over Leg*, ¶ 4.9.9, pp. 4:135.

38. Johnson, "Introduction," xxix.

39. Rastegar, *Literary Modernity*, 104–5. If the Fāriyāqiyyah were simply a feminine version of the Fāriyāq, it would be sufficient to append an *-a* to his name in order to derive her name: the Fāriyāqa. The *-iyya* suffix implies a categorical noun.

40. Rastegar, *Literary Modernity*, 105; see al-Shidyāq, *Leg over Leg*, ¶ 0.2.12, pp. 1:14–15.

41. Al-Shidyāq, *Leg over Leg*, ¶ 4.18.15–20, pp. 4:290–99.

42. In Arabic, the word *Frank* refers to Latin Christians in a general and imprecise way. The Fāriyāqiyyah turns her back on western Europe and returns to the Ottoman Empire following her farewell.

43. Al-Shidyāq, *Leg over Leg*, ¶ 4.18.20, pp. 4:296–99. The book goes on for another 200 pages (in Davies's translation). But these pages don't extend the plot; they consist mainly of poetry, much of it nominally written by the Fāriyāq, word lists, and pages detailing errors made by the Franks, or western Europeans.

44. See al-Shidyāq, *Leg over Leg*, ¶ 4.14, pp. 4:202–17. This episode is based on Shidyāq's loss of his own son, according to the chronology provided by Davies (4:501).

45. Arberry, "Fresh Light on Ahmad Faris al-Shidyaq," 155.

46. Lane, *An Arabic-English Lexicon*, 1:xxi–xxii.

47. Thompson, *Edward William Lane*, 623; Haywood, *Arabic Lexicography*, 127.

48. Al-Shidyāq, *Leg over Leg*, 4:485.

49. Alwan, *Aḥmad Fāris ash-Shidyāq*, 207–211.

50. See the Library of Arabic Literature at NYU Press, https://nyupress.org/search-results/?series=library-of-arabic-literature (accessed July 25, 2019). See also chapter 13 below for discussion of another recent publication from the Library of Arabic Literature.

51. El-Ariss, Review of *Leg over Leg*, 286.

52. On this dimension of al-Shidyāq's career as lexicographer, see Sawaie, "An Aspect of 19th Century Arabic Lexicography," 162, and Alwan, *Aḥmad Fāris Ash-Shidyāq and the West*, 14.

53. See above, chapter 8, n. 30, on p. 203.

54. See Dalton, "Caveat Emptor." For another, thoroughly tongue-in-cheek version of the pan-European language, see Marani's article-cum-manifesto "EUROPANTO: From Productive Process to Language."

CHAPTER ELEVEN

1. This statement was made of the Rev. John Palmer, who was "Professor of Arabick" at St. John's College at Cambridge from 1804 to 1819; see Wood, "The Missing Fragment of the Fourth Book of Esdras," 265.

2. For a more detailed discussion of the life cycles of the two languages, with references, see chapter 1.

3. The literature on multilingualism and code-switching between languages in the Arabophone world is vast. For two very different perspectives, from opposite ends of the Mediterranean, see McDougall, "Dream of Exile" (on language politics in Algeria) and Seigneurie, "The Institution and the Practice of Comparative Literature in Lebanon" (on the study of comparative literature in Lebanese universities; especially 392–94).

4. On Giustinian's funeral oratory, see McManamon, *Funeral Oratory*, 88–91. For Giustinian's Venetian Italian lyrics, see Carocci, *Non si odono altri canti*. Giustinian's Latin translations from Plutarch's *Lives* were also popular, much copied and printed, and much imitated; see Pade, *The Reception of Plutarch's Lives in Fifteenth-Century Italy*, 1:202–9.

5. Dante, *Vita nova*, 150.

6. On vernacular translation in Italy, see Cornish, *Vernacular Translation in Dante's Italy*; for a discussion of the vernacular as literary register for a feminine audience in particular, see her chapter 1, "Dressing down the muses."

7. Perry, *Secundus*, 102.

8. From the Greek version, with Perry's translation; Perry, *Secundus*, 74–75.

9. This is my translation of a mash-up of the Greek and two Latin versions edited by Perry. See the Greek version, Perry, *Secundus*, 74; the Latin version by Willelmus in Perry, *Secundus*, 94; and the Latin version by Vincent of Beauvais in Perry, *Secundus*, 102.

10. *Nomos* in the Greek; see Perry, *Secundus*, 74; in Latin, *lex*, 94; in Arabic, *al-nāmūs*, 18. See also Syriac, 106, and Armenian, 109.

11. From the Greek, Perry's translation; Perry, *Secundus*, 78–79.

12. From the Latin, my translation; Perry, *Secundus*, 94.

13. The third question, in both Greek and Latin, is "What is God?" The Armenian duplicates those three questions but switches the order of the last two (Perry, *Secundus*, 111–12). The Arabic version begins, "What is God?" "What is the universe?" (English 137–38, Arabic 27–28).

14. For Perry's discussion of the mistranslations in the twelfth-century Latin, see Perry, *Secundus*, 34–36.

15. There is an example of noun soup in the extract from the Latin quoted above: "the impudence of the road" translates "audacia vie." Some manuscripts give an alternate reading: "audaciae via," "the path of audacity," which makes better sense.

16. The Arabic version, uniquely among those extant, introduces syntax: it includes verbs and simple sentences in its definitions. In all cases, I rely on the edited modern version. The manuscript history could tell a different story.

17. The Arabic and Ethiopic versions are unique in that they draw out the seduction scene to great length, and they explain and excuse the mother's transgression in the son's explanation to the king, when at last he begins to write out his self-explanation. See Arabic version, chapter 14; Perry, *Secundus*, English, 135–37, and Arabic, 23–26. For a Latin translation of the Ethiopic version, see Perry's appendix IV, chapter 14, 29–30.

18. For Philip's biography, see Léopold Devillers in *Nouvelle Biographie Nationale*, vol. 20, col. 310–13; and Sijen, "Philippe de Harveng."

19. Philip of Harveng, *De silentio clericorum*, col. 946a–b.

20. Philip of Harveng, *De silentio clericorum*, col. 1012c–d.

21. Philip of Harveng, *De silentio clericorum*, col. 1013a.

22. Philip of Harveng, *De silentio clericorum*, col. 1012c.

23. Philip of Harveng, *Epistolae*, col. 154b.

24. Philip of Harveng, *Epistolae*, col. 154a. Note that Philip writes before the metaphor of the "living language" has been coined. Hebrew and Greek are "rumors" (not dead); Latin is "present" (not alive). On the metaphor of the "living language," see below, chapter 13.

25. Thomas à Kempis, *Opera Omnia*, 7:118.

26. Borst, *Der Turmbau von Babel*, 2.2:728; emphasis added. For another perspective on "Latin silence," see O'Rourke and Holcroft, "Latin and the Vernacular." They argue that in Bruni's *Dialogi ad Petrum Histrum* (1406), the possibility of debate in Latin is made the topic of a Latin debate. An embarrassed silence opens the debate, illustrating the position of those who believe that spoken Latin is a lost art. But by the book's end, "medium and message have merged, and it is clearly established that conversational debate in Latin about contemporary topics is first of all possible, and secondly, really rather entertaining" (44).

27. Hutchins's translation, *Nine Essays of al-Jahiz*, 16; al-Jāḥiẓ, *Rasā'il al-Jāḥiẓ*, 100.

28. Al-Jāḥiẓ, *Rasā'il al-Jāḥiẓ*, 112; cf. *Nine Essays of al-Jahiz*, 25.

29. Death Cab for Cutie, "I Will Possess Your Heart," by Ben Gibbard, Nick Harmer, Jason McGerr, and Chris Walla, track 2 on *Narrow Stairs*, Atlantic 7567-89946-5, 2008, compact disc.

30. The video for this song (which won the MTV Video Music Award for Best Editing) emphasizes the linguistic imagery of these opening lines by tracking the winsome heroine through a number of foreign landscapes and cityscapes, many of them marked by foreign languages and writing systems. Like the cosmopolitan language, the love celebrated in "I Will Possess Your Heart" is soaring and seductive, but also shades into something sinister and ominous. The lover's obsession with the beloved is stalker-adjacent. The song appeared in a *Paste* magazine list of the "25 Creepiest Songs about Love" (by Tyler Kane; https://www.pastemagazine.com/blogs/lists/2011/09/25-creepy-songs-about-love.html?p=2, accessed July 29, 2019).

CHAPTER TWELVE

1. From an Esperanto translation of the Qur'an by Italo Chiussi, *La Nobla Korano*, 238.

2. For overview and bibliography on the origination of language, see Nuessel, "Language: Semiotics." On invented languages, see Eco, *The Search for the Perfect Language*.

3. Discussed above; see chapter 4, n. 22, on p. 195.

4. For overviews of the lingua franca, in addition to the works cited below, see Mallette, "Lingua Franca"; and Schuchardt, "Lingua Franca" (a seminal essay of historical

interest in lingua franca studies). Cremona, "'Acciocché ognuno le possa intendere'" and "Italian-Based Lingua Francas around the Mediterranean," study the use of Italian as bureaucratic (written) lingua franca. Stahuljak's "Multilingualism and Translation in the Mediterranean" is a lively, incisive, and inventive book review essay on multilingualism in the premodern Mediterranean and the strategies that medieval men and women used to mediate between languages, including the lingua franca.

5. Kahane, "Lingua Franca: The Story of a Term"; Cifoletti, *La lingua franca mediterranea* (1989), 5–6.

6. For "franco piccolo," see della Valle, *Viaggi di Pietro della Valle*, 1:320; for "italien corroumpu," see Savary de Brèves, *Relation des voyages de monsieur de Brèves*, 39; for "italien baragouïné," see Savary de Brèves, *Relation des voyages de monsieur de Brèves*, 325; for "italiano corrotto," see Scudéry, *Il perfetto Ibrahim* (an Italian translation of a book originally written in French), 237–38.

7. Dakhlia, *Lingua franca*, 267.

8. Savary de Brèves, *Relation des voyages de monsieur de Brèves*, 39. The French *iargon* (*jargon* in modern French) might mean "corrupt language"; antilanguage or argot ("Un langage concerté, que l'on fait pour n'estre entendu que de ceux avec qui on a intelligence"), or it might be used contemptuously to refer to languages which one does not understand ("Il se dit aussi abusivement, & par une espece de mespris des Langues estrangeres qu'on n'entend pas"; *Dictionnaire de l'Académie Française*, s.v. *jargon*).

9. Spanish text reprinted in Cifoletti, *La lingua franca mediterranea*, 157; Cifoletti, *La lingua franca barbaresca*, 197; see also Sosa, *An Early Modern Dialogue with Islam*, 185. The author of this passage, long thought to be Diego Haedo, has recently been identified as Antonio de Sosa.

10. Della Valle describes the lingua franca as "Italian—that is, that bastard Italian . . . which in these parts of the Orient they call *franco piccolo*"; *Viaggi di Pietro della Valle*, 1:320.

11. Savary de Brèves, *Relation des voyages de monsieur de Brèves*, 39.

12. Sosa, *An Early Modern Dialogue with Islam*, 185.

13. Cf. Cifoletti, *La lingua franca mediterranea*, 38; Cifoletti, *La lingua franca barbaresca*, 23.

14. *Informacon for pylgrymes*, 27–28.

15. Alcarotti, *Del viaggio di terra santa*, introduction, page P. Yet later, in Damascus, Alcarotti is introduced to a guide who "learned a little Italian from some Spaniards, during the time when he was in the Indies" (59): what language could this possibly be, other than lingua franca?

16. Lamanskiĭ, *Secrets d'État de Venise*, 2:573. Pietro della Valle, in Damascus, describes the last moments of a dying companion who has to confess himself as best he can in "franco piccolo," because he does not know the local languages (*Viaggi di Pietro della Valle*, 1:322).

17. Lanfreducci and Bosio, "Costa e Discorsi di Barberia," 440.

18. Carey, *A Short Account of Algiers*, 14.

19. Tyler, *The Algerine Captive*, 2:67.

20. Galt, *Letters from the Levant*, 22.

21. Some early modern witnesses viewed the lingua franca as pastiche or parody of more formal languages. A late eighteenth-century Italian author mocks the language of an Italian opera he has seen performed in London: "Generally in all his Works [the

librettist] uses the verb *sortire* instead of *uscire* [to go out], following the rules of the lingua franca" (Nemesini, *Il tributo della coglionatura*, 5). In a utopian work, George Berkeley describes the linguistic education of his hero: "The knowledge of languages being of great use as well as ornament to young gentlemen, he himself [i.e., the boy's tutor], by way of recreation, taught me that mixed language called *Lingua Franca*, so necessary in Eastern countries. It is made up of Italian, Turkish, Persian, and Arabian, or rather a jargon of all languages together. He scarce ever spoke to us but in that language, saying we might learn Latin from our masters, and our mother-tongue from our play fellows" (Berkeley, *Adventures*, 5).

22. For examples of European travelers defining the ethnonym "franco," see Alcarotti, *Del viaggio di terra santa*, 61; Ceverio de Vera, *Viaie de la Tierra Santa*, 40v; Frescobaldi, *Viaggio*, 77–78.

23. See, e.g., Genina, *Lo squadrone bianco*. This typical line of dialogue captures both the sentiment and linguistic spirit of the pseudo–lingua franca of Italian empire cinema: "Tutto bene. Nostra vita stare nel deserto. Nel deserto uomo dimenticare tutto" ("Everything good. Our life is in the desert. In the desert a man forgets everything"). See Bertellini, "Colonial Autism," 262–67, for an interesting discussion of the use of sound (including language) in empire cinema. Bertellini does not address the use of pidgin Italian but rather talks about the transition from silent to sound movies in fascist Italy and the strategic deployment of silence, and operatic scenes with symphonic accompaniment and no dialogue, in *Lo squadrone bianco*. I am grateful to Ruth Ben-Ghiat for talking with me about the pidgin Italian used in empire cinema and in *Lo squadrone bianco* in particular.

24. See the European Commission's official press release on European languages, September 26, 2013: http://europa.eu/rapid/press-release_MEMO-13-825_en.htm (accessed July 29, 2019).

25. Savary de Brèves, *Relation des voyages de monsieur de Brèves*, 325.

26. Brasca, *Relazione del suo viaggio a Gierusalemme*, 15v.

27. Pesenti, *Peregrinaggio di Giervsalemme*, 21–22.

28. For the topos of the unreliable dragoman, see, e.g., Frescobaldi, *Viaggio*, 99–100. That the distrust of the dragoman persisted into the era of the modern empires is attested in Ruth Ben-Ghiat's discussion of the shadowy figure of the native translator in the Italian fascist colonies; see *Italian Fascism's Empire Cinema*, 119.

29. See, e.g., Selbach, "The Superstrate Is Not Always the Lexifier," 53.

30. Lewis et al., "Manifesto," 22. The manifesto first "blasts," "curses," and "damns" enemies of the emergent aesthetic and social formations which the Vorticists are calling forth from 1914 Britain, then "blesses" those people and phenomena which the authors see as exemplary. This is the first of four Vorticist manifestoes that open the inaugural issue of *Blast*. The adversarial energy of the movement was, of course, typical of the avant-garde movements that preceded World War I in Europe.

CHAPTER THIRTEEN

1. Levinas, "Le moi et la totalité," 371; cp. Levinas, "The Ego and the Totality," 43.

2. Arendt, *Portable Hannah Arendt*, 3.

3. See, for instance, Noha Radwan's seminal study of colloquial poetry in twenty-first-century Egypt, which begins with a passionate (if historically tenuous) account of the extirpation of linguistic competitors to Arabic: "Unfortunately all the extant records

from the seventh to the tenth century carry none of these noncanonical poetic forms [i.e., poetry in colloquial forms of Arabic] but only traces of their elision, a reminder that the poetry attested in these records was part of an elite rather than the popular culture, and that other poetic expressions had been condemned to silence" (Radwan, *Egyptian Colloquial Poetry*, 3).

4. My account of Alessandro Paganini and the printed Qur'an draws on Nuovo, "Il Corano arabo ritrovato," "A Lost Arabic Koran Rediscovered," and "La scoperta del Corano arabo"; Nallino, "Una cinquecentesca edizione del Corano"; and *Senza ammenda e con più vaghezza*.

5. Barbieri, "I libri di Alessandro Paganini a Toscolano," 6. On the press's activities, in particular under Alessandro's leadership, see *Senza ammenda e con più vaghezza*.

6. Borrmans, "Présentation," 99–104.

7. See Bodin, *Colloquium heptaplomeres*, 225, and *Colloquium of the Seven*, 294. On Bodin as witness to the fate of the Paganini Qur'an in Constantinople, see Nuovo, "La scoperta del Corano arabo," 17–18; Malcolm, "Jean Bodin and the Authorship of the 'Colloquium Heptaplomeres,'" 115.

8. For centuries, the only known extant copy of the Paganini Qur'an lay undiscovered in the library of the Frati Minori di San Michele in Isola, and it was thought that the book had been destroyed during the Inquisition—or that it had never existed at all. It was rediscovered in 1987. See Nuovo, "Il Corano arabo ritrovato," the publication which announced the discovery of the Qur'an to the scholarly public; Nuovo, "A Lost Arabic Koran Rediscovered," the English publication of the discovery; and Nuovo, "La scoperta del Corano arabo," for an updating of the research into the Paganini press, the Paganini family connections, and the creation (and loss) of the Arabic Qur'an.

9. The Paganini Qur'an has been published digitally in *Early Western Korans Online: Koran Printing in the West*. Ambrogio's annotations are visible, if not entirely legible, in the digital publication.

10. These were the *Heroides* of Ovid and Giovanni Antonio Tagliente's book of model love letters; *Senza ammenda e con più vaghezza*, 15.

11. On the *Kitāb ṣalāt al-sawāʿī*, printed either in Fano or, possibly, in Venice, see Hitti, "The First Book Printed in Arabic"; and Krek, "The Enigma of the First Arabic Book Printed from Movable Type."

12. Copying the Qur'an presented unique difficulties because of its length and complexity, the difficulties of Qur'anic Arabic (a register distinct from both literary and spoken Arabic), and the extremely high aesthetic expectations with which the Muslim public approached the written Qur'an. For discussion of the written Qur'an as aesthetic object and magnificent reproductions of a variety of Qur'ans from different eras and different parts of the Muslim world, see Farhad and Rettig, eds., *The Art of the Qur'an*.

13. Earlier presses in Istanbul had printed in Armenian and Greek. See Nallino, "Una cinquecentesca edizione del Corano stampata a Venezia," 12.

14. Verdery, "The Publications of the Būlāq Press," 129. Verdery explains the nature of this first publication—an Italian-Arabic dictionary—by explaining that "Italian was still *the* 'lingua franca,' although soon to be replaced by French" (ibid.).

15. Albin, "Printing of the Qur'ān." The second printed Arabic Qur'an, after Paganini's monstrosity, was also produced by non-Arabs. Tsarina Catherine the Great commissioned its printing as a service to the Muslims (mainly of Turkic descent) of her kingdom. See Albin, "Printing of the Qur'ān," and van Dijk, "Early Printed Qur'ans," 142.

16. On Citolini as creator of the metaphor of the "living language," see Faithfull, "The Concept of 'Living Language.'" Faithfull's discussion of the meaning of the term "living" (*vivo*, opposed to *morto*) in Cinquecento Italy is fascinating, and it informs my discussion of the "posthuman" ontology of the cosmopolitan language below; see especially ibid., 282–83. For a discussion of the flip side of this metaphor—the "dead language"—see Considine, "*De ortu et occasu linguae latinae.*"

17. Citolini, *La lettera d'Alessandro Citolini in difesa della lingua uolgare*, 6r.

18. See Edwards, *Language and Identity*, 80; and Baugh, "Ebonics and Its Controversy." Already, in the run-up to the Oakland Ebonics debacle, some participants in the language debate claimed that Ebonics was not "genetically related" to English (Baugh, "Ebonics and its Controversy," 310–11). At this point, the metaphor has been pushed past its capacity to produce a meaningful representation of linguistic actualities.

19. The word *hocus-pocus*, which connotes trickery or deception, is a corruption of Latin. The notion that it is a corruption specifically of the phrase *hoc est corpus meum* ("this is my body"), pronounced by the Catholic priest at the moment of transubstantiation of the communion host, is a long-standing folk etymology which may or may not be true; see *OED Online*, s.v. "hocus-pocus."

20. See above, chapter 6, n. 7, on p. 197.

21. On Arabic colloquial poetry in Egypt, see Radwan, *Egyptian Colloquial Poetry*.

22. Dante, *De vulgari eloquentia*, I, i, 3, pp. 30–32. For the reference to the waters of the Arno, see Dante, *De vulgari eloquentia*, I, vi, 3, p. 52, and *Dante, De vulgari eloquentia*, trans. Steven Botterill, 13.

23. For a comprehensive and compassionate discussion of the possibilities and difficulties raised by the global reach of English in the twenty-first century, see Crystal, *English as a Global Language*. Crystal is particularly good at expressing compassion for the different positions from which one might approach English, and the possessiveness felt by native speakers; see chapter 1 and pp. 186–89.

24. See above, chapter 4, n. 3, on p. 193.

25. Arendt, *The Portable Hannah Arendt*, 3 and 12. Quoted in Agamben, *Remnants of Auschwitz*, 159, and *Quel che resta di Auschwitz*, 148. On Arendt's interview and her reflections on language in particular, see also Derrida, *Monolingualism of the Other*, 85–90; and Yildiz, *Beyond the Mother Tongue*, 16–17 and 220 n. 47.

26. Arendt, *The Portable Hannah Arendt*, 12; and Rokem, "Hannah Arendt and Yiddish."

27. See above, chapter 10, n. 49, on p. 207.

28. In his introduction, Cooperson tells the reader that Shawkat Toorawa suggested the English translation of the title (al-Ḥarīrī, *Impostures*, xix).

29. For Cooperson's summary of al-Ḥarīrī's stylistic calisthenics, see al-Ḥarīrī, *Impostures*, xxiii. The verbal performances that include only words with undotted letters, or that alternate words with all undotted and all dotted letters, are exceptionally witty in that they assume an audience who *sees* the speaker's words as they *listen*, in order to appreciate his rhetorical skill.

30. Al-Ḥarīrī, *Impostures*, 50.9, p. 474.

31. Al-Ḥarīrī, *Impostures*, 19.2, p. 164.

32. Al-Ḥarīrī, *Impostures*, xxvi.

33. Al-Ḥarīrī, *Impostures*, 169. As Cooperson notes, Wodehouse himself, during the time he lived in New York, became infatuated with American slang (al-Ḥarīrī, *Impostures*, 163).

34. See *maqāma* 6.

35. The Library of Arabic Literature has made the Arabic-language edition of the *Maqāmāt* available for free download, as it does with all the Arabic editions it prints in English translation; see https://www.libraryofarabicliterature.org/ar/books_ar/ مقامات-أبي-زيد-السروجي (accessed July 2, 2020).

36. Dante's representation of the literary Italian he seeks as a panther is discussed in chapter 5; see chapter 5, n. 25, on p. 196.

Bibliography

Adorno, Theodor W. "Late Style in Beethoven." In *Essays on Music*, edited by Richard Leppert, translated by Susan H. Gillespie, 564–68. Berkeley: University of California Press, 2002.

Agamben, Giorgio. *Quel che resta di Auschwitz: L'archivio e il testimone*. Turin: Bollati Bolinghieri, 1998.

———. *Remnants of Auschwitz: The Witness and the Archive*. Translated by Daniel Heller Roazen. New York: Zone Books, 1999.

Agius, Dionisius. "Arabic under Shidyāq in Malta, 1833–1848." *Journal of Maltese Studies* 19–20 (1989–1990): 52–57.

Ahmed, Shahab. *What Is Islam? The Importance of Being Islamic*. Princeton, NJ: Princeton University Press, 2016.

Albert, Mathias. "On Boundaries, Territory and Postmodernity: An International Relations Perspective." *Geopolitics* 3, no. 1 (1998): 53–68.

Albin, Michael W. "Printing of the Qur'ān." In *Encyclopaedia of the Qur'ān*, edited by Jane Dammen McAuliffe. Washington, DC: Georgetown University, 2001. http://dx.doi.org/10.1163/1875-3922_q3_EQCOM_00158.

Alcarotti, Giovanni Francesco. *Del viaggio di terra santa*. Novara, Italy: Heredi di Fr. Sesalli, 1596.

Alwan, Mohammed Bakir. "Aḥmad Fāris ash-Shidyāq and the West." PhD diss., Indiana University, 1970.

Anderson, Benedict. *Imagined Communities: Reflections on the Origin and Spread of Nationalism*. London: Verso, 1983.

Antrim, Zayde. *Routes and Realms: The Power of Place in the Early Islamic World*. Oxford: Oxford University Press, 2012.

Arberry, A. J. "Fresh Light on Ahmad Faris al-Shidyaq." *Islamic Culture* 25–26 (1951–1952): 155–68.

Arendt, Hannah. *The Portable Hannah Arendt*, edited by Peter Baehr. New York: Penguin Books, 2000.

Ariss, Tarek el-. Review of *Leg over Leg, or the Turtle in the Tree, Concerning the Fariyaq, What Manner of Creature Might He Be*. *Arab Studies Journal* 24, no. 1 (Spring 2016): 286–90.

Aristotle. *Kitāb Aristūtālīs fī al-shi'r*. Translated by Abū Bishr Mattā ibn Yūnus. Cairo: Dar al-Kātib al-Arabī, 1967.

Aristotle, Longinus, and Demetrius. *Aristotle: Poetics. Longinus: On the Sublime. Demetrius: On Style*. Translated by Stephen Halliwell, W. Hamilton Fyfe, Doreen C. Innes, and W. Rhys Roberts. Revised by Donald A. Russell. Cambridge, MA: Harvard University Press, 1995.

Auerbach, Erich. *Literary Language and Its Public in Late Latin Antiquity and in the Middle Ages*. Translated by Ralph Manheim. Princeton, NJ: Princeton University Press, 1993.

Aytürk, Iker. "Script Charisma in Hebrew and Turkish: A Comparative Framework for Explaining Success and Failure of Romanization." *Journal of World History* 21, no. 1 (March 2010): 97–130.

Baalbaki, Ramzi. *The Legacy of the Kitāb: Sībawayhi's Analytical Methods within the Context of the Arabic Grammatical Theory*. Boston: Brill, 2008.

Bacon, Roger. *Compendium Studii Philosophiae*. Edited by J. S. Brewer. Vol. 1 of *Fratris Rogeri Baconis opera quaedam hactenus inedita*. London: Longman, Green, Longman and Roberts, 1859.

Bagdadi, Nadia al-. "Print, Script and Free-Thinking in Arabic Letters of the Nineteenth Century: The Case of al-Shidyāq." *Al-Abhath* 48–49 (2000–2001): 99–122.

Banniard, Michel. *Viva voce: Communication écrite et communication orale du IVe au IXe siècle en occident latin*. Paris: Institut des études augustiniennes, 1992.

Barbeu du Rocher, A. "Ambassade de Pétrarque auprès du Roi Jean le Bon." *Mémoires, Académie des inscriptions et belles-lettres de l'Institut Impérial de France*, 2nd series, vol. 3 (1854): 172–228.

Barbieri, Edoardo. "I libri di Alessandro Paganini a Toscolano." In *Senza ammenda e con più vaghezza: Alessandro Paganini, tipografo a Toscolano (1517–1538)*, 5–9. Toscolano, Italy: Centro di Eccellenza, Polo Cartario di Maina Inferiore, 2008.

Barfield, Thomas J. *The Perilous Frontier: Nomadic Empires and China*. Cambridge, MA: Blackwell, 1989.

Bashshār ibn Burd. *Dīwān Bashshār ibn Burd*. Edited by Muḥammad Rifʿat Maḥmūd Fatḥ Allāh and Muḥammad Shawqī Amīn. 3 vols. Cairo: Lajnat al-Taʾlīf wa-al-Tarjamah wa-al-Nashr, 1950–1966.

Baugh, John. "Ebonics and Its Controversy." In *Language in the USA: Themes for the Twenty-First Century*, edited by John R. Rickford and Edward Finegan, 305–18. Cambridge, UK: Cambridge University Press, 2004.

Beckner, Clay, et al. "Language Is a Complex Adaptive System: Position Paper." *Language Learning* 59, suppl. 1 (December 2009): 1–26.

Ben-Ghiat, Ruth. *Italian Fascism's Empire Cinema*. Bloomington: Indiana University Press, 2015.

Berend, Nora. "Medievalists and the Notion of the Frontier." *Medieval History Journal* 2 (1999): 55–72.

Bergé, Marc. "Abū Ḥayyān al-Tawḥīdī." In *The Cambridge History of Arabic Literature: Abbasid Letters*, edited by Julia Ashtiany et al., 112–24. Cambridge, UK: Cambridge University Press, 1990.

Berkeley, George [Simon Berington, pseud.]. *The Adventures of Sig. Gaudentio di Lucca*. Glasgow: James Knox, 1765.

Bertalanffy, Ludwig von. "An Outline of General System Theory." *British Journal for the Philosophy of Science* 1, no. 2 (1950): 134–65.

———. "Problems of General System Theory." *Human Biology* 23, no. 4 (December 1951): 302–12.

Bertiau, Christophe. "Neo-Latin Literature in Nineteenth-Century Europe: An Overview." *History of European Ideas* 43, no. 5 (2017): 416–26.

Bertellini, Giorgio. "Colonial Autism: Whitened Heroes, Auditory Rhetorics, and National Identity in Interwar Italian Cinema." In *A Place in the Sun: Africa in Italian*

Colonial Culture, edited by Patrizia Palumbo, 255–78. Berkeley: University of California Press, 2003.

Billanovich, Giuseppe. *Tradizione e fortuna di Livio tra medioevo e umanesimo*. Vol. 1 of *La tradizione del testo di Livio tra medioevo e umanesimo*. Padua: Antenore, 1981.

Bīrūnī, Muḥammad ibn Aḥmad al-. *The Determination of the Coordinates of Positions for the Correction of Distances between Cities*. Translated by Jamil Ali. Beirut: American University of Beirut, 1967.

Black, Robert. *Humanism and Education in Medieval and Renaissance History: Tradition and Innovation in Latin Schools from the Twelfth to the Fifteenth Century*. Cambridge, UK: Cambridge University Press, 2001.

Bodin, Jean. *Colloquium heptaplomeres de rerum sublimium arcanis abditis*. Edited by Ludwig Noack. Schwerin, Germany: F. G. Baerensprung, 1857.

———. *Colloquium of the Seven about Secrets of the Sublime*. Translated by Marion Leathers Daniels Kuntz. Princeton, NJ: Princeton University Press, 1975.

Boggess, William F. "Aristotle's *Poetics* in the Fourteenth Century." *Studies in Philology* 67, no. 3 (July 1970): 278–94.

Bonner, Michael. "The Naming of the Frontier: ʿAwāṣim, Thugūr, and the Arab Geographers." *Bulletin of the School of African and Oriental Studies* 57, no. 1 (1994): 17–24.

Borrmans, Maurice. "Présentation de la première édition imprimée du Coran à Venise." *Quaderni di studi arabi* 9 (1991): 93–126.

Borst, Arno. *Der Turmbau von Babel: Geschichte der Meinungen uber Ursprung und Vielfalt der Sprachen und Völker*. 2 vols. Stuttgart: Hiersemann, 1957.

Bosworth, C. E. "The Persian Impact on Arabic Literature." In *Cambridge History of Arabic Literature*: *Arabic Literature to the End of the Umayyad Period*, edited by A. F. L. Beeston et al., 483–96. Cambridge, UK: Cambridge University Press, 1983.

Brasca, Santo. *Relazione del suo viaggio a Gierusalemme*. Milan: Leonard Pachel and Ulrich Scinzenzeler, 1481.

Braudel, Fernand. *The Mediterranean and the Mediterranean World in the Age of Philip II*. 2 vols. Translated by Siân Reynolds. Berkeley: University of California Press, (1949) 1995.

Brauer, Ralph W. *Boundaries and Frontiers in Medieval Muslim Geography*. Philadelphia: American Philosophical Society, 1995.

Bresc, Henri. *Arabes de langue, juifs de religion: L'évolution du judaïsme sicilien dans l'environnement latin, XIIe–XVe siècles*. Paris: Bouchène, 2001.

Brustad, Kristen. "The Iconic Sībawayh." In *Essays in Islamic Philology, History, and Philosophy*, edited by Alireza Korangy, 141–65. Berlin: De Gruyter, 2016.

Bull, Hedley. *The Anarchical Society*. 3rd ed. New York: Columbia University Press, 2002.

Burnett, Charles. "Arabic into Latin: The Reception of Arabic Philosophy into Western Europe." In *Cambridge Companion to Arabic Philosophy*, edited by Peter Adamson and Richard C. Taylor, 370–404. Cambridge Companions Online. Cambridge, UK: Cambridge University Press, 2006.

Carey, Mathew. *A short account of Algiers, and of its several wars against Spain, France, England, Holland, Venice, and other powers of Europe*. 2nd ed. Philadelphia: Mathew Carey, 1794.

Carocci, Anna. *Non si odono altri canti: Leonardo Giustinian nella Venezia del Quattrocento*. Rome: Viella, 2014.

Carter, Michael. "The Ethical Basis of Arabic Grammar." *Al-Karmil* 12 (1991): 9–23.

———. *Sībawayhi*. London: Tauris, 2004.

———. "Sībawayhi." In *Arabic Literary Culture, 500–925*, edited by Michael Cooperson and Shawkat Toorawa, 325–31. Vol. 311 of *Dictionary of Literary Biography*. Farmington Hills, MI: Thomson Gale, 2005.

———. "Sībawayhi." In *Encyclopaedia of Islam, Second Edition*, edited by P. Bearman et al. Brill Online, 2013. http://referenceworks.brillonline.com/entries/encyclopaedia-of-islam-2/sibawayhi-COM_1068.

Caviedes, Alexander. "The Role of Language in Nation-Building within the European Union." *Dialectical Anthropology* 27, no. 3–4 (2003): 249–68.

Cereti, Carlo G. "Middle Persian Literature: i. Pahlavi Literature." *Encyclopaedia Iranica*, online edition, 2009. http://www.iranicaonline.org/articles/middle-persian-literature-1-pahlavi.

Certeau, Michel de. "Walking in the City." In *The Practice of Everyday Life*, translated by Steven Rendall, 91–110. Berkeley: University of California Press, 1984.

Ceverio de Vera, Juan. *Viaie de la Tierra Santa*. Pamplona: Mathias Mares, 1598.

Chahine, Youssef, dir. *Al-Maṣīr (Destiny)*. 1997; Paris: Editions Montparnasse, 1998. DVD.

Cheikh, Nadia Maria El-. *Byzantium Viewed by the Arabs*. Cambridge, MA: Harvard University Press, 2004.

Chejne, Anwar G. *The Arabic Language: Its Role in History*. Minneapolis: University of Minnesota Press, 1969.

Cifoletti, Guido. *La lingua franca barbaresca*. Rome: Il Calamo, 2004.

———. *La lingua franca mediterranea*. Padua: Unipress, 1989.

Citolini, Alessandro. *La lettera d'Alessandro Citolini in difesa della lingua uolgare; e i luoghi del medesimo*. Venice: Al segno del pozzo [Andrea Arrivabene], 1551.

Claval, Paul. *Espace et pouvoir*. Paris: Presses Universitaires de France, 1978.

Considine, John. "*De ortu et occasu linguae latinae*: The Latin Language and the Origins of the Concept of Language Death." In *Latinity and Alterity in the Early Modern Period*, edited by Yasmin Haskell and Juanita Feros Ruys, 55–77. Tempe: Arizona Center for Medieval and Renaissance Studies, 2010.

Copeland, Rita. *Rhetoric, Hermeneutics, and Translation in the Middle Ages: Academic Traditions and Vernacular Texts*. Cambridge, UK: Cambridge University Press, 1991.

Cornish, Alison. *Vernacular Translation in Dante's Italy: Illiterate Literature*. Cambridge, UK: Cambridge University Press, 2011.

Cornish, Vaughan. *Waves of the Sea and Other Water Waves*. London: T. Fisher Unwin, 1910.

Cremona, Joseph. "'Acciocché ognuno le possa intendere': The Use of Italian as a Lingua Franca on the Barbary Coast of the Seventeenth Century. Evidence from the English." *Journal of Anglo-Italian Studies* [Malta] 5 (1997): 52–69.

———. "Italian-Based Lingua Francas around the Mediterranean." In *Multilingualism in Italy: Past and Present*, edited by Anna Laura Lepschy and Arturo Tosi, 24–30. Oxford: Legenda, 2002.

Cresswell, Tim. *Place: An Introduction*. Chichester, UK: Wiley Blackwell, 2015.

Cross, Richard. "Medieval Theories of Haecceity." In *The Stanford Encyclopedia of Philosophy*, edited by Edward N. Zalta. https://plato.stanford.edu/archives/sum2014/entries/medieval-haecceity/.

Crystal, David. *English as a Global Language*. Cambridge, UK: Cambridge University Press, 2012.

Curatola, Giovanni. "Four Carpets in Venice." *Oriental Carpet and Textile Studies* 2 (1986): 123–30.

———. "A Sixteenth-Century Quarrel about Carpets." *Muqarnas* 21 (2004): 129–37.

Dagron, Gilbert. "Formes et fonctions du pluralisme linguistique à Byzance (IXe–IIe siècle)." *Travaux et mémoires du Centre de recherche d'histoire et civilisation byzantines* 12 (1994): 219–40.

Dakhlia, Jocelyne. *Lingua franca*. Arles: Actes Sud, 2008.

Dalton, Matthew. "Caveat Emptor: Lovers of Latin Try to Sell a Dead Tongue." *Wall Street Journal*, November 29, 2013.

Damrosch, David. "Scriptworlds." *Modern Language Quarterly* 68, no. 2 (2007): 195–219.

Dandolo, Andrea. *Chronica per extensum descripta*. Edited by Ester Pastorello. Rerum Italicarum Scriptores, n.s., 12, part. 1. Bologna: Zanichelli, 1938.

Dante Alighieri. *La Commedia secondo l'antica vulgata*. Edited by Giorgio Petrocchi. 2nd ed. 4 vols. Florence: Le Lettere, 1994.

———. *Convivio*. Edited by Franco Brambilla Ageno. 3 vols. Florence: Le Lettere, 1995.

———. *De vulgari eloquentia*. Edited by Pier Vincenzo Mengaldo. Vol. 2, *Opere minori*. Milan: Ricciardi, 1979–1988.

———. *De vulgari eloquentia*. Translated by Steven Botterill. Cambridge, UK: Cambridge University Press, 1996.

———. *Vita nova*. Edited by Guglielmo Gorni. Turin: Einaudi, 1996.

Darrouzès, Jean. "Le mémoire de Constantin Stilbès contre les Latins." *Revue des études byzantines* 21 (1963): 50–100.

Database of Latin Dictionaries. Turnhout, Belgium: Brepolis, 2017.

Davis, Charles T. "Education in Dante's Florence." *Speculum* 40, no. 3 (July 1965): 415–35.

Debord, Guy. "Theory of the Dérive." *Internationale Situationniste* 2 (December 1958): n.p.

Dekker, Kees. "Pentecost and Linguistic Self-Consciousness in Anglo-Saxon England: Bede and Ælfric." *Journal of English and Germanic Philology* 104, no. 3 (July 2005): 345–72.

Deleuze, Gilles, and Félix Guattari. *Kafka: Toward a Minor Literature*. Translated by Dana Polan. Minneapolis: University of Minnesota Press, 1986.

———. *A Thousand Plateaus: Capitalism and Schizophrenia*. Translated by Brian Massumi. Minneapolis: University of Minnesota Press, 1987.

Della Valle, Pietro. 1843. *Viaggi di Pietro della Valle: Il pellegrino*. 3 vols. Brighton, UK: Gancia.

Denny, Walter B., and Norma Jean Jourdenais. *Sotheby's Guide to Oriental Carpets*. New York: Simon & Schuster, 1994.

Derrida, Jacques. *Monolingualism of the Other, or, The Prosthesis of Origin*. Stanford: Stanford University Press, 1998.

De sanctis episcopis Slavorum apostolis Cyrillo et Methodio Olomucii in Moravia vita cum translatione S. Clementis. Bibliotheca Hagiographica Latina 2073. Acta Sanctorum Database, 1999. http://acta.chadwyck.com/all/fulltext?action=byid&id=Z400056916.

Dictionnaire de l'Académie Française. 1st ed. The ARTFL Project, Department of Romance Languages, University of Chicago. http://artfl-project.uchicago.edu/content/dictionnaires-dautrefois. Originally published in 1694.

Dijk, Arjan van. "Early Printed Qur'ans: The Dissemination of the Qur'an in the West." *Journal of Qur'anic Studies* 7, no. 2 (2005): 136–43.

Dronke, Peter. *Fabula: Explorations into the Uses of Myth in Medieval Platonism.* Leiden: Brill, 1974.

Dvornik, Francis. *Byzantine Missions among the Slavs: SS. Constantine-Cyril and Methodius.* New Brunswick, NJ: Rutgers University Press, 1970.

Early Western Korans Online: Koran Printing in the West, 1537–1857. Edited by Hartmut Bobzin and August den Hollander. Brill, 2004. https://primarysources.brillonline.com/browse/early-western-korans.

Eco, Umberto. *The Search for the Perfect Language.* Translated by James Fentress. Oxford: Blackwell, 1995.

Edwards, John. *Language and Identity: Key Topics in Sociolinguistics.* Cambridge, UK: Cambridge University Press, 2009.

Elden, Stuart. "Missing the Point: Globalization, Deterritorialization and the Space of the World." *Transactions of the Institute of British Geographers* 30, no. 1 (March 2005): 8–19.

Ellenblum, Ronnie. "Were There Borders and Borderlines in the Middle Ages? The Example of the Latin Kingdom of Jerusalem." In *Medieval Frontiers: Concepts and Practices,* edited by David Abulafia and Nora Berend, 105–19. Burlington, VT: Ashgate, 2002.

Enciclopedia Dantesca. Edited by Umberto Bosco. 6 vols. Rome: Istituto della Enciclopedia Italiana, 1970.

Endress, Gerhard. "Mattā ibn Yūnus." In *Encyclopedia of Arabic Literature,* edited by Julie Scott Meisami and Paul Starkey, 2:517. London: Routledge, 1998.

Faithfull, R. Glynn. "The Concept of 'Living Language' in Cinquecento Vernacular Philology." *Modern Language Review* 48, no. 3 (July 1953): 278–92.

Fārābī, al-. *Catálogo de las ciencias.* Edited and translated by Angel González Palencia. Madrid: Estanislao Maestre, 1932.

Faral, Edmond. *Les arts poétiques du XIIe et du XIIIe siècle: Recherches et documents sur la technique littéraire du Moyen Âge.* Paris: Librairie H. Champion, 1962.

Farhad, Massumeh, and Simon Rettig, eds. *The Art of the Qur'an: Treasures from the Museum of Turkish and Islamic Arts.* Washington, DC: Smithsonian Institution, 2016.

Feeney, Denis. *Beyond Greek: The Beginnings of Latin Literature.* Cambridge, MA: Harvard University Press, 2016.

Fleisch, Henri. "Esquisse d'un historique de la grammaire arabe." *Arabica* 4, no. 1 (January 1957): 1–22.

Frankfurter, David. "The Magic of Writing and the Writing of Magic: The Power of the Word in Egyptian and Greek Traditions." *Helios* 21, no. 2 (1994): 189–221.

Frend, W. H. C. "Coptic, Greek and Nubian at Q'asr Ibrim." *Byzantinoslavica* 33 (1972): 224–29.

Frescobaldi, Lionardo di Nicolò. *Viaggio di Lionardo di Nicolò Frescobaldi in Egitto e in Terra Santa.* Parma: P. Fiaccadori, 1845.

Gabrieli, Francesco. "Appunti su Baśśār b. Burd." *Bulletin of the School of Oriental Studies* 9, no. 1 (1937): 151–63.

Gal, Susan. "Migration, Minorities and Multilingualism: Language Ideologies in

Europe." In *Language Ideologies, Policies, and Practices: Language and the Future of Europe*, edited by Clare Mar-Molinero and Patrick Stevenson, 13–27. Baskingstoke, UK: Palgrave, 2006.

———. "Multiplicity and Contention among Language Ideologies: A Commentary." In *Language Ideologies: Practice and Theory*, edited by Bambi B. Schieffelin, Kathryn A. Woolard, and Paul V. Kroskrity, 317–31. New York: Oxford University Press, 1998.

Galt, John. *Letters from the Levant*. London: Cadell and Davies, 1813.

Garbini, Giovanni. *Le lingue semitiche*. Naples: Istituto Orientale, 1972.

Genina, Augusto. *Il squadrone bianco*. Directed by Augusto Genina. Rome: Roma Films, 1936.

Géraud, H., ed. *Chronique latine de Guillaume de Nangis de 1113 à 1300 avec les continuations de cette Chronique de 1300 à 1368*. 2nd ed. 2 vols. Paris: Jules Renouard, 1843.

Gibb, Hamilton A. R. "The Social Significance of the Shuubiyya." In *Studies on the Civilization of Islam*, edited by Stanford J. Shaw and William R. Polk, 62–73. Boston: Beacon, 1962.

Giovanni Diacono. "La cronaca veneziana." In *Cronache veneziane antichissime*, edited by Giovanni Monticolo, 1:58–171. Rome: Forzani, 1890.

Giuffrida, Antonino, and Benedetto Rocco. "Una bilingue arabo sicula." *Annali dell'Istituto Orientale di Napoli* 24 (1974): 109–22.

Goldziher, Ignác. "Al-Dasūḳī, al-Sayyid Ibrāhīm b. Ibrāhīm." In *Encyclopaedia of Islam, Second Edition*, edited by P. Bearman et al. Brill Online, 2013. http://dx.doi.org/10.1163/1573-3912_islam_SIM_1735.

Gould, Rebecca. "The *Poetics* from Athens to al-Andalus: Ibn Rushd's Grounds for Comparison." *Modern Philology* 112, no. 1 (August 2014): 1–24.

Green, Nile, ed. *The Persianate World: The Frontiers of a Eurasian Lingua Franca*. Oakland: University of California Press, 2019.

Griffith, Sidney H. "From Aramaic to Arabic: The Languages of the Monasteries of Palestine in the Byzantine and Early Islamic Periods." *Dumbarton Oaks Papers* 51 (1997): 11–31.

Grondeux, Anne. "La notion de langue maternelle et son apparition au Moyen Âge." In *Zwischen Babel und Pfingsten: Sprachdifferenzen und Gesprächsverständigung in der Vormoderne (8.–16. Jahrhundert)*, edited by Peter von Moos, 339–56. Vienna: Lit, 2008.

Gutas, Dimitri. *Greek Thought, Arabic Culture: The Graeco-Arabic Translation Movement in Baghdad and Early 'Abbāsid Society (2nd–4th/8th–10th Centuries)*. London: Routledge, 1998.

Haag, Michael. *Alexandria: City of Memory*. New Haven: Yale University Press, 2004.

Haeri, Niloofar. *Sacred Language, Ordinary People: Dilemmas of Culture and Politics in Egypt*. New York: Palgrave Macmillan, 2003.

Hanna, Nelly. *Ottoman Egypt and the Emergence of the Modern World*. Cairo: American University of Cairo Press, 2014.

Hanna, Sami A., and George H. Gardner. "'Al-Shu'ūbiyyah' Up-Dated: A Study of the 20th Century Revival of an Eighth Century Concept." *Middle East Journal* 20, no. 3 (Summer 1966): 335–51.

Ḥarīrī, al-. *Impostures*. Translated by Michael Cooperson. New York: New York University Press, 2020.

Harvey, David. *Justice, Nature and the Geography of Difference*. Cambridge, MA: Blackwell, 1996.

Hasse, Dag Nikolaus. "The Social Conditions of the Arabic- (Hebrew-) Latin Translation Movements in Medieval Spain and in the Renaissance." In *Wissen über Grenzen: Arabisches Wissen und lateinisches Mittelalter*, edited by Andreas Speer and Lydia Wegener, 68–88. Berlin: De Gruyter, 2006.

———. *Success and Suppression: Arabic Sciences and Philosophy in the Renaissance*. Cambridge, MA: Harvard University Press, 2016.

Hava, J. G. *Arabic-English Dictionary for the Use of Students*. Beirut: Catholic Press, 1921.

Haywood, John A. *Arabic Lexicography: Its History, and its Place in the General History of Lexicography*. Leiden: Brill, 1960.

Helander, Hans. "Neo-Latin Studies: Significance and Prospects." *Symbolae Osloenses* 76 (2001): 5–102.

Hermannus Alemannus. *De arte poetica*. In William de Moerbeke, *De arte poetica*, edited by Lorenzo Minio-Paluello, 40–74. 2nd ed. Brussels: Desclee de Brouwer, 1968.

Hexter, Ralph J., and David Townsend, eds. *The Oxford Handbook of Medieval Latin Literature*. Oxford: Oxford University Press, 2012.

Hitti, Philip K. "The First Book Printed in Arabic." *Princeton University Library Chronicle* 4, no. 1 (1942): 5–9.

Hollevoet, Christel. "Wandering in the City—*Flânerie* to *Dérive* and After: The Cognitive Mapping of Urban Space." In *The Power of the City/The City of Power*, edited by Christel Hollevoet, Karen Jones, and Timothy Nye, 25–55. New York: Whitney Museum of Art, 1992.

Hopkins, Gerard Manley. *The Major Works*. Edited by Catherine Phillips. Oxford: Oxford University Press, 2002.

Horden, Peregrine, and Nicholas Purcell. *The Corrupting Sea: A Study of Mediterranean History*. Oxford: Blackwell, 2000.

Ibn Manzūr, Muḥammad ibn Mukarram. *Lisān al-ʿarab*. Edited by ʿAbd Allāh ʿAlī Kabīr, Muḥammad Aḥmad Ḥasab Allāh, and Hāshim Muḥammad Shādhilī. Cairo: Dār al-Maʿārif, 1981.

Ibn Rushd. *Averroes' Middle Commentary on Aristotle's "Poetics."* Edited and translated by Charles Butterworth. Princeton, NJ: Princeton University Press, 1986.

———. *Talkhīṣ kitāb al-shiʿr*. Edited and translated by Charles Butterworth and Aḥmad ʿAbd al-Majīd Harīdī. Cairo: al-Hayah al-Miṣrīyah al-ʿĀmmah lil-Kitāb, 1986.

Ibn Sīnā. *Al-mantiq al-shiʿr*. Edited by ʿAbd al-Raḥmān Badāwī. Vol. 9 of *Al-Shifāʾ*. Cairo: al-Dār al-Miṣrīyah lil-Taʾlīf wa-al-Tarjamah, 1966.

Informacon for pylgrymes unto the Holy Londe. London: Wynkyn de Word, 1500?

Irvine, Judith T., and Susan Gal. "Language Ideology and Linguistic Differentiation." In *Linguistic Anthropology: A Reader*, edited by Alessandro Durante, 402–34. 2nd ed. Malden, MA: Wiley Blackwell, 2009.

Iṣfahānī, Abī al-Faraj al-. *Kitāb al-Aghānī*. Edited by ʿAbd al-Salām Muḥammad Hārūn. 16 vols. Cairo: Maṭbaʿat Dār al-Kutub al-Miṣrīyah, 1927–.

Jāḥiẓ, Abū ʿUthmān ʿAmr ibn Baḥr al-. *Al-Bayān wa-al-tabyīn*. Edited by ʿAbd al-Salām Muḥammad Hārūn. 4 vols. Cairo: Maktabat al-Khānijī, 1968.

———. *The Life and Works of al-Jāḥiẓ*. Translated by Charles Pellat and D. M. Hawke. London: Routledge and Kegan Paul, 1969.

———. *Nine Essays of al-Jahiz*. Translated by William M. Hutchins. New York: P. Lang, 1989.

———. *Rasāʾil al-Jāḥiẓ, Abī ʿUthmān ʿAmr ibn Baḥr ibn Maḥbūb al-Baṣrī: Al-fuṣūl al-*

mukhtārah min kutub al-Jāḥiẓ. Edited by Muḥammad Bāsil ʿUyūn al-Sūd. 2 vols. Beirut: Dār al-Kutub al-ʿIlmīyah, 2000.

Jakobson, Roman. "The Byzantine Mission to the Slavs. Report on the Dumbarton Oaks Symposium of 1964 and Concluding Remarks about Crucial Problems of Cyrillo-Methodian Studies." *Dumbarton Oaks Papers* 19 (1965): 257–65.

Jallad, Ahmad al-. "The Earliest Stages of Arabic and Its Linguistic Classification." In *The Routledge Handbook of Arabic Linguistics*, edited by Elabbas Benmamoun and Reem Bassiouney, 315–31. Florence: Taylor and Francis, 2017.

Janson, Tore. *A Natural History of Latin*. Translated by Merethe Damsgård Sørensen and Nigel Vincent. Oxford: Oxford University Press, 2004.

Johnson, Rebecca C. "Foreword." In Aḥmad Fāris al-Shidyāq, *Leg over Leg, or: The Turtle in the Tree*, edited and translated by Humphrey Davies, 1:xi–xxx. New York: New York University Press, 2013.

Kahane, Henry Romanos. "Lingua Franca: The Story of a Term." *Romance Philology* 30, no. 1 (August 1976): 25–41.

Kāshgharī, Maḥmūd al-. *Compendium of the Turkic Dialects (Dīwān lughāt al-Turk)*. Translated by Robert Dankoff and James Kelly. 3 vols. Cambridge, MA: Harvard University Printing Office, 1982–85.

Keane, Webb. "Language and Religion." In *A Companion to Linguistic Anthropology*, edited by Alessandro Duranti, 431–48. Malden, MA: Blackwell, 2004.

Kilito, Abdelfattah. *Les Séances: Récits et codes culturels chez Hamadhânî et Harîrî*. Paris: Sindbad, 1983.

———. *Thou Shalt Not Speak My Language*. Translated by Waïl S. Hassan. Syracuse, NY: Syracuse University Press, 2008.

Kilpatrick, Hilary. *Making the Great Book of Songs: Compilation and the Author's Craft in Abū al-Faraj al-Iṣfahānī's "Kitāb al-Aghānī."* London: Routledge, 2003.

Kim, David Young. "Lotto's Carpets: Materiality, Textiles, and Composition in Renaissance Painting." *Art Bulletin* 98, no. 2 (June 2016): 181–212.

Kinoshita, Sharon. "Almería Silk and the French Feudal Imaginary: Toward a 'Material' History of the Medieval Mediterranean." In *Medieval Fabrications: Dress, Textiles, Clothwork, and other Cultural Imaginings*, edited by E. Jane Burns, 165–76. New York: Palgrave Macmillan, 2004.

———. *Medieval Boundaries: Rethinking Difference in Old French Literature*. Philadelphia: University of Pennsylvania Press, 2006.

Kirkham, Victoria, and Armando Maggi, eds. *Petrarch: A Critical Guide to the Complete Works*. Chicago: University of Chicago Press, 2012.

Krek, Miroslav. "The Enigma of the First Arabic Book Printed from Movable Type." *Journal of Near Eastern Studies* 38, no. 3 (July 1979): 203–12.

Lamanskiĭ, Vladimīr Ivanovich. *Secrets d'État de Venise; Documents, extraits, notices, et études servant à éclaircir les rapports de la seigneurie avec les Grecs, les Slaves, et la Porte ottomane à la fin du XVe et au XVIe*. 2 vols. Reprint. New York: B. Franklin, 1968.

Lane, Edward William. *An Arabic-English Lexicon*. 8 vols. Reprint ed. Beirut: Librairie du Liban, 1997. Originally published by Williams and Norgate in 1863–1893.

Lanfreducci, Francesco, and Giovanni Otho Bosio. "Costa e discorsi di Barberia." Edited by Charles Monchicourt. *Revue Africaine* 66 (1925): 419–549.

Larkin, Margaret. "Popular Poetry in the Post-Classical Period, 1150–1850." In *The Cambridge History of Arabic Literature: Arabic Literature in the Post-Classical Period*, edited by R. Allen and D. Richards, 189–242. Cambridge, UK: Cambridge University Press, 2006.

Larsson, Göran. *Ibn García's Shuʿūbiyya Letter*. Leiden: Brill, 2003.

Lectiones ecclesiasticae de iisdem Sanctis Cyrillo et Methodio. Bibliotheca Hagiographica Latina 2075. Acta Sanctorum Database, 1999. http://acta.chadwyck.com/all/fulltext?action=byid&id=Z400056920.

Lev, Yaacov. *The Administration of Justice in Medieval Egypt: From the Seventh to the Twelfth Century*. Edinburgh: Edinburgh University Press, 2020.

Levin, Aryeh. "Sībawayhi's Attitude to the Spoken Language." *Jerusalem Studies in Arabic and Islam* 17 (1994): 204–43.

Levinas, Emmanuel. "The Ego and the Totality." In *Collected Philosophical Papers*, translated by Alphonso Lingis, 25–46. Dordrecht: M. Nijhoff, 1987.

———. "Le moi et la totalité." *Revue de Métaphysique et de Morale* 59 (1954): 353–73.

Lewis, Charlton T., and Charles Short. *A Latin Dictionary*. Perseus Digital Library, Tufts University, 2005–. http://www.perseus.tufts.edu/hopper.

Lewis, Wyndham, et al. "Manifesto." *Blast* 1 (June 20, 1914): 11–28.

Lunt, Horace. "Thoughts, Suggestions, and Questions about the Earliest Slavic Writing Systems." *Wiener Slavistisches Jahrbuch* 46 (2000): 271–86.

Luquet, G. H. "Hermann l'Allemand." *Revue de l'histoire des religions* 44 (1901): 407–22.

Macfarlane, Robert. *The Wild Places*. New York: Penguin, 2008.

Machiavelli, Niccolò. *Discorso o dialogo intorno alla nostra lingua*. Edited by Bortolo Tommaso Sozzi. Turin: Einaudi, 1976.

Makdisi, Ussama Samir. *Artillery of Heaven: American Missionaries and the Failed Conversion of the Middle East*. Ithaca, NY: Cornell University Press, 2008.

Malcolm, Noel. "Jean Bodin and the Authorship of the 'Colloquium heptaplomeres.'" *Journal of the Warburg and Courtauld Institutes* 69 (2006): 95–150.

Mallette, Karla. "Beyond Mimesis: Aristotle's *Poetics* in the Medieval Mediterranean." *PMLA* 124, no. 2 (March 2009): 583–91.

———. *European Modernity and the Arab Mediterranean: Toward a New Philology and a Counter-Orientalism*. Philadelphia: University of Pennsylvania Press, 2010.

———. "Lingua Franca." In *Companion to Mediterranean History*, edited by Peregrine Horden and Sharon Kinoshita, 330–44. Malden, MA: Wiley Blackwell, 2014.

———. "Translation in the Pre-modern World." *Middle Eastern Literatures* 20 (2017): 18–30.

———. "Vernacular and Cosmopolitan Language in Late Medieval Europe: Petrarch at Sea." *Interfaces* 1, no. 1 (July 2015). http://riviste.unimi.it/interfaces/article/view/4931.

Mansel, Philip. *Levant: Splendour and Catastrophe on the Mediterranean*. London: John Murray, 2010.

Mantino, Jacob. *Averrois paraphrasis in librum Poeticae Aristotelis*. Edited by Frederich Heidenhain. Leipzig: Teubner, 1890.

Manzano Moreno, Eduardo. "The Creation of a Medieval Frontier: Islam and Christianity in the Iberian Peninsula, Eighth to Eleventh Centuries." In *Frontiers in Question: Eurasian Borderlands, 700–1700*, edited by Daniel Power and Naomi Standen, 32–54. Houndmills, UK: Macmillan, 1999.

Marani, Diego. "EUROPANTO: From Productive Process To Language; or, How to Cause International English to Implode." http://www.europanto.be/gram.en.html.

Margoliouth, D. S. "The Discussion between Abū Bishr Mattā and Abū Saʿīd al-Sīrāfī on the Merits of Logic and Grammar." *Journal of the Royal Asiatic Society of Great Britain and Ireland* 37, no. 1 (January 1905): 79–129.

Marti, Roland. "Philologia in the *Slavia Cyrillo-Methodiana*: From Constantine the Philosopher to Constantine the Philosopher." In *Love of Learning and Devotion to God in Orthodox Monasteries: Selected Proceedings of the Fifth International Hilandar Conference*, edited by Miroljub Joković, Daniel Collins, M. A. Johnson, and Predrag Matejić, vol. 1, 11–25. Belgrade: Raška škola, 2006.

Martin, Richard C. "Inimitability." In *Encyclopaedia of the Qur'ān*, edited by Jane Dammen McAuliffe. Washington, DC: Georgetown University, 2001. http://dx.doi.org/10.1163/1875-3922_q3_EQCOM_00093.

Massey, Doreen B. *For Space*. London: Sage, 2005.

———. *Space, Place, and Gender*. Minneapolis: University of Minnesota Press, 1999.

———. "Landscape as a Provocation: Reflections on Moving Mountains." *Journal of Material Culture* 11, no. 1–2 (2006): 33–48.

Matthew of Vendôme. *The Art of Versification*. Translated by Aubrey Galyon. Ames: Iowa State University Press, 1980.

———. *Mathei Vindocinensis opera*. Edited by Franco Munari. 3 vols. Rome: Edizioni di storia e letteratura, 1977–1988.

Mayhew, Henry. *London Labour and the London Poor: A Cyclopaedia of the Condition and Earnings of Those That Will Work, Those That Cannot Work, and Those That Will Not Work*. 3 vols. London: Woodfall, 1851.

McDougall, James. "Dream of Exile, Promise of Home: Language, Education, and Arabism in Algeria." *International Journal of Middle East Studies* 43, no. 2 (May 2011): 251–70.

McManamon, John M. *Funeral Oratory and the Cultural Ideals of Italian Humanism*. Chapel Hill: University of North Carolina Press, 1989.

McNally, R. E. "The 'Tres Linguae Sacrae' in Early Irish Bible Exegesis." *Theological Studies* 19, no. 3 (September 1958): 395–403.

Mejdell, Gunvor. "Diglossia." In *The Routledge Handbook of Arabic Linguistics*, edited by Elabbas Benmamoun and Reem Bassiouney, 332–44. Florence: Taylor and Francis, 2017.

Miéville, China. *The City & the City*. London: Macmillan, 2009.

Monfrin, Jacques. "Humanisme et traductions au Moyen Âge." *Journal des savants* 1963, no. 3 (July–September 1963): 161–90.

Moreh, Shmuel. *Live Theatre and Dramatic Literature in the Medieval Arab World*. Edinburgh: Edinburgh University Press, 1992.

Mortensen, Lars Boje. "European Literature and Book History in the Middle Ages, c. 600–c. 1450." *Oxford Research Encyclopedia of Literature*, 2018. https://dx.doi.org/10.1093/acrefore/9780190201098.013.284.

Moul, Victoria, ed. *A Guide to Neo-Latin Literature*. Cambridge, UK: Cambridge University Press, 2017.

Mubārak, ʿAlī Bāshā. *Al-Khiṭaṭ al-tawfīqīyah al-jadīdah li-Miṣr al-Qāhirah wa-mudunihā wa-bilādihā al-qadīmah wa-al-shahīrah*. 20 vols. Bulaq, Egypt: al-Maṭbaʿah al-Kubrā al-Amīrīyah, 1886–1889.

Nagel, Alexander, and Christopher S. Wood. *Anachronic Renaissance*. New York: Zone Books, 2010.

Nallino, Maria. "Una cinquecentesca edizione del Corano stampata a Venezia." *Atti dell'Istituto Veneto di scienze, lettere ed arti* 124 (1965–1966): 1–12.

Nemesini, Vittorio. *Il tributo della coglionatura dell'abate Vittorio Nemesini.* [London?]: n.p., 1793.

La Nobla Korano. Translated by Italo Chiussi. Copenhagen: TK, 1970.

Norris, H. T. "Shuʿūbiyyah in Arabic Literature." In *Cambridge History of Arabic Literature: ʿAbbasid Belles-Lettres,* edited by Julia Ashtiany, T. M. Johnstone, J. D. Latham, R. B. Serjeant, and G. Rex Smith, 31–47. Cambridge, UK: Cambridge University Press, 1990.

Norwich, John Julius, and Quentin Blake. *The Illustrated Christmas Cracker.* London: Doubleday, 2002.

Nouvelle Biographie Nationale. 14 vols. Brussels: Académie royale des sciences, des lettres et des beaux-arts de Belgique, 1988.

Nuessel, Frank. "Language: Semiotics." *Encyclopedia of Language and Linguistics.* 2nd ed. Louisville: University of Louisville Press, 2006. https://dx.doi.org/10.1016/B0-08-044854-2/01422-X.

Nuovo, Angela. "Il Corano arabo ritrovato (Venezia, Paganino e Alessandro Paganini, tra l'agosto 1537 e l'agosto 1538)." *La Bibliofilía* 89 (1987): 237–71.

———. "A Lost Arabic Koran Rediscovered." *The Library,* 6th series, 12, no. 4 (December 1990): 273–92.

———. "La scoperta del Corano arabo, ventisei anni dopo: Un riesame." *Nuovi annali della scuola speciale per archivisti e bibliotecari* 27 (2013): 9–23.

OED Online. 3rd ed. Oxford University Press, 2000–. https://www.oed.com.

Ornston, Darius. "Cathexis." In *The Freud Encyclopedia: Theory, Therapy, and Culture,* edited by Edward Erwin, 69–72. New York: Routledge, 2002.

O'Rourke, Siobhan, and Alison Holcroft. "The Silence at the Beginning of Bruni's *Dialogi ad Petrum Histrum.*" In *Latinity and Alterity in the Early Modern Period,* edited by Yasmin Haskell and Juanita Feros Ruys, 35–53. Tempe: Arizona Center for Medieval and Renaissance Studies, 2010.

Ostler, Nicholas. *Ad Infinitum: A Biography of Latin.* New York: Walker, 2007.

Ouyang, Wen-chin. "Literature and Thought: Re-reading al-Tawḥīdī's Transcription of the Debate between Logic and Grammar." In *The Heritage of Arabo-Islamic Learning Studies Presented to Wadad Kadi,* edited by Maurice A. Pomerantz and Aram Shahin, 444–60. Leiden: Brill, 2016.

Pade, Marianne. *The Reception of Plutarch's Lives in Fifteenth-Century Italy.* 2 vols. Copenhagen: Museum Tusculanum Press, University of Copenhagen, 2007.

Pamuk, Orhan. *Istanbul: Memories and the City.* Translated by Maureen Freely. New York: Knopf, 2005.

Panella, Emilio. *Dal bene comune al bene del comune: I trattati politici di Remigio dei Girolami (d. 1319) nella Firenze dei bianchi-neri.* Florence: Nerbini, 2014.

Pannier, Léopold. "Notice biographique sur le bénédictin Pierre Bersuire, premier traducteur français de Tite-Live." *Bibliothèque de l'école des chartes* 33 (1872): 325–64.

Pavić, Milorad. *Dictionary of the Khazars: A Lexicon Novel in 100,000 Words.* Translated by Christina Pribićević-Zorić. New York: Knopf, 1988.

Pellat, Charles. "Ḥikāya." In *Encyclopaedia of Islam, Second Edition,* edited by P. Bearman et al. Brill Online, 2013. https://referenceworks.brillonline.com/entries/encyclopaedia-of-islam-2/hikaya-COM_0285.

Penney, John. "Archaic and Old Latin." In *A Companion to the Latin Language,* edited by James Clackson, 220–35. Chichester, UK: Wiley Blackwell, 2011.

Perry, Ben Edwin. *Secundus the Silent Philosopher*. Ithaca, NY: American Philological Society, 1964.

Pesenti, Giovanni Paolo. *Peregrinaggio di Giervsalemme fatto e descritto dal sr. cavalier Gio. Paolo Pesenti*. Brescia: Bartolomeo Fontana, 1628.

Peters, F. E. *Aristoteles Arabus*. Leiden: Brill, 1968.

Petrarch, Francesco. *Canzoniere*. Edited by Marco Santagata. Milan: Mondadori, 2004.

———. *Il codice Vaticano Lat. 3196*. Edited by Manfredi Porena. Rome: G. Bardi, Tipografo della Reale Accademia d'Italia, 1941.

———. "Collatio coram Domino Johanne, Francorum Rege." In *Opere Latine*, edited by Antonietta Bufano, 2:1285–1309. Turin: Unione Tipografico-Editrice Torinese, 1975.

———. *Le familiari*. Edited by Vittorio Rossi. 4 vols. Florence: Le Lettere, 1997.

———. *Petrarch's Guide to the Holy Land: Itinerary to the Sepulcher of Our Lord Jesus Christ (Itinerarium ad sepulchrum Domini nostri Yehsu Christi)*. Translated by Theodore J. Cachey Jr. Notre Dame, IN: University of Notre Dame Press, 2002.

———. *Rerum familiarium libri: Letters on Familiar Matters*. Translated by Aldo S. Bernardo. 3 vols. Baltimore: John Hopkins University Press, 1975.

———. *Rerum memorandum libri*. Edited by Giuseppe Billanovich. Florence: Sansoni, 1945.

Philip of Harveng. *De silentio clericorum. Patrologia Latina*, vol. 203, col. 943–1206. Paris: Garnieri Fratres, 1855.

———. *Epistolae. Patrologia Latina*, vol. 203, col. 1–180. Paris: Garnieri Fratres, 1855.

Pollock, Sheldon. "Cosmopolitan and Vernacular in History." *Public Culture* 12, no. 3 (Fall 2000): 591–625.

Pollock, Sheldon, Homi K. Bhabha, Carol A. Breckenridge, and Dipesh Chakrabarty. "Cosmopolitanisms." *Public Culture* 12, no. 3 (Fall 2000): 577–89.

Power, Daniel, and Naomi Standen, "Introduction." In *Frontiers in Question: Eurasian Borderlands, 700–1700*, edited by Power and Standen, 1–31. Houndmills, UK: Macmillan, 1999.

Pred, A. R. "Place as Historically Contingent Process: Structuration and the Time-Geography of Becoming Places." *Annals of the Association of American Geographers* 74, no. 2 (June 1984): 279–97.

Principe, Walter H. "Bishops, Theologians and Philosophers in Conflict at the Universities of Paris and Oxford: The Condemnations of 1270 and 1277." *Proceedings of the Catholic Theological Society of America* 40 (1985): 114–26.

Rabin, C. "The Origin of the Subdivisions of Semitic." In *Hebrew and Semitic Studies Presented to G.R. Driver*, edited by D. Winton Thomas and W. D. McHardy, 104–15. Oxford: Clarendon, 1963.

Radwan, Noha M. *Egyptian Colloquial Poetry in the Modern Arabic Canon: New Readings of Shi'r Al-'Āmmiyya*. New York: Palgrave Macmillan, 2012.

Rastegar, Kamran. *Literary Modernity between the Middle East and Europe: Textual Transactions in Nineteenth-Century Arabic, English, and Persian Literatures*. London: Routledge, 2007.

Reiss, Tom. *The Orientalist: Solving the Mystery of a Strange and Dangerous Life*. New York: Random House, 2005.

Renan, Ernst. *Qu'est-ce qu'une nation?* 2nd ed. Paris: Lévy, 1882.

Reynolds, Dwight. "Popular Prose in the Post-Classical Period." In *Cambridge History of Arabic Literature: Arabic Literature in the Post-Classical Period*, edited by Roger

Allen and D. S. Richards, 245–69. Cambridge, UK: Cambridge University Press, 2006.

Richards, D. S. "Edward Lane's Surviving Arabic Correspondence." *Journal of the Royal Asiatic Society*, 3rd series, 9, no. 1 (April 1999): 1–25.

Rocco, Benedetto. "Le tre lingue usate dagli ebrei in Sicilia dal sec. XII al sec. XV." In *Italia Judaica: Gli ebrei in Sicilia sino all'espulsione del 1492*, 355–69. Atti del V convegno internazionale, Palermo, 15–19 giugno 1992. Palermo: Ministero per i beni culturali e ambientali e Ufficio centrale per i beni archivistici, 1995.

Rochette, Bruno. "Language Policies in the Roman Republic and Empire." In *Companion to the Latin Language*, edited by James Clackson, 549–63. Chichester, UK: Wiley, 2011.

Rodenbeck, John. "Edward Said and Edward William Lane." In *Travellers in Egypt*, edited by Paul Starkey and Jane Starkey, 233–43. London: I. B. Tauris, 1998.

Rokem, Na'ama. "Hannah Arendt and Yiddish." Hannah Arendt Center for Politics and Humanities at Bard College, 2013. https://hac.bard.edu/amor-mundi/hannah-arendt-and-yiddish-2013-02-18.

Romanov, Maxim. "Islamic Urban Centers, 661–1300 C.E." *Al-Raqmiyyāt*, 2014. https://alraqmiyyat.github.io/2014/08-23.html.

Roper, Geoffrey. "Texts from Nineteenth-Century Egypt: The Role of E. W. Lane." In *Travellers in Egypt*, edited by Paul Starkey and Jane Starkey, 244–54. London: I. B. Tauris, 1998.

Rothman, Natalie. *Brokering Empire: Trans-imperial Subjects between Venice and Istanbul.* Ithaca, NY: Cornell University Press, 2007.

Sacks, Jeffrey. "Falling into Pieces, or Aḥmad Fāris al-Shidyāq and Literary History: A Love Letter." *Middle Eastern Literatures* 16, no. 3 (2013): 317–33.

Said, Edward. *Orientalism*. New York: Vintage, 1979.

Sakhai, Essie. *Oriental Carpets: A Buyer's Guide*. Wakefield, RI: Moyer Bell, 1995.

Saleh, Walid A. "Reflections on Muslim Hebraism: Codex Vindobonensis Palatinus and al-Biqa'i." In *A Sea of Languages: Rethinking the Arabic Role in Medieval Literary History*, edited by Suzanne Conklin Akbari and Karla Mallette, 71–81. Toronto: University of Toronto Press.

Salvatori, Enrica. "Corsairs' Crews and Cross-Cultural Interactions: The Case of the Pisan Trapelicinus in the Twelfth Century." *Medieval Encounters* 13, no. 1 (January 2007) 32–55.

Sanders, Ruth H. *German: Biography of a Language*. Oxford: Oxford University Press, 2010.

Santagata, Marco. *Dante: The Story of His Life*. Translated by Richard Dixon. Cambridge, MA: Harvard University Press, 2016.

Savary de Brèves, François. *Relation des voyages de monsieur de Brèves, tant en Grèce, Terre Saincte et Aegypte, qu'aux Royaumes de Tunis et Arger*. Paris: Nicolas Gasse, 1628.

Sawaie, Mohammed. "An Aspect of 19th Century Arabic Lexicography: The Modernizing Role and Contribution of Faris al-Shidyaq (1804?–1887)." In *History and Historiography of Linguistics*, edited by Hans-Josef Niederehe and Konrad Koener, 157–74. Amsterdam: John Benjamins, 1990.

Schoeler, Gregor. "Bashshār b. Burd, Abū 'l-'Atāhiya and Abū Nuwās." In *The Cambridge History of Arabic Literature: Abbasid Letters*, edited by Julia Ashtiany et al., 275–99. Cambridge, UK: Cambridge University Press, 1990.

Schuchardt, Hugo. "The Lingua Franca." In *Pidgin and Creole Languages: Selected Essays by Hugo Schuchardt*, edited and translated by Glenn G. Gilbert, 65–88. London: Cambridge University Press, 1980.

Scudéry, Georges de. *Il perfetto Ibrahim, ovvero l'Illustre Bassa*. Venice: Abbondio Menafogli, 1668.

Seigneurie, Ken. "The Institution and the Practice of Comparative Literature in Lebanon." *Comparative Literature Studies* 51, no. 3 (2014): 373–96.

Selbach, Rachel. "The Superstrate Is Not Always the Lexifier: Lingua Franca in the Barbary Coast, 1530–1830." In *Roots of Creole Structures: Weighing the Contribution of Substrates and Superstrates*, edited by Susanne Michaelis, 29–58. Amsterdam: John Benjamins, 2008.

Selove, Emily. *Ḥikāyat Abī al-Qāsim: A Literary Banquet*. Edinburgh: Edinburgh University Press, 2016.

Senza ammenda e con più vaghezza: Alessandro Paganini, tipografo a Toscolano (1517–1538). Toscolano, Italy: Centro di Eccellenza, Polo Cartario di Maina Inferiore, 2008.

Ševčenko, Ihor. *Byzantium and the Slavs in Letters and Culture*. Cambridge, MA: Harvard Ukrainian Research Institute, 1991.

———. "Three Paradoxes of the Cyrillo-Methodian Mission." *Slavic Review* 23, no. 2 (June 1964): 220–36.

Shapiro, Marianne. "Dante and the Grammarians." *Zeitschrift für romanische Philologie* 105, no. 5–6 (1989): 498–528.

———. *De vulgari eloquentia: Dante's Book of Exile*. Lincoln: University of Nebraska Press, 1990.

Sharkawi, Muhammad al-. *The Ecology of Arabic: A Study of Arabicization*. Leiden: Brill, 2010.

Shidyāq, Aḥmad Fāris al-. *Leg over Leg, or, The Turtle in the Tree: Concerning the Fāriyāq, What Manner of Creature Might He Be*. Translated by Humphrey Davies. 4 vols. New York: New York University Press, 2013.

———. *Sirr al-layāl fī al-qalb wa-al-ibdāl fī ʿilm maʿānī al-alfāẓ al-ʿArabīyah*. Edited by Muḥammad al-Hadī al-Maṭwī. Beirut: Dār al-Gharb al-Islāmī, 2006.

Sībawayh, ʿAmr ibn ʿUthmān. *Kitāb Sībawayh*. Edited by Hartwig Derenbourg. 2 vols. Paris: al-Maṭbaʿ al-ʿĀmmī al-Ashraf, 1881–1885.

Sijen, G. P. "Philippe de Harveng, abbé de Bonne-Espérance: Sa biographie." *Analecta Praemonstratensia* 14 (1938): 37–52.

Sims-Williams, Nicholas. "Bactrian Letters from the Sasanian and Hephthalite Periods." In *Proceedings of the 5th Conference of the Societas Iranologica Europæa Held in Ravenna, 6–11 October 2003*, edited by Antonio Panaino and Andrea Piras, 701–13. Milan: Mimesis, 2007.

———. *New Light on Ancient Afghanistan: The Decipherment of Bactrian*. London: School of Oriental and African Studies, University of London, 1997.

———. "The Sasanians in the East: A Bactrian Archive from Northern Afghanistan." In *The Sasanian Era*, edited by Vesta Sarkhosh Curtis and Sarah Stewart, 88–102. London: I. B. Tauris, 2008.

Smail, Daniel Lord. *Imaginary Cartographies: Possession and Identity in Late Medieval Marseille*. Ithaca, NY: Cornell University Press, 2000,

———. "The Linguistic Cartography of Property and Power in Late Medieval Marseille." In *Medieval Practices of Space*, edited by Barbara A. Hanawalt and Michael Kobialka, 37–63. Minneapolis: University of Minnesota Press, 2000.

Solmsen, Friedrich. "Boethius and the History of the Organon." *American Journal of Philology* 65, no. 1 (1944): 69–74.

Sophocles, E. A., J. H. Thayer, and Henry Drisler. *Greek Lexicon of the Roman and Byzantine Periods (from B.C. 146 to A.D. 1100)*. Cambridge, MA: Harvard University Press, 1914.

Sosa, Antonio de. *An Early Modern Dialogue with Islam: Antonio de Sosa's "Topography of Algiers" (1612)*. Edited by María Antonia Garcés. Translated by Diana de Armas Wilson. Notre Dame, IN: University of Notre Dame Press, 2011.

Spallanzani, Marco. *Oriental Rugs in Renaissance Florence*. Florence: SPES, 2007.

Stahuljak, Zrinka. "Multilingualism and Translation in the Mediterranean." *Exemplaria* 26, no. 4 (2014): 389–400.

Steinberg, Justin. *Accounting for Dante: Urban Readers and Writers in Late Medieval Italy*. Notre Dame, IN: University of Notre Dame Press, 2007.

Strange, Susan. "The Defective State." *Daedalus* 124, no. 2 (Spring 1995): 55–75.

Stukeley, William. *The Family Memoirs of the Rev. William Stukeley, M.D.* 3 vols. Durham, UK: Andrews & Co., 1882–1887.

Suleiman, Yasir. "Arabic Folk Linguistics: Between Mother Tongue and Native Language." In *The Oxford Handbook of Arabic Linguistics*, edited by Jonathan Owens, 264–80. Oxford: Oxford University Press, 2013.

———. "Arabic Language Reforms, Language Ideology, and the Criminalization of Sībawayhi." In *Grammar as a Window onto Arabic Humanism: A Collection of Articles in Honour of Michael G. Carter*, edited by Lutz Edzard and Janet Watson, 66–83. Wiesbaden, Germany: Harrassowitz, 2006.

Tachios, Anthony-Emil N. *Cyril and Methodius of Thessalonica: The Acculturation of the Slavs*. Crestwood, NY: St. Vladimir's Seminary Press, 2001.

Tarán, Leonardo, and Dimitri Gutas. *Aristotle Poetics: Editio Maior of the Greek Text with Historical Introductions and Philological Commentaries*. Leiden, Boston: Brill, 2012.

Tati, Jacques, dir. *Playtime*. 1967; New York: Criterion, 2006. DVD.

Tawḥīdī, Abū Ḥayyān al-. *Kitāb al-imtā' wa-al-mu'ānasah*. Edited by Aḥmad Amīn and Aḥmad al-Zayn. 3 vols. Cairo: Lajnat al-Ta'līf wa-al-Tarjamah wa-al-Nashr, 1939.

Thomas à Kempis. *Opera omnia*. Edited by Michael Joseph Pohl. 7 vols. Freiburg: Herder, 1922.

Thompson, Jason. *Edward William Lane, 1801–1876: The Life of the Pioneering Egyptologist and Orientalist*. Cairo: American University in Cairo Press, 2010.

Tkatsch, Jaroslaus. *Die arabische Ubersetzung der "Poetik" des Aristoteles und die Grundlage der Kritik des griechischen Textes*. 2 vols. Vienna: Holder-Pichler-Tempsky, 1928.

Toscani, Xenio. "Analfabetismo e alfabetizzazione." *Enciclopedia dell'italiano*. Treccani, 2010. http://www.treccani.it/enciclopedia/analfabetismo-e-alfabetizzazione_%28Enciclopedia-dell%27Italiano%29/.

Troupeau, Gérard. *Lexique-index du "Kitāb" de Sībawayhi*. Paris: Klincksieck. 1976.

Tuan, Yi-Fu. *Space and Place: The Perspective of Experience*. Minneapolis: University of Minnesota Press, 1977.

Turner, Frederick Jackson. "The Significance of the Frontier in American History." *American Historical Association Annual Report for the Year 1893*, 199–227.

Tyler, E. M., ed. *Conceptualizing Multilingualism in England, c.800–c.1250*. Turnhout, Belgium: Brepolis, 2011.

Tyler, Royall. *The Algerine Captive*. 2 vols. Walpole, NH: Carlisle, 1797.

Urvoy, Dominique. *Ibn Rushd, Averroes.* Translated by Olivia Stewart. London: Routledge, 1991.

Van Bladel, Kevin. "The Bactrian Background of the Barmakids." In *Islam and Tibet: Interactions along the Musk Routes,* edited by Anna Akasoy, Charles Burnett, and Ronit Yoeli-Tlalim, 43–88. Farnham, UK: Ashgate, 2011.

Verde, Tom. "Threads on Canvas." *Saudi Aramco World* 61, no. 1 (January–February 2010). http://www.saudiaramcoworld.com/issue/201001/threads.on.canvas.htm.

Verdery, Richard N. "The Publications of the Būlāq Press under Muḥammad ʿAlī of Egypt." *Journal of the American Oriental Society* 91, no. 1 (January–March 1971): 129–32.

Verkholantsev, Julia. *The Slavic Letters of St. Jerome: The History of the Legend and its Legacy, or, How the Translator of the Vulgate Became an Apostle of the Slavs.* De Kalb: Northern Illinois University Press, 2014.

Versteegh, Kees. *The Arabic Language.* Edinburgh: Edinburgh University Press, 2001.

———. "Linguistic Contacts between Arabic and Other Languages." *Arabica* 48, no. 4 (2001): 470–508.

Vita eorundem Sanctorum Cyrilli et Methodii. Bibliotheca Hagiographica Latina 2074. Acta Sanctorum Database, 1999. http://acta.chadwyck.com/all/fulltext?action=byid&id=Z400056918.

The Vita of Constantine and the Vita of Methodius. Translated by Marvin Kantor and Richard S. White. Ann Arbor: Michigan Slavic Publications, 1976.

Wallace, David, ed. *Europe: A Literary History, 1348–1418.* 2 vols. Oxford: Oxford University Press, 2016.

Wansbrough, John. *Lingua Franca in the Mediterranean.* Surrey, UK: Curzon, 1996.

Werbner, Pnina. "Vernacular Cosmopolitanism." *Theory, Culture & Society* 23, no. 2–3 (2006): 496–98.

Wheelock, Wade T. "Language: Sacred Language." In *Encyclopedia of Religion,* edited by Lindsay Jones, 2nd ed., vol. 8, 5301–8. Gale Virtual Reference Library, 2005. http://link.galegroup.com/apps/doc/CX3424501784/GVRL?u=lom_umichanna&sid=GVRL&xid=8d2b4f44.

White, Joshua M. *Piracy and Law in the Ottoman Mediterranean.* Stanford, CA: Stanford University Press, 2018.

Whitehead, Colson. *Zone One.* New York: Anchor, 2012.

Wilkins, Ernest Hatch. *Life of Petrarch.* Chicago: University of Chicago Press, 1961.

Williams, Joy. *Ninety-Nine Stories of God.* Portland: Tin House, 2016.

Wood, J. S. "The Missing Fragment of the Fourth Book of Esdras." *Journal of Philology* 7, no. 13 (1877): 264–78.

Woolard, Kathryn A. "Bernardo de Aldrete and the Morisco Problem: A Study in Early Modern Spanish Language Ideology." *Comparative Studies in Society and History* 44, no. 3 (July 2002): 446–80.

Woolard, Kathryn A., and Bambi B. Schieffelin. "Language Ideology." *Annual Review of Anthropology* 23 (1994): 55–82.

Wright, Roger. *A Sociophilological Study of Late Latin.* Turnhout, Belgium: Brepolis, 2002.

Yildiz, Yasemin. *Beyond the Mother Tongue: The Postmonolingual Condition.* New York: Fordham University Press, 2012.

Index